The Reminiscences

of

Vice Admiral Charles L. Melson,

U. S. Navy (Retired)

U. S. Naval Institute
Annapolis, Maryland
1974

Preface

This volume is the result of a series of thirteen taped interviews with Vice Admiral Charles L. Melson at his home in Providence, Annapolis, Maryland. These interviews were conducted by John T. Mason, Jr., for the Oral History program of the U. S. Naval Institute over a period from February, 1971 to June, 1972.

A comprehensive index has been prepared for the benefit of the reader.

Admiral Melson read the original transcript and made some minor corrections. For the sake of clarity, the entire manuscript has been re-typed. The reader is reminded that (as usual with oral history manuscripts) this is truly a record of the spoken word and makes no pretense at being a literary effort.

VICE ADMIRAL CHARLES L. MELSON
UNITED STATES NAVY, RETIRED

Charles Leroy Melson was born in Richmond, Virginia, on May 25, 1904, son of Mrs. O. L. Brownlee (formerly Mrs. Edith Allen Melson) and the late Elijah Zenith Melson. He attended John Marshall High School and the University of Richmond, prior to his appointment to the U. S. Naval Academy, Annapolis, Maryland, from the Third District of his native state in 1923. Graduated and commissioned Ensign on June 2, 1927, he subsequently advanced in rank, attaining that of Vice Admiral, to date from February 1, 1960.

Following graduation from the Naval Academy in 1927, he remained there for the summer course in aviation, and in August of that year joined the USS TRENTON, operating on the East Coast and the West Coast and finally on Asiatic Station. He continued duty on Asiatic Station, serving in the USS PENGUIN (February-May 1929); the USS NAPA; the USS McCORMICK (August 1929-January 1931); and the USS PITTSBURGH. In August 1931 he reported on board the USS DUPONT, attached to the Scouting Force, and for two months, October-December 1932, was an Instructor NAPC, Naval Operating Base, Norfolk, Virginia.

In December 1932 he joined the USS DICKERSON as Engineer Officer and in June 1933 transferred to the USS NORTHAMPTON to serve as Division Officer until June 1934. Following instruction in naval engineering at the Postgraduate School, Annapolis, Maryland, he reported in June 1936, on board the USS PENNSYLVANIA. Detached from that battleship in June 1937, he next served as Engineer Officer in the USS PATTERSON and in June 1940 was assigned to the Division of Fleet Training, Office of the Chief of Naval Operations, Navy Department, Washington, D. C.

After the United States' entry into World War II, December 8, 1941, he transferred (December 28, that year) to Headquarters of the Commander in Chief, United States Fleet, Navy Department, and in March 1942 became Assistant Operations Officer on the Staff of the Commander in Chief, U. S. Fleet. On September 2, 1942, he assumed command of the USS CHAMPLIN, and for outstanding services in that command was awarded a Gold Star in lieu of a Second Legion of Merit with Combat "V," and also received two Letters of Commendation, with authorization to wear the Commendation Ribbon and Bronze Star (each with Combat "V"), from the Secretary of the Navy and the Commander EIGHTH Fleet, respectively. The citations follow in part:

Gold Star in lieu of the Second Legion of Merit: "For exceptionally meritorious conduct...as Commanding Officer of the USS CHAMPLIN during operations against enemy forces in the Mediterranean and Atlantic War Areas on March 12 and 13, 1943. While escorting a convoy of merchant ships from the United States to Mediterranean ports, (he) directed his ship in a vigorous attack against an enemy submarine after dusk on March 12 and, firing his guns and releasing depth charges throughout the night, aided in the sinking of the submarine, which was unable to inflict any damage on friendly ships. By his skillful handling of his ship and his direction and training of the personnel under his command, he contributed materially to the success of our forces in the area..."

Letter of Commendation (SecNav): "For heroic conduct...as Commanding Officer of the USS CHAMPLIN during the amphibious invasion of the Island of Sicily from July 10 to 12, 1943. Expertly maneuvering his ship and directing her fire, Lieutenant Commander Melson provided excellent gunfire support for our assaulting troops in the initial landing at Scoglitti, Sicily and, by his skillful leadership in shore bombardment of enemy positions, materially assisted the rapid advance of our invading troops..."

Letter of Commendation (Com8th Fleet): "For outstanding performance of duty as Commanding Officer of the USS CHAMPLIN while performing convoy escort duty in the Central Mediterranean on November 7, 1943..."

Detached from command of the CHAMPLIN, he reported in January 1944 as Commander Destroyer Division THIRTY-TWO, USS BOYLE, flagship. For meritorious duty in this assignment he was awarded two Letters of Commendation, with Bronze Stars in lieu of the Ribbon, from the Commander in Chief, U. S. Atlantic Fleet, the Legion of Merit, each with Combat "V," and the Silver Star Medal. The citations follow by date of action:

Letter of Commendation: "For...performance of duty as Commander of a submarine killer group during the period from March 29, 1944 to April 13, 1944. During the period that Task Unit 27.6.2 operated in search of a reported enemy submarine, (he) cooperated to the fullest extent with other search groups on a similar mission, thereby achieving maximum coverage of the area and preventing the U-boat from escaping. When a ship of (his) command made contact with the submarine (he) directed a coordinated attack which resulted in the destruction of the enemy. Later, in spite of unfavorable sea conditions and severe damage to one of (his) ships, (he) directed the rescue of the survivors of the destroyed submarine..."

Legion of Merit: "For exceptionally meritorious conduct...as Commander Destroyer Division THIRTY-TWO, in action against enemy forces during advanced operations in support of the Allied Armies in Italy, from May 15 to August 5, 1944. Skillfully directing the operations of his ship from the time of the break-through to the Anzio Beachhead and continuing through the coastal advance northward, (he) directed successful shore bombardments against enemy concentration and installations; protected Allied coastal shipping lanes against enemy submarine and surface attacks; and supported advance minesweeping formations engaged in clearing heavily mined approaches to ports occupied by our forces despite repeated hostile aerial attacks. By his leadership, initiative and devotion to duty throughout, Captain Melson rendered invaluable assistance to the Allied armies in overcoming enemy resistance in their advance into northern Italy..."

Silver Star Medal: "For conspicuous gallantry and intrepidity in action...during the amphibious invasion of Southern France between August 18 and 30, 1944. By skillfully maneuvering his ships and accurately directing their gunfire, (he) provided effective support for the advancing ground forces in clearing the enemy from coastal positions on the right flank of the central assault area. Braving strong return fire, he conducted the shore bombardment with competence and vigor, silenced several enemy shore batteries, saturated enemy troop and tank concentrations and harassed the interior supply lines. His able participation in this action materially assisted in the expulsion of the enemy from Southern France..."

Letter of Commendation: "For meritorious service as Commanding Officer of a United States warship, and later as Commander of a unit of ships engaged in escort of convoy operations in the Atlantic during the Second World War..."

In November 1944 he joined the Staff of Commander Destroyers, U. S. Atlantic Fleet, USS DENEBOLA, flagship, and for "meritorious service as Operations Officer and Assistant Chief of Staff to Commander Destroyers, United States Atlantic Fleet in support of sustained operations against enemy forces from November 1944 to August 1945..." he was awarded the Bronze Star Medal. The citation further states:

"Confronted with the many problems involved in the maintenance and improvement of a vigorous training schedule, Captain Melson ably handled the complex details of his assignment and, by his expert scheduling and control of the movements of the ships of his command, enabled them to obtain vital training while meeting their many and varied operations commitments. In addition, he rendered valuable assistance to the Commander Destroyers, Atlantic Fleet, in fulfilling his many and widespread administrative responsibilities..."

He reported in September 1945 as Chief of Staff to Commander Battleship Division FIVE, USS TEXAS, flagship. In December of that year he was assigned to the SIXTEENTH Fleet (Atlantic Reserve Fleet) as Operations and Plans Officer. From July 1947 to May 1948 he attended the Senior Course at the Naval War College, Newport, Rhode Island, and upon completion of instruction, remained there for duty on the Staff until July 1949. He next commanded Destroyer Squadron TWENTY, USS BARTON, flagship, and in July 1950 became Administrative Aide to the Superintendent of the U. S. Naval Academy.

In October 1952 he assumed command of the USS NEW JERSEY, and for "exceptionally meritorious conduct...as Commanding Officer of (that battleship), Flagship of Commander SEVENTH Fleet, and as Commander Task Group 70.1 during operations against enemy aggressor forces in Korea from April 8 to July 27, 1953..." he was awarded a Gold Star in lieu of the Third Legion of Merit, with Combat "V." The citation states further:

"Throughout this period, Captain Melson discharged his many responsibilities with exceptional professional skill and leadership and effectively directed the gunfire of his vessel and the Task Group under his command during repeated shore bombardment missions against enemy installations along both coasts of Korea, inflicting widespread damage and destruction on supply

V. Adm. C. L. Melson, USN, Ret.   Page 4

lines, shore batteries, industrial centers and troop concentrations. During the months of June and July when the tempo of fighting increased along the main line of resistance, he skillfully maneuvered the NEW JERSEY to lend close gun support to the friendly forces on the eastern terminus of the front lines which prohibited the enemy from launching successful attacks ...(and) contributed immeasurably to the success of friendly forces in Korea..."

Detached from command of the NEW JERSEY in October 1953, he reported as Chief of Staff and Aide to Commander Battleship-Cruiser Force, U. S. Atlantic Fleet, and in February 1955 joined the Staff of the Commander in Chief, U. S. Atlantic Fleet as Assistant Chief of Staff for Plans. While so serving he had additional duty on the Joint Staff of the Commander in Chief, Atlantic, and the Commander in Chief, Western Atlantic Area. Later, from October 1955, he served as Deputy Chief and Staff, and Deputy Chief of Staff for Plans and Operations, on the Staff of the Commander in Chief, U. S. Atlantic Fleet.

On March 17, 1957, he assumed command of Cruiser Division FOUR, comprised of the USS ALBANY (CA-123) and USS MACON (CA-132) home-ported in Boston, Massachusetts. On June 27, 1958, he became Superintendent of the U. S. Naval Academy, Annapolis, Maryland, with additional duty as Commandant of the Severn River Naval Command. He was Commander FIRST Fleet, from July 14, 1960 until May 1962, after which he commanded the United States Taiwan Defense Command. He was awarded the Joint Service Commendation Medal for "meritorious service...from May 8, 1962 to June 30, 1964..." The citation further states in part:

"...(He) exhibited exceptional qualities of leadership and professional competence in discharging duties of vital importance to the security of the Republic of China and the United States. Admiral Melson's endeavors to coordinate military commands and to secure the willing cooperation of Chinese forces were marked with a high degree of success, as attested time and again by the combat readiness of operational units in joint exercises and maneuvers observed in Taiwan. He manifested keen insight in identifying and eliminating potential problem areas and was unremitting in his effort to effect reductions in operating costs through the consolidation of functions, streamlining of procedures, and elimination of duplicative and nonessential tasks. His executive capability, thorough knowledge of the mission of the Taiwan Defense Command, and unceasing vigilance in safeguarding United States and Republic of China interests were key factors in the high level of effectiveness established and maintained by military forces under his command throughout the period of his tenure..."

In July 1964 he reported as President of the Naval War College, Newport, Rhode Island and in July 1965 was assigned additional duty as Commander Naval Base, Newport, Rhode Island. "For exceptionally meritorious service...(in that capacity) from August 1964 to January 1966..." he was awarded the Distinguished Service Medal. The citation continues in part:

V. Adm. C. L. Melson, USN, Ret.

"Dedicated to maintaining the academic reputation and prestige of the Navy's highest educational institution, Vice Admiral Melson conducted several studies and made a number of significant representations to his superiors in the Navy Department which resulted in a redefinition of the mission and functions of the Naval War College; notable improvements in the curricula of the resident schools, academic planning procedures, educational methods, student research, and the structure and quality of the faculty; clarification and redirection of planning for facilities development; and promotion of an overall Navy policy on professional education. At his urgent suggestion, a Committee of Advisors on the Naval War College has been appointed to conduct an annual objective examination of the College programs..."

He was transferred to the Temporary Disability Retired List of the U. S. Navy, effective January 25, 1966.

In addition to the Distinguished Service Medal, the Silver Star Medal, the Legion of Merit with two Gold Stars and Combat "V," the Bronze Star Medal, the Joint Service Commendation Medal and the Commendation Ribbon with three bronze stars and Combat "V," Vice Admiral Melson has the Yangtze Service Medal; the American Defense Service Medal, Fleet Clasp; American Campaign Medal; European-African-Middle Eastern Campaign Medal, with silver star (five engagements); Asiatic-Pacific Campaign Medal; World War II Victory Medal; China Service Medal (extended); Navy Occupation Service Medal, Europe Clasp; National Defense Service Medal; Korean Service Medal with two stars; the United Nations Service Medal; and the Korean Presidential Unit Citation Badge. He also has the Medal of Cloud and Banner with Grand Cordon awarded by the Republic of China.

Vice Admiral Melson's official home address is Richmond, Virginia. He is married to the former Vadah Lee Jenkins of Charleston, West Virginia, and has one daughter, Mrs. Nancy Lee McHugh, and two stepsons, Commander Arthur H. Cummings, USN, a Naval Aviator, and John A. Cummings, who served as a First Lieutenant (aviator) in the U. S. Marine Corps.

Navy Office of Information
Internal Relations Division (OI-430)
8 August 1966

DECLARATION OF TRUST

The undersigned does hereby appoint and designate as his (her) Trustee herein, the Secretary-Treasurer and Publisher of the United States Naval Institute to perform and discharge the following duties, powers, and privileges in connection with the possession and use of a certain taped interview between the undersigned and the Oral History Department of the United States Naval Institute.

1. Classification of Transcript.

   (✓) a. If classified OPEN, the transcript(s) may be read or the recording(s) audited by the qualified personnel upon presentation of proper credentials, as determined by the Secretary-Treasurer of the U. S. Naval Institute.

   ( ) b. If classified PERMISSION REQUIRED TO CITE OR QUOTE, the user will be required to obtain permission in writing from the interviewee prior to quoting or citing from either the transcript(s) or the recording(s).

   ( ) c. If classified PERMISSION REQUIRED, permission must be obtained in writing from the interviewee before the transcribed interview(s) can be examined or the tape recording(s) audited.

   ( ) d. If classified CLOSED, the transcribed interview(s) and the tape recording(s) will be sealed until a time specified by the interviewee. This may be until the death of the interviewee or for any specified number of years.

2. It is expressly understood that in giving this authorization, I am in no way precluded from placing such restrictions as I may desire upon use of the interview at any time during my lifetime, nor does this authorization in any way affect my rights to the copyright of my literary expressions that may be contained in the interview.

Witness my hand and seal this 5th day of December 1973.

Charles L. Melson

I hereby accept and consent to the foregoing Declaration of Trust and the powers therein conferred upon me as Trustee:

Vice Admiral Charles L. Melson, USN, Ret.   by John T. Mason, Jr.
Annapolis, Maryland   February 15, 1971

Mr. Mason: Admiral, I've been looking forward to this series with you. You've had a notable career, it certainly is something that should be preserved in the records of the Navy.

Would you begin in the proper way for a biography by telling me the date and place of your birth. Also tell me something about your parents, your father's business, the background to your family.

Admiral Melson: I was born in Richmond, Virginia on May the 25th, 1904. My father was Elijah Zenith Melson originally from Elizabeth City, North Carolina and my mother Edith Allen was from Allentown, Pennsylvania.

Mason: Was she a decendent of the founder?

Admiral Melson: No, she was not, that was just her family home.

They met in Richmond, Virginia and were married there in later years.

My father was born in Elizabeth, North Carolina. His family originally had been in the shipping business, which, of course, failed as a result of the Civil War. His family were in very poor straits and he had very little training in any field. He went to Richmond, Virginia, in his early twenties and became a machinist helper in the Tredgar Iron Works.

Mason: So he was kind of an apprentice engineer.

Admiral Melson: Yes.

He met my mother and they were married and lived in Richmond, Virginia where I was born.

In my younger years I went to grammar school in Richmond, later followed up by going to Binford Junior High School, and then John Marshall High School from where I was graduated in 1921.

After a year of doing postgraduate high school work, and attending University of Richmond for one year, I received an appointment to the Naval Academy.

Mason: You anticipated the appointment?

Admiral Melson: Yes, I did. I entered the Naval Academy on July the 6th, 1923, a day I'll never forget.

Mason: Tell me how you happened to seek a naval career, and what inspired you to do that.

Admiral Melson: In my younger life, particularly during junior high school and high school, I was much interested in military matters and was a member of the High School Cadet Corps and later a member of the Richmond Light Infantry Blues before I went to the Naval Academy. I had developed an ambition to go to sea in the Navy, and actually the Naval Academy was the place that I really wanted to attend.

Mason: Did you know something about the Naval Academy?

Admiral Melson: I knew very little. I knew more about West Point.

My ambition was to go to the Naval Academy, that's where I set my sights, and that's where I ended up.

Mason: Did you parents support you in this ambition or did they try --

Admiral Melson: They supported me, but very reluctantly.

Mason: What did you father actually want you to do?

Admiral Melson: He wanted me to stay in Richmond and go to Richmond College and become a lawyer. Actually I attended Richmond College for one year before going to the Naval Academy. (Richmond College is now known as the University of Richmond.)

At Richmond College I was a day student while preparing

to enter the Naval Academy.

Mason: What did you take especially, mathematics, in preparation?

Admiral Melson: Mathematics mostly.

Later in that period I attended Bobbie Werntz's Prep School here in Annapolis for about two months for a final briefing on the Naval Academy entrance exams.

Mason: From whom did you get your appointment to the Academy?

Admiral Melson: My appointment was from Mr. Robert L. Montague, the Representative of the third district of Virginia, a democrat.

Mason: When you were at Bobbie Werntz's this was an intensive kind of a prep thing. Was this for the examination which was held?

Admiral Melson: The work at Bobbie Werntz's was preparing for the entrance exams to the Naval Academy, and consisted primarily of studying old exams. At very frequent intervals we would take the old exams to see how we made out. In those days the exams had a way of repeating themselves, or maybe I should say that individual questions had a way of reappearing on the examination. So if you mastered most questions you might get by. That's the way it went.

Mason: How did you stand in your high school classes?

Admiral Melson: About the middle of the class, if that's a good way to express it. I was not a great student.

At Bobbie Werntz's we had opportunity to visit the Naval Academy frequently. I remember particularly meeting Admiral Henry B. Wilson one afternoon on a walk in front of Bancroft Hall; he was Superintendent of the Naval Academy at that time. We were all quite struck by his appearance. He had adopted some of the English characteristics of uniform dress. He wore a large white cap, carried a cane, hankerchief in his pocket, many ribbons on his chest. He made quite an impression on all the fellows that were around then. I've never forgotten that meeting.

Mason: Your entering class was a large one, wasn't it?

Admiral Melson: It was the largest class up to that time. Since then there have been larger classes. At that time it was the largest, numbering over a thousand.

I might say, of that thousand, about five hundred and seventy-five graduated, and five hundred and twenty-five were commissioned. Those are round figures.

Mason: And you people chose to call your class 'the vintage class', did you not?

Admiral Melson: No, I don't remember that.

Mason: That's what Don Griffin calls it.
   Tell me something about your Academy days.

Admiral Melson: I enjoyed my four years at the Academy immensely.

   Plebe year was difficult, but it never bothered me. I'm speaking now in relationship with other Midshipmen, upper classmen. And hazing didn't bother me. No one really hurt me in any way. I had the usual verbal hazing and things like that, but it was something that I didn't mind. I guess I was set to go through the Academy and just wouldn't be bothered with it. I enjoyed Plebe year immensely.

   The academic courses were not too difficult, because I had much preparatory work, for the first year. Later I was to find out that I would have a little difficulty.

Mason: That's of great importance, isn't it, to make the first year easier? Then you can face the difficulties of the advanced study.

Admiral Melson: My background of studies before going there

were a lifesaver and eased me through the first year at the Academy. From then on it was quite different. If I hadn't had that advanced preparation I sometimes wonder whether I would have passed in Plebe year.

Mason: That first year is not only a matter of study, but it's a matter of adjusting to a new kind of life.

Admiral Melson: Adjusting to a new life, and study along with it, and it can be very difficult.

The first year I was in the first company, the first battalion, where I remained for all four years. It so happened that the year that I entered they decided not to rotate Midshipmen between companies and battalions which had been done in previous years, so that midshipmen would become better acquainted with their classmates and with other people in naval service. So I remained four years in this one company and battalion.

Plebe summer was a very interesting summer because I made my first Midshipmen cruise. It was my first voyage on the broad Atlantic. We made a trip to Europe, which was doubly worthwhile. I not only enjoyed it, but I'm sure all my classmates did - our first European trip.

Mason: First European trip, and was it the event that caused you to be very solid in your determination to be a naval officer?

Admiral Melson: Yes, I think so.

Although I shoveled coal a good part of the way, it seemed to fit into the picture that I expected at that time, I was not unhappy with it. Of course, I didn't like shoveling coal any more than anybody else, but nevertheless I think I expected it.

The European trip, of course, made it doubly interesting. At the end of Plebe summer and the cruise, I had my normal thirty days leave which you had every year at the Naval Academy, which I spent at my home in Richmond.

Youngster year, or third class year, hasn't made any great impression on me, except that I had a very difficult time with Electricity, but I survived. I went to extra instruction several times in the afternoon, but I made it.

Our Second Class cruise was to the West Coast of the United States, not quite as interesting as the previous year, Plebe cruise, but we did visit places that I hadn't been before. I had not traveled much before I entered the Naval Academy. I found the Panama Canal to be of great interest, as well as the West Coast of the United States.

When we returned from Second Class cruise, we again went on thirty days leave which I spent at my home in Richmond.

Second class year wasn't too different from Youngster year as far as my life and what we did. Again I was very happy that I had had some previous advanced education before entering the Naval Academy. Most courses were not too difficult, but Electrical Engineering was still my problem child and I had difficulties there.

Mason: How did you do with languages?

Admiral Melson: I had had three years of Spanish before I entered the Naval Academy. Spanish was therefore the language that I chose. I passed but not well. I was not a star pupil in Spanish. I'm not today either.

The cruise after Second class year, First class cruise, was to the East Coast of the United States. It was interesting as far as going to sea is concerned, but not particularly interesting from the point of view of places we visited. Being First Classmen we had a great many more privileges than before. For that reason it was quite interesting and pleasant.

Mason: By this time I suppose you began to see the implementation of some of the things you'd learned in classes, the theories.

Admiral Melson: For instance at sea as first classmen we had to navigate. We had navigation, a training course, in second class year. At sea we had to take our sextant sights and work out our position which was checked by the ship's navigator.

Along other lines we had some experience with the radio and electrical parts of the ship and the engineering spaces.

We'd had some of this training before, but on the other two cruises more in the capacity of seamen or firemen doing the dirty work, the hand work.

On first class cruise you were in a sense more in the officer's status. We did observe how our studies were applied. It was quite worthwhile.

First class year was a wonderful year at the Naval Academy. I didn't have any trouble academically. I didn't star, but I didn't have any trouble. I was a three striper, first battalion sub-commander for the whole year, which to me was very rewarding.

I was in a place in life where I looked at things a little differently I guess. I did not worry much about what happened day by day, but I thought more about what we were going to do, what the future had to offer.

Little things like a round trip to Chicago for the Army-Navy game, which was a 26-26 tie, played in Soldier's Field, I made the trip being a three striper. I had a stateroom on the train to myself. We had three Thanksgiving Day dinners enroute and coming back. These things sound silly now I guess, but nevertheless they were a big thing to me at that time.

In Chicago the midshipmen marched down Michigan Boulevard to Soldier's Field to dedicate Soldier's Field. This was the reason we were out there. I'll never forget it was so damned cold. We went under arms, I was carrying a sword, and I think my hand is still around that sword, it damned near froze.

Mason: In retrospect, what is your estimate of the course of study at the Academy in that time?

Admiral Melson: In looking back I think that the course of study prepared us for what we were going to be - naval officers. I think it was fine. Of course we're talking about forty years ago, and times have changed a lot since. But I do think the course was so devised that they turned out dedicated and capable naval officers, not necessarily students, but naval officers, which was the prime mission of the Naval Academy. Of course, there have been many changes and for very good reasons. But I do think the Academy did quite well in training us.

Mason: I'm fond of citing what Admiral Tommy Hart told me once upon a time - how in his day the objective was to turn out officers who would be leaders and men who were gentlemen, the twofold intention of the course of study.

Admiral Melson: If you read the mission of the Naval Academy today as set forth in the plaque in front of the Superintendent's office, a bronze plaque down on the walk, I don't think it's any different from the one in the various publications.

We developed that mission here while I was Superintendent, and that mission was developed from the one which was in effect when I was a Midshipman. It's not much changed, just a slight difference in the wording if you compare the two. The only reason it was changed was purely to update the old mission.

The course is supposed to prepare young men to become dedicated naval officers and gentlemen, as Admiral Hart said. Incidentally, I was here with Admiral Hart for a short time, so I have slight knowledge of him.

One very amusing episode happened in first class year. We had all received our class rings at the end of second class year, which is routine. First class year, being a three striper, Admiral Hart entertained the stripers at dinner in his quarters. He had certain groups certain nights, he couldn't have them all at once.

I remember the dinner. The Harts had very beautiful dinner china. A lovely plate was in front of me. Everything was quiet, subdued conversation going on, and I raised my hand. I don't know why I did, but I raised my hand. When it came up my ring hit that plate and it rang like a bell. All conversation ceased. Everybody looked at me, and I was just thankful that I didn't break it.

Mason: Somewhere along the line you did get interested in aviation too, didn't you?

Admiral Melson: Yes, I did, but I had high blood pressure, slight hypertension, and I was not cleared for aviation, although I had some preliminary aviation training. I might hit upon that now.

After graduation I went on leave for thirty days, and

#1 Melson - 13

then I came back to the Naval Academy and spent I believe six weeks here in aviation training. We used to operate flying boats right off the river here in the Bay, and I enjoyed it very much. But I never really had a great desire to be an aviator because I knew that I probably couldn't. No one ever told me I couldn't and I passed the exam, but I always had a feeling that I couldn't. I never tried for it.

Mason: But all your peers were interested in it at that moment.

Admiral Melson: I just never had any great ambition to be an aviator, I just didn't have the desire.

After the six weeks aviation summer, I was ordered to the USS TRENTON, my first ship. I reported to her in Norfolk, Virginia.

The skipper of the TRENTON at that time was Captain J. K. Taussig, and the executive officer was Commander D. E. Cummings, who became a very close friend. He and his wife sort of mothered me during my first few weeks on the TRENTON. I had a very enjoyable time on the TRENTON.

Mason: The first tour of duty is always an important one, if you're lucky enough to get a good skipper it's very helpful.

Admiral Melson: Well, I had a good one.

When I first reported to the TRENTON I was ordered as assistant navigator, the navigator being at that time Commander R. M. Hinckley, now deceased.

With the assignment of assistant navigator I found that I knew more about what the ship was doing and where we were going and what was developing in the fleet than I would in a job down below decks, and I enjoyed it immensely. Fortunately I kept this assignment the whole time I was on the TRENTON. That involved much cruising on the East Coast, a trip to Guantenamo, passage through the Panama Canal, and a long trip to the Far East via San Diego, Honolulu, from Honolulu direct to Chefoo, China, which was the first port that I visited on the Asiatic mainland.

Mason: Did she go out to the Asiatic Station to join the fleet there?

Admiral Melson: After arrival the TRENTON was assigned permanently to the Asiatic Fleet. The time she was there wasn't just a trip, in other words.

Mason: That again was a very fortunate thing. That was a sought after tour of duty, wasn't it?

Admiral Melson: While on the TRENTON we visited numerous

Asiatic ports - Tsingtao, Takubar, Shanghai, and finally down to Manila.

While in Manila the Mayon volcano in Gaspe became active and we took the then Governor General of the Philippines, Henry L. Stimson, on a fast trip down through the Bernadino Straits to the town of Gaspe where Governor Stimson and his party went ashore to view the damage of the volcano. We then returned to Manila by the same route at a very high speed all the way to get Mr. Stimson back. It was to be a down and back quick trip.

Gaspe was just over the mountain from Manila. Going by ship you had to go all the way around and you couldn't go by car for many reasons - one being there weren't any roads. The second reason is the Huk guerrilas were even active in those days. So you had to go by water.

In February of 1929 I was detached from the TRENTON and ordered to the USS PENGUIN, another unit of the Asiatic Fleet. The reason for this detachment was that the TRENTON was being ordered home, having been on the Asiatic Fleet a little over a year.

When the ship was ordered back, they detached all the Lieutenants, junior Lieutenants, and Ensigns and left them on the China Station. They were ordered to various units of the Asiatic Fleet. They took on board some of the short timers out there that were due to come back. This all would save the government transportation.

#1   Melson - 16

Mason: And most of you young officers were unmarried still?

Admiral Melson: We were all unmarried, because the two year rule was in effect then.

I was ordered at that time to the USS PENGUIN, a submarine rescue vessel which had been converted to a gunboat for service in China; for the Yangtze and Hong Kong. But the PENGUIN was really not a river gunboat because her draft was too great for most of the river navigation.

I reported to the PENGUIN in Manila at the time. We were ordered to take the eclipse expedition to Iloilo to observe the next eclipse of the sun. We took all the eclipse party on board, went down to Iloilo, (these were scientists from the United States) where they set up their cameras and other equipment for watching the eclipse. We tied up to the dock in Iloilo and remained there for some two months.

Mason: What was their particular objective? What did they hope to learn from the observation?

Admiral Melson: Frankly I can't tell you. They would take pictures, I know, and take them back. I wasn't cut in on that part of it, so I didn't know. Because there were only two officers on the ship and we were quite busy running the ship, we had no part of that. They had their own party they did all of the work. I must admit at this time I don't know the objective.

Before the eclipse occurred the PENGUIN was ordered back to Manila.

So we started out from Manila in the PENGUIN with me, a young Lieutenant J.G., as the navigator. We made passage down through the Bernadino Straits and found our way out to Guam. I might add that it was a great relief when I saw that island come up over the horizon.

Mason: You mean you were apprehensive about your abilities as a navigator?

Admiral Melson: I was really on my own because the Commanding Officer was a Lieutenant, an extemporary, and he had very little training in navigation. The other two officers on board were both Warrant Officers, neither one of them knew how to navigate. So it was up to me and the strain was on me at that time.

When we arrived in Guam the crew of the PENGUIN went to the NAPA, which was then the tug in Guam, and the crew of the NAPA came to the PENGUIN. Then we set sail to come back on the NAPA, the seagoing tug.

After arriving in Manila, the NAPA was ordered placed out of commission. So I was ordered detached and ordered to report to the USS McCORMICK, destroyer 223, part of the Asiatic Fleet.

I left Manila on the USS CANOPUS, a submarine tender, for transportation from Manila to Shanghai where I joined up with the McCORMICK.

Mr. Mason: This certainly gave you a diversity of experience.

Admiral Melson: I reported to the McCORMICK in Tsingtao, China. The skipper of the McCORMICK was F. C. Denebrink, who later became a Vice Admiral. He was quite well known in the fleet at that time.

On the McCORMICK I was the torpedo officer and assistant engineer for my full tour of duty. On the McCORMICK I think we visited almost every seaport on the China coast. We went to Chinwangtao, Takubar, Chefoo, Wei-hai-wei, Tsingtao, Amoy, Forchow, Shanghai, Hong Kong, Singapore and Saigon.

Mason: What would be the purpose of these various calls?

Admiral Melson: It was customary at that time to have our destroyers patrol the whole China coast and touch these various ports for visits to become acquainted with the ports and also to show our flag in these various ports. We had American consular representatives in all ports that we visited. It was just part of the basic duties of the

Asiatic Fleet.

Mason: Was the country in a state of turmoil?

Admiral Melson: It was.

I left out one place - we went up the river Nanking. We were up there at the time that they were having a great deal of difficulty. This was at the time when Chiang-kai-chek and the Nationalist forces were trying to take over all of China.

I didn't know at that time that later years I was going to get to know Chiang-kai-chek much better and see him much more often than I saw him in Nanking, which was not at all.

Mason: Actually in a sense our fleet was protecting American citizens there.

Admiral Melson: Yes.

We had the Asiatic Fleet out there at that time. The PITTSBURGH was the Fleet flag ship. We had cruisers that came out occasionally, like the TRENTON and the MILWAUKEE, to bolster the Fleet from time to time. Then we had three squadrons of the old four-stack destroyers. We also had a squadron of submarines. We had, I'm not sure of the number, a few airplanes - seaplane type at that time.

Later while still on the McCORMICK we visited Saigon

and Singapore and made a dip across the line so that we'd become confirmed salt water sailors, after we left Saigon on our way back to Manila. We also paid visits to two or three other Philippine ports.

Mason: What was the attitude of the Asiatic Fleet toward the Japanese in that period? Did you have very friendly relations with them or what?

Admiral Melson: We were, I would say, on friendly terms with them.

I personally had made several boarding calls on Japanese vessels and had been there when they returned their calls. These were just social calls to meet with the Japanese.

Not only the Japanese, but the British and French also had ships there. We were not the only nation that had many ships there.

I know of no case where there was any problem at all. We did see a lot of Japanese activity. For instance in Chinwangtao the Japanese were landing troops and supplies which they pushed on into Manchuria, but we had no conflict with them, they just landed there.

Mason: Had we begun yet to consider them as a potential enemy?

Admiral Melson: I don't think so, no.

I think we considered everybody a potential enemy from the point of view of trying to judge what they could do and couldn't do, but we certainly were on friendly terms at that time, at least the navies were. I can't say about the State Department and other departments of the government, but we were.

It was a very interesting time, and it's just too bad that at that time and my age I didn't realize what might come in the future - I might have paid a little bit more attention to it.

Mason: You were still in the process of growing up.

Admiral Melson: That's right. I hadn't graduated yet.

Mason: Were you fortunate in getting other good skippers in other ships you went to besides the TRENTON?

Admiral Melson: To begin with I mentioned Captain Taussig on the TRENTON when I first arrived. He was later relieved by Captain Taylor, who was a very fine officer.

Then on the PENGUIN I had a Lieutenant Dick Tuggle, who I think was a very fine officer, who's retired and now lives down in Florida.

Then Denebrink on the McCORMICK was an outstanding officer.

He was later made Vice Admiral, he was aide to the Commander-in Chief of the Pacific Fleet, a very capable individual. He's retired now and lives in California.

Denebrink was relieved by Lieutenant Commander J. H. Lawson just before I left. We were all very fond of Joe Lawson. He'd been aide to the Secretary of the Navy. I didn't know him too well, because I wasn't there long enough.

On the CANOPUS, I wasn't on the CANOPUS long enough to even know who the Commanding Officer was.

In January of 1931, while we were in Manila on the McCORMICK, I was ordered to report to the PITTSBURGH for transportation home, having been on the Asiatic Station now since the middle of 1928. My skipper on the PITTSBURGH was Captain Halsey Powell.

I reported to the PITTSBURGH and was very promptly made the assistant navigator again. Denebrink, who'd been my skipper on the McCORMICK, was the navigator. He was coming home, too. So it all worked out very nicely.

The first event involving the ship, the PITTSBURGH, was when we were ordered to take the Governor General of the Philippines, who by now was Dwight Davis, and his daughter on a tour of the southern islands. We left on the PITTSBURGH and visited Saigon, Singapore, Medan (the name of the city, but I can't think of the name of the seaport) in Sumatra. From there we went to Bali and up to Zamboanga. There was a short stop in one of the islands on the way up. We stopped off at Zamboanga and then came back to the Philippines. That was an extremely interesting cruise because it was a political cruise, showing the flag among those islands. There was a great deal of entertaining. Although I was not directly involved because I was too junior, we did see a lot of top people come and go. Occasionally we were included in parties which made the trip doubly interesting.

Then after returning to Manila the PITTSBURGH was ordered home, having been relieved just prior to that by the HOUSTON, the new heavy cruiser which had just been commissioned. We set sail for home, going to Saigon again - that was the third time in three months - then Singapore, Ceylon, Suez, Alexandria, Naples, Gibraltar, and then Norfolk.

Mason: What was the purpose of coming back that way?

Admiral Melson: Everybody on the Asiatic Station, when they can, like to come back the other way around. I just put it as simply as that.

Really I think there was another purpose for this trip, of showing the flag again. The PITTSBURGH had been in the Mediterranean before, and she'd visited both these ports in years before.

It's about the same distance, it might have been a little shorter since we were coming to the East Coast. I just think it was a damn good reason.

It was a wonderful trip back and I enjoyed it, and it got us back to Norfolk.

Mason: Who was CinC out there with the Asiatic Fleet when you were there?

Admiral Melson: Charles B. McVay.

It was his son that had the cruiser, INDIANAPOLIS, torpedoed in the last few days of the war with a very important cargo.

When I first arrived out in the China Station Mark Bristol was Commander-in-Chief of the Asiatic Station.

Mason: Tell me about the incident of the Japanese flag.

Admiral Melson: While I was in Tsingtao on the TRENTON we had to dress ship in honor of the Japanese national day. The custom of that day was to full dress ship and hoist the flag of the nation that's being honored at the fore and then fire a national salute to that country.

On this particular occasion the ship was dressed at eight o'clock and the national flag of Japan was hoisted, but instead of going all the way to the foretop it jammed halfway up the mast. This was an error or a mistake on our part, and called for our taking action to appease the Japanese in case they took exception to it.

I might add that in the meantime while the flag was only halfway up the salute which had been scheduled had gone off according to schedule.

I was assigned the job of going around and apologizing to the various Japanese ships and explaining to the other foreign men-of-war what happened and what action we proposed to take to correct it.

I dressed in my cocked hat, frock coat, epaulettes, sword, white gloves, and in the Admiral's barge made the rounds of all the foreign men-of-war present.

In the course of these calls it was customary to be greeted aboard formally on each foreign ship and escorted to the wardroom, where you explained the purpose of your visit and then usually had a sip of the national drink before you departed.

As this particular trip involved visiting some ten foreign men-of-war I had to be very careful to make sure that I did not imbibe too much and not be able to go up or down the last gangway. Fortunately, it worked out all right.

Mason: The Japanese weren't offended by this --

Admiral Melson: The Japanese, if they were offended, didn't show any signs of it after I'd arrived to apologize. After I went back to the ship we went through the drill all over again and did it properly.

Mason: You returned home on the PITTSBURGH to Norfolk -

Admiral Melson: Upon being detached from the PITTSBURGH in July of 1931 I was ordered to the USS DUPONT, DD-152, a four-stacker. On the DUPONT we did normal cruising up and down the East Coast with one trip to the West Coast visiting various ports enroute. In the fall of 1932 the DUPONT was ordered back to the East Coast and went into the Navy Yard at Norfolk in October.

In October 1932 I was detached from the DUPONT and ordered to the Training Station at Norfolk as instructor at the Naval Academy Preparatory School. I reported there for duty and in my preliminary conversation with the Commanding Officer I indicated I would be willing to instruct in anything but English. I heard the following Monday when I reported was that I was to instruct in English.

Mason: Tell me about this preparatory school at Norfolk.

Admiral Melson: The preparatory school at Norfolk was a school run by the Navy for members of the naval service who aspired to go to the Naval Academy to receive instruction to prepare them for examination for entrance and their first year at the Naval Academy.

There is a similar school at Bainbridge today, except it's a much enlarged version of the school we had in Norfolk.

I reported to the school and I did my best in instructing in English, but I'm afraid it was not a particularly good job - writing composition, trying to teach Shakespeare's works, taking home themes every night to be corrected. It just wasn't my dish of tea.

Mason: The boys who came there, how did they achieve an appointment to that school?

Admiral Melson: They were selected by the various Commanding Officers and approved by the Bureau of Personnel. A certain number, the outstanding ones, of the group were ordered to the school for this additional education to help them to get into the Naval Academy. And I think the school did a very good job.

Mason: Was the other system of appointment by Congressmen and so forth inadequate for supplying --

Admiral Melson: That was in effect. This was to give the enlisted men in the Navy who didn't know a Congressman or couldn't get a Congressional appointment a chance to go to the Naval Academy.

I've forgotten the exact number, but there was an established quota each year for enlisted men from the service to go to the Naval Academy, but they had to pass the entrance exam like everybody else.

So that was the purpose of the school - to try to help these boys who presumably hadn't had the education of the ones they were competing with on the outside to get into the Naval Academy.

Mason: This was to make the whole system somewhat more democratic.

Admiral Melson: That is correct, and I think did a good job.

I know that over the years I've had officers come up and speak to me and say, "You may not remember me, but you taught me English at the Naval Academy Preparatory School in Norfolk." It sounds good to hear them say I taught them English, but I don't believe I did.

Mason: How long a course was this?

Admiral Melson: It was about seven months. They reported in October and stayed through the examinations for the Naval Academy, which were usually in April. At the end of April if they passed the exams they were ordered to the Naval Academy. If they didn't pass the exams they went on back to sea as sailors as they had been before.

While I was at the Preparatory School on Christmas Eve I received a phone call from Washington saying as long as my ship was in the yard for overhaul of which I was the engineer and in view of the fact that Lieutenant Wall, a classmate of mine, the engineer officer of the USS DICKENSON, also in the shipyard, had been ordered to the hospital with tuberculosis, and also in view of the fact that the DICKENSON was supposed to sail the day after New Year's, that I was going to be ordered to the DICKENSON as engineer officer.

So that ended my short tour of duty at the Naval Academy Preparatory School and I went to the DICKENSON.

Mason: What happened to all your students?

Admiral Melson: I guess they got somebody else. This was right at Christmas. Maybe they were trying to get rid of me.

I went to the DICKENSON as engineer officer and we sailed on the day after New Year's for the West Coast.

I remained on the DICKENSON until June of 1933, during which time we as before made the usual visits up and down the West Coast.

One thing that stands out in my mind during this period on the West Coast on the DICKENSON was a visit we made to Puget Sound. It was customary during this period for ships to have annual inspections, one ship sending groups of officers over to inspect another ship of their division or squadron.

The officers of the DICKENSON were going over to inspect another ship in the division leaving me behind as the only officer on board. We were then at anchor in the waters off of Seattle. During the time that they were gone it became necessary to move the DICKENSON because of other ship movements in the harbor and it fell upon me as the lone officer, and I might add for the first time, the responsibility to get the ship underway and move it to a new anchorage which I did. We felt very fortunate when I had her safely anchored in the new spot. It was the first time in my naval career that I'd ever had the complete responsibility for a ship underway.

In June of 1933 I was detached from the DICKENSON and ordered to the USS NORTHAMPTON, a heavy cruiser, CA-125.

The NORTHAMPTON was attached to the Pacific Fleet. Very little happened on my tour on her other than routine fleet maneuvers and operating in and out of the Los Angeles area.

Mason: This was at the height of the depression.

Admiral Melson: And I had a fifteen percent pay cut.

Mason: Yes, you had that. But did you not have limited personnel on board, too?

Admiral Melson: I don't remember that. On the NORTHAMPTON

I was the first division officer and had the number one turret. I don't remember the depression in any respect that way.

I do remember it in the sense that living for my wife and myself was quite difficult. At that time I was still a Lieutenant and didn't get very much to begin with, and on top of it a fifteen percent pay cut.

Mason: You didn't tell me when you were married.

Admiral Melson: I was married on October 1st, 1932 while I was an officer on the USS DUPONT. My wife and I were married in Yuma, Arizona.

Mason: This was shortly after you came back from the Far East.

Admiral Melson: Yes. She had been previously married and had two sons.

While I was on the NORTHAMPTON I had put in for the Postgraduate School, asking for an engineering course. I was accepted for the Postgraduate School and in April of 1934 I was ordered back to the P.G. School, then in Annapolis.

My wife at the time was pregnant, as a matter of fact very close to expecting. The Commanding Officer of the

NORTHAMPTON was very kind to detach me and let me drive across the continent at my own expense because the NORTHAMPTON was scheduled to come to the East Coast and he could have provided government transportation. So my wife and I and the two step boys drove across the continent.

Mason: This was an ideal time for you to come back for a land duty, wasn't it?

Admiral Melson: Yes.

Mason: Tell me about P. G. School.

Admiral Melson: I reported to the Postgraduate School in June of 1934, having been on leave since being detached from the NORTHAMPTON. I was assigned to the operating engineering course, which was a two year course.

There were two courses in engineering at the P. G. School at that time. One was two years, and one was three years. The courses were the same for the first year. At the end of the first year certain students were selected for a third year to go to another school, like California or MIT, for a third year in engineering. Then you continued on in your second year taking practically the same courses, except the people who had been selected for a third year took more math the second year.

I was not selected for a third year at another school, much to my regret. So I stayed on for the two years in the operating course. I found it to be a very good and very interesting course and it served me well in the following years.

Mason: Was there much of a contrast between the P. G. School and undergraduate work at the Academy?

Admiral Melson: Oh, very much. It was much more advanced. In the operating course, as we called it at the time, it was much more practical and not quite as much theory. And we had the advantage of having been at sea, and I had been in engineering at sea prior to that. So it all meant a little bit more to me at that time.

The third year course went into even more theoretical engineering in the latter part of the second year and before they went on to another technical school, where they received their Master's Degrees.

We were not awarded degrees from the two year course.

When I left the Postgraduate School I went to the Boiler Laboratory in Philadelphia for a short course in boilers, which was really a continuation of my course at the P. G. School.

When I left the P. G. School to go to the Boiler Laboratory I had orders to the USS PATTERSON, a new destroyer then being built in the Bremerton Shipyard. She was a new high pressure very modern destroyer.

While at the Boiler Laboratory I received change in orders because the PATTERSON's date of completion had been delayed. So they ordered me to the USS PENSYLVANIA as engineering officer with the understanding that a year later I would still be ordered to the PATTERSON when she was due to go into commission.

I reported to the PENNSYLVANIA in Long Beach, she being then the flag ship of the United States Fleet. That was a very good assignment.

Captain Milo Draemal was then the skipper and Commander Hinckley, who had been the navigator of the PITTSBURGH while I was on her, was then the executive officer of the PENNSYLVANIA. So I knew some people when I reported aboard.

I think I made some very fine friends among those who later became senior officers due to being on the flag ship where you get a chance to meet these people. All the other ships I'd been on had been rather small.

Nothing of any great note occurred on the PENNSYLVANIA, other than again the cruises up and down the West Coast and fleet exercises at sea.

Mason: Things were beginning to shape up in the Pacific in that time, were they not? Do you want to talk about that a little bit?

Admiral Melson: I'm afraid I didn't know enough about it to really talk about it at that point. I think just a little bit later I'll hit a better place for it.

In June of 1937, after having been on the PENNSYLVANIA a year, the Bureau of Personnel kept their word and ordered me to the headquarters of the 13th Naval District as perspective engineering officer of the USS PATTERSON.

Mason: I would think you would have been reluctant to go to her at that point.

Admiral Melson: I liked destroyers and had been in destroyers a long time, and I liked the engineering part of destroyers. This is what my training had been for up to this point. And I'd be in a little bit more important job, I'd be the Chief Engineer, where I'd just been a division officer on the PENNSYLVANIA. This was a brand new type, and it was a very much sought after assignment - duty on these new ships.

I reported to the PATTERSON September of 1937 and remained with the PATTERSON until May 1940, almost three full years.

During that time again we did a lot of cruising on the East and West Coasts, out to Honolulu and back. I found it extremely interesting in view of the fact that we were still experimenting with high pressure steam propulsion.

The PATTERSON's class is four hundred pound steam pressure

ship, and they had just moved up to six hundred pound ships which came later with the CRAVEN and GRIDLEY, the forerunners of the real high pressure steam.

The problems we had in keeping the plants going, preventing leaks which may sound funny at this point, but that's a great problem - we were just learning how to control high pressure steam. Of course, today we deal in twelve hundred and sixteen hundred pounds pressure with no problem.

Mason: What made this vast increase possible - different metals?

Admiral Melson: New techniques and new metals - people experimented with this in the laboratory.

Of course, aboard ship you have a little different problem. In a shore plant, where you have high pressure steam, everything's static, nothing is moving. In the ship you've got the ship moving back and forth, your joints vibrate, there's always a tendency to leak. And it's a particular danger to a leak because four hundred or six hundred pounds of steam at 850 to 875 degrees temperature - if it hit your hand would just cut it off. We never had many accidents like that fortunately, but it does happen.

Mason: What were you using in the PATTERSON and similar ships that was new in terms of metals? Had aluminum come in?

Admiral Melson: Aluminum had just been started, we just started using aluminum. We had a great deal of aluminum in the topside of the ship to cut down topside weight, to avoid becoming top heavy, where the older ships were built very sturdy with iron all the way up. The PENNSYLVANIA had steel practically up to the crow's nest. But in the PATTERSON everything was made out of light weight metal. Later years as they developed new metals they were used in newer ships, too.

Mason: Can you cite some interesting incidents on the PATTERSON?

Admiral Melson: The PATTERSON was one of the few ships built with only one engine room. Both the starboard and the port engines were all in the one space, where most ships before that and later ships built had two engine rooms to give better accessibility to the machinery for one thing. In the case of being hit or something it would provide more stability when flooded.

She had one engine room, and when the officer in charge of the plant sat at the throttle he could see both throttles right in front of him. He could reach out and touch the throttle practically, so you had better control in that respect. But the machinery was jammed into the engine room so compactly and close together that it was very difficult to maintain it and keep it going.

Mason: What was the real rationale for doing it that way?

Admiral Melson: To gain space in other ways, in other parts of the ship. If you could combine the two engine rooms here, you had much more space forward and aft than if you had all the space devoted to engine room.

Mason: But in wartime how vulnerable if a torpedo hit in that spot.

Admiral Melson: If a torpedo hit in that engine room you were gone, because that would finish you off.

Everything was in this one engine room - the main engines, both your generators, and everything you need to survive on. The only thing you really had outside of that generator was an emergency auxiliary diesel generator which could be cut in.

Mason: Was this type of ship continued in construction?

Admiral Melson: No. They built probably sixteen altogether of that one engine room type.

Mason: They naturally were operating in World War II.

Admiral Melson: Oh, yes, they operated and most of them were sunk sooner or later, not all of them, but most of them were.

The PATTERSON went down and the BLUE went down, the sister ship. I don't know about the CRAVEN. Not necessarily because of this one engine room, but it probably contributed to it.

I was detached in May of 1940 from the PATTERSON and ordered to the office of the Chief of Naval Operations in Washington.

My wife and I found a place to live in Arlington which was quite satisfactory, and to this day we regret we didn't buy the house, but we didn't.

I was assigned to the office of Fleet Training in the office of the Chief of Naval Operations. Admiral Herbert Fairfax Leary was the head of Fleet Training and his Deputy was then Captain Willis A. Lee. My immediate superior in the office of Fleet Training was a Lieutenant Commander Shultz. A classmate of mine, Johnny Waterman, was in the office with me. He had the submarine desk and I had the surface craft desk, with Shultz in overall charge. We ran the engineering competition for the United States Navy at that time. It was interesting but in some ways very dull work.

Mason: What was the objective of the engineering competition? What were you hoping to achieve?

Admiral Melson: The ships were all supposed to economize in the use of fuel oil. The competition was based entirely on the use of fuel oil. The ship that was the most economical, that used the smallest amount of fuel oil in her class, received the engineering E. That's stating it very broadly and very briefly.

The purpose of this office was to take the reports that were sent in and summarize and check them for accuracy, and see how each ship was doing in her engineering competition, then issue the award later.

Mason: Were there any lessons to be learned from any of these competitions, in terms of different design and so forth?

Admiral Melson: I cannot state for a certainty, but I'm sure that some changes in design came out as an outgrowth of this competition. I know that all the engineer officers aboard ships at sea, I had been one of them before that, did everything they could to try and reduce the amount of fuel oil that they had to use to accomplish their mission. I'm sure that these reports were analysed in the Bureau of Engineering to determine characteristics of new pieces of machinery and so forth to improve their efficiency and performance.

We had several people in the office who would audit the reports. Our job was to collect them and sort them out and determine who was the winner each year in each class. The competition was within your own class of ships. A destroyer did not have to compete with a battleship. Two destroyers of an entirely different age and type didn't compete against each other, they'd compete with those of the same class.

A lot of things entered into this - the amount of water you used, because you had to make your own water to re-evaporate it and that took fuel oil. If you didn't keep your evaporate scale down then you took more fuel oil to transfer the heat and make more water.

I was there until Pearl Harbor.

Mason: One enterprising engineering officer told me that in anticipation of this competition within his class he, while the ship was refitting, seized that opportunity to get improvements in the machinery so that he would be in a better position to compete, and then won the E.

Admiral Melson: There were so many things an engineer officer could do to improve his position - like draining his boilers, draining his evaporators, keeping the machinery operating at top efficiency all the time. All these things would reduce the amount of oil he had to use.

Occasionally somebody would think up a new wrinkle which would save oil. Some of them weren't always strictly above board, we had to ferret those out once in a while.

Mason: Was the Navy still under an economy blanket, so to speak, at that point in 1940?

Admiral Melson: Yes. We ran the engineering competition right up to the day the war started.

The day of Pearl Harbor, which was Sunday December the 7th, 1941, I had taken the two boys to a movie in Falls Church. While in the movies they announced that Pearl Harbor had been attacked and the fleet had been badly damaged. I took the two children and went to the ticket booth of the theater and called home. My wife told me what was on the radio, that perhaps I'd better come home right away, which I did.

Of course, all the grim details were being broadcast, not too accurately perhaps, but enough to indicate that something serious had happened.

I called Lieutenant Waterman, who was my associate in the office. We thought the best thing we could do was get in uniform and go down to the Navy Department, which we did. We got down to Main Navy and found it as dead as a doornail, except up at the front office and there nobody would talk. After hanging around for a time we decided we'd better go home, this still being Sunday afternoon.

Then later that night the radio message was broadcast, "All officers report in Monday morning in uniform," which we did.

That day I received orders to report to the Staff of the Commander-in-Chief United States Fleet, which was then being set up in the Munitions Building. Admiral Ernest J. King was coming in as Commander-in-Chief, but he had not arrived. This was all being organized.

I reported to that office for duty and did very little the first few days because they weren't organized. It was no longer war games, it was war.

Captain Lee, knowing that I wasn't busy at the time, got me and had me go over and collect some of the pictures that had been made in Pearl Harbor and flown back to Washington, to sort of get them in order and organized to be gone over in the CNO's office. That I did that week.

The latter part of that week the office began to get organized, and I was assigned with a Captain Derby of the Coast Guard to head up a Sea Frontier branch of that office. Captain Frog Low was overall head of the operations section.

Mason: Would you tell me something about Willis Lee? You got to know him well there?

#1   Melson - 44

Admiral Melson: Willis and Mabel Lee were among our very close friends. I had never met the gentleman until I reported to this office. I think he was one of the finest gentlemen in this Navy, very quiet, unassuming, very deliberate in his actions, and a very brilliant man. I had fairly close association with him in this office in CNO at that time.

I was in touch with him a number of times after I'd left the office, and also after he'd left and gone on out to the Pacific.

Later in the war, which I'll cover the rest of it later, he came back to the United States, apparently ordered back for rest because he had a very strenuous time in the Pacific. At that time I was on the staff of Commander Destroyers Atlantic, this was 1944. At that time he lived not very far from us there in Portland, Maine. We lived actually in the Portland Country Club, and they lived in a little house a little further up the road.

I used to see him almost every day because his flag ship was anchored out in the bay, the ship which provided his accomodations at that time when he was head of ComDevFor in Casco Bay. We used to see him quite frequently, had a drink with him once in a while, and enjoyed being with him. At this time I was the operations officer of ComDesLant in Casco Bay.

One morning I was down at the office early and had a

phone call from his flag ship saying that - Admiral Lee had had a stroke and they were sending him ashore in the barge, and would I arrange to have him met by an ambulance. When he arrived on the barge he was dead, he died on the barge on the way in to the beach.

He was a very very fine gentleman and quite brilliant.

Vice Admiral Charles L. Melson, USN, Ret.   by John T. Mason, Jr.
Annapolis, Maryland   March 10, 1971

Mr. Mason: Admiral, it's good to see you today. For the second chapter I think you want to begin at the outset of World War II, when you were assigned to the staff of Admiral King.

Admiral Melson: I was assigned to the staff of the Commander-in-Chief U. S. Fleet in February of 1942, just three months after the beginning of the war.

Mason: Where were you in the interim?

Admiral Melson: In the interim I went up one floor. The office of CNO that I was in was in the old Munitions Building. When Admiral King first set up his staff as Commander-in Chief U. S. Fleet it was set up in the same building with a number of people we know today as his aides, among them being Admiral George Dyer and Admiral George Russell.

I transferred from the office of Fleet Training up one floor to the office of Commander-in-Chief United States Fleet, Admiral King.

My assignment up there was as the assistant operations officer assigned primarily to duties in connection with the

Eastern Sea Frontier. My immediate superior was Captain Derby, United States Coast Guard.

At this particular period the situation on the East Coast was very bad as the submarines were sinking tankers one after another up and down the East Coast and in the Caribbean. It was indeed a very tough time for the U. S. as there were insufficient escort ships available to escort ships along the Coast and provision had to be made for convoys to get maximum advantage out of the small number of escorts available. The escorts were a few old four-stack destroyers, PC-boats, and SC-boats. This did not stop the sinkings, but it did reduce the number of torpedoings on our coastline.

Mason: What was your particular job in connection with the convoys?

Admiral Melson: Assistant to the operations officer for the Eastern Sea Frontier. As a Lieutenant Commander I was just a member of the staff of Admiral King who held the overall responsibility.

This particular section of the staff was charged with the responsibility of overseeing operations on the Eastern Sea Frontier. This, of course, was parallel to New York and under the command of the Eastern Sea Frontier and his staff.

My job was to represent or to keep track of all that was going on on the East Coast for the Commander-in-Chief.

Mason: Did you have anything to do with organizing the convoys?

Admiral Melson: Not directly, no. That was done mostly by the Eastern Sea Frontier itself, command in New York.

This meant keeping track of all the sinkings, all the actions that took place, setting up various bases for the submarine vessels to go into to replenish, and in general overseeing the operations on just the East Coast myself. There were other officers who took care of the Western Sea Frontier, Pacific, and other areas.

Mason: This was something that Cominch himself was very much interested in.

Admiral Melson: He had to be because we couldn't afford to have all these sinkings. In the first place we couldn't afford to lose the ships, and we couldn't afford to lose the fuel oil that was being lost in the ships. Later the submarines got into our other convoys carrying troops and supplies to Europe which all originated on the East Coast. To prevent a blockade of our coast we had to take some very positive action.

As I said before this meant establishing convoys, escorts of the convoys, and the various things associated with that type of operation.

Mason: What sort of tonnage was being lost monthly in these coastal convoys?

Admiral Melson: I don't remember, I can't quote, but I know it was very high. At one point it was so high, in 1942, that it became very critical as to how we were going to make out with the war.

Most of our oil was coming at that time from South America - Aruba, and areas down there. A large part of it, it was true, was coming from overseas, but a large part came from Venezuela. Convoys from Venezuela carrying fuel oil had to get through or we would have been very short on oil.

Also some of our oil was transshipped around through the Gulf to the East Coast. Of course, that was subject to attack by submarines. That was part of the Eastern Sea Frontier.

Mason: And what kind of connection or cooperation did you have with Admiral Hoover in Puerto Rico?

Admiral Melson: As far as I know it was very excellent, we had no close contact with him.

Mason: His job also was in that area, it involved convoys coming up out of the Gulf.

Admiral Melson: There were three frontiers. Eastern Sea Frontier was in most of the East Coast of the United States. The Caribbean Sea Frontier, which as it's name says, took care of the Caribbean area. And then the Gulf Sea Frontier took in the coast of Florida around New Orleans towards Tampico. All three joined down in the Caribbean area. There were three Sea Frontiers all together.

Mason: Did you have a chart room where you posted the data that you collected? Tell me about that.

Admiral Melson: We certainly did. It wasn't a chart room with all the features of the ones we know today with all the automatic things that they have, but it consisted primarily of just a series of charts on the wall with pins stuck on which showed the convoy and the submarines locations when we knew them.

Of all things we did know, and kept a record of, sinkings were the data that we knew fairly accurately. So we had a pretty good chart of that. It showed the area in which most sinkings were taking place, which indicated that submarines were active in that area.

One of the most active areas was off the coast of Florida

not far out from Miami. Another area was off Cape Hatteras. Of course there were a number of sinkings up off the New York - Long Island area. Those were the three principal areas in which there were sinkings.

There were scattered sinkings in the Gulf itself, and some to the south of Cuba towards Aruba in Venezuela. But they were concentrated mostly along the coast of Florida and Cape Hatteras as I remember.

Mason: Did the Sea Frontier command get involved also with the British naval command in Bermuda? They too were concerned about it.

Admiral Melson: There was some contact, but as I remember it not very much, not on the Sea Frontier side anyway. Bermuda really was a little far out from the coast. They had their own problems around Bermuda. We didn't have a great deal of contact with them.

Mason: Were they using PBYs for reconnaissance to spot the subs?

Admiral Melson: Yes, they were using them, but the PBYs weren't used a great deal at that time. They were based in places like Norfolk and Jacksonville and down off the Gulf. Patrols were flown with them and occasionally one of them managed to find a submarine.

I think you remember the old saying, "Saw sub, sank same." I think that's the correct thing he said. That was, I believe, a PBY.

Mason: You said your immediate superior was a Coast Guard Captain. How did the Coast Guard tie in with this picture?

Admiral Melson: The Coast Guard had a great number of ships in the escort group on the coast. As you know when we declared war they came over and became part of the Navy.

The Coast Guard officer was in there for the Coast Guard to coordinate the activities between the Navy and the Coast Guard in this Sea Frontier area, which they did very well.

Of course, the Coast Guard was not limited entirely to the coastal escorts. They had a number of escorts on the North Atlantic runs later as you will remember, the larger cutters.

The small Coast Guard cutters were invaluable in this work along the shore.

Mason: When the thing got pretty hot were there any problems with merchant seamen? Did they show a lack of interest in sailing vessels in that dangerous area?

Admiral Melson: No. As far as I know I don't remember any great reluctance on the part of the men to sail except they all wanted extra pay, which they got when they went into the war zone. Actually, if there were any difficulties it would have been in the New York office and we probably would never have heard of it, unless it was a large strike or something of that nature. I don't remember any thing like that that happened.

Of course, I was only in this particular office for about six months, when I left to take command of a destroyer.

Mason: In that brief time I was the counterpart of yours in ONI since I posted the sinkings too in Captain Bode's office.

You wanted to add something to the Sea Frontier story -

Admiral Melson: During the time that I was on Admiral King's staff as assistant to Sea Frontier operations the anti-submarine school set up down in Miami, Florida with Captain McDaniels as the head, in which they trained crews and officers for the PC-boats that were doing escorting along the coast. These were mostly reservists, a few regulars, but not very many. The regulars were getting very thin at that stage.

Mason: Tell me about this anti-submarine school. What was

it's scope? How large was it and what was the objective?

Admiral Melson: The school was set up to try and turn out a group of officers and men who were trained in anti-submarine warfare. They were manning PCs and SCs, primarily anti-submarine vessels. We just had to train a lot of people in a short time.

Captain McDaniels, who incidentally was a classmate of mine at the Naval Academy, was the one who set it up. He was a very strict disciplinarian and really did quite well in this particular job.

Mason: How heavily for this school did you borrow on the experience of the British?

Admiral Melson: If you mean by that, "Did we have any British officers there," I don't believe we did.

Of course, we did have people who had been to sea with the British and had some training and observation in British methods, but we didn't draw on them too strongly. This was new to all of us at the time.

It's true that the British had been involved earlier. I'm not quite sure when I say it, because I can't quite recollect the dates involved, but the British did not have the new anti-submarine gear which was coming out at that time, the stuff that we developed.

They had their own anti-submarine devices, and we came out with new ones. Actually while we drew on their experience we had to train them in a sense to use our equipment in cases where they got it for their ships.

I'm not sure, for instance, whether the fifty destroyers we turned over to England had the new anti-submarine gear or not. I know they had things like depth charges.

Mason: What was the new gear that we had developed? I know about the British asdic and the paravanes and so forth.

Admiral Melson: It was a development of the asdic as a matter of fact - sonar. It was new in the sense that it was more refined.

Of course, equipment like depth charges and depth charge throwers I think we all had at the beginning of the war. There were further developments as we went along, like the S. G. radar, which while strictly not an anti-submarine device was very useful in detecting submarines.

I can recollect an instance where we picked up a submarine on the surface by S. G. which resulted in it's sinking. I'll cover that story in more detail later. I'm just indicating the use of the equipment.

Of course, we relied heavily on direction finders in

#2 Melson - 56

locating submarines in operating at sea.

I can't say that these were really new, except that we had developed them more than the British and were continuing our development, where they'd been at in two years and should have been much farther ahead of us than they were.

Mason: We were not using carriers, were we, in escorting?

Admiral Melson: Not at this particular stage. That came along very quickly thereafter, using baby carriers.

As you know they were set up in attack groups and went to sea - a carrier and five or six destroyers, and operated individually in different areas. They didn't as a rule operate with convoys. They tried to operate in the areas of the greatest concentration of submarines.

Mason: When the baby flattops came along I know that a technique for night flying and observation of German submarines on the surface came into being. Was there anything of this sort at the time connected with the Sea Frontier in terms of PBYs - did they fly at night?

Admiral Melson: I feel pretty certain that they did. The PBYs operated at night I'm sure, because their endurance was quite long and they flew quite a long ways out. It was not just a daylight operation. Of course, they didn't have the equipment and the ability they developed as the war went along.

Mason: Did the german submarines in the coastal areas resort to what was known as the 'wolf-pack' or were they single submarines?

Admiral Melson: In the coastal areas, as I remember, they operated singly. The wolf-packs were generally further at sea. As a matter of fact they were used in the area just to the west of Iceland and that general area. Then later in the war they did move down south. But in the Sea Frontier areas it was almost always individual boats.

Mason: And where were they refueling? What sort of bases did they have?

Admiral Melson: I'm not sure I can answer that. I think most of them actually did not refuel during this early period of the war. They came over, stayed on the station as long as they could, and then went home.

I know that later they set up refueling from other submarines, some tanker submarines, and also even later they had tankers they rendevouzed with in certain areas. Just when this type of refueling started I don't know.

At the first part of the war I'm sure they operated on the basis of a round trip, operating out of some place on the European coast.

I know that we tried, later in the war, to set traps and pick them up as they came down around Iceland and north of England coming out in the open sea and catch them before they got over here.

At this period we didn't catch very many, they got through.

Mason: In this period that you were connected it was a very discouraging picture, wasn't it?

Admiral Melson: Very discouraging and there wasn't very much hope as far as getting convoys through.

This was the first six months of our engagement in the war and we were far from being ready. We needed ships, we needed men, we needed everything that you need to fight a war. It wasn't until a few months after that that we really got into the swing of things.

Mason: In the light of this discouraging situation, how did the high command act? What was their reaction to all of this - King and the others?

Admiral Melson: From my very limited point of view on this,

in that I was not in close contact with these people - King and the others, I think there was a great determination to go ahead and win the war. There was no sign of any giving up or quiting. It was just a question of finding out what you had to do to win and getting on with it. There was never any sign of discouragement that I could note.

In the leaders that we had at that time, again I'm talking about the first six months because that is the period which we were in, there were not any weak individuals in command positions at that time. If they were, they didn't last very long with Ernie King.

I just think that we were very fortunate in having an excellent and outstanding group of senior officers who took charge at this time, and I include Ernie King in that group.

He picked a staff, I'm not talking about myself because he picked me out of the woods, of people like Frog Low and Dick Edwards and Russell Wilson and many others that you can name of really outstanding officers.

Mason: Was Cook there when you were there?

Admiral Melson: And Cook, yes. There are any number that I could name that really were, I think, a very fine group of officers. Of course, I have to admit that they were in a sense hand picked to come to the job to begin with. They were just not there, they were all brought in.

Mason: They were largely men whom King had known.

Admiral Melson: Oh, yes, people that he had known and who had worked with him before.

People like Admiral Edwards - who really did an outstanding job, I think. I speak of him in the sense of being his subordinate. My observations were probably different from people who were higher up in the chain of command, but just watching him and his people who worked this business was tremendous. He did a tremendous job, along with the other members of the staff. Hours meant nothing when they had work to do.

And I guess that's true today of people who get involved in current problems.

Mason: During the time that you were with the Sea Frontier, since it was such a frightening situation for us with so many sinkings and so many convoys disrupted, was the Press not anxious to have information of this? And what was the attitude in the Department toward the release of unfavorable information to the Press?

Admiral Melson: I don't believe I can answer that question, other than give an opinion, because I was not in any way connected with the Public Relations outfit at that time.

Mason: Did any of the sinkings which you recorded appear in the Press?

Admiral Melson: A lot of them appeared in the Press. How they got it I don't know. It could have come from sources other than the Navy Department.

The ships were sunk, many survivors were picked up and they were all brought into ports along the coast. I'm sure that newspaper people were very much on hand to greet all these people and to get first hand accounts of what had happened.

I don't believe there was any attempt to try to hold back any of this information. As far as I know there was no censorship - there again I'm speaking from memory.

I know that my office didn't give out any. If it went out, it went out through a higher office.

If you remember the papers in those days - pages were just covered with these submarines activities, some pictures, and big headlines of what was happening along the coast. A lot of that probably came from local news agencies along the coast which interviewed these survivors being brought in. That you couldn't hold back very well.

I don't know just what was released officially. I knew people knew there was much submarine activity and sinkings along the coast because it was in the paper, but how they got it, I don't know for certain. George Russell might be able to tell you that, he was flag secretary at that time, and probably George Dyer, too.

Mason: I know that within a short time you went to sea as Commanding Officer of the CHAMPLIN. Were you anxious to get out to sea?

Admiral Melson: During this period in Cominch's office all the young officers that I knew in Washington were anxious to get out and get in the war, and I think that I was one of them.

I went to Admiral Wilson, the Chief of Staff, and indicated that I would like to be released to go to sea, preferably in destroyers. He knew how I felt, but he suggested that I wait a little while.

Mason: What was the actual policy in Cominch at that time?

Admiral Melson: I don't know that they had a policy, but after all the staff had just been organized and they were trying to get officers to keep the staff going. They were reluctant to let somebody go unless they had a replacement for him.

Admiral Wilson told me that he thought it would be beneficial for me if I'd just wait a little while. So with those remarks I went back to my office.

Shortly thereafter, in September of 1942, I received orders to put the USS CHAMPLIN, DD-601, in commission. The CHAMPLIN was being built in Fall River shipyard close to Boston, Massachusetts.

My wife and I drove to Boston and we started hunting for a place to live during this commissioning period. Considering that we had three small children it was not easy in this shipbuilding town and this war period. We finally ended up by staying at the Blackhorse Inn, which was just outside of Fall River. I might say that we were very very happy during that period.

Mason: How long a period was involved in waiting for her commissioning?

Admiral Melson: About four months from the time I reported.

During that time I was attached to the Supervisor of Shipbuilding in Quincy, Massachusetts which is all in the same area. I spent my days becoming acquainted with my new command to be.

I actually reported to the Supervisor of Shipbuilding in August, and in September the ship was commissioned with me as the Commanding Officer at the Boston Naval Shipyard.

Mason: You had to assemble the crew and train the crew and all of that?

Admiral Melson: The crew, of course were ordered in ahead of time to the Supervisor of Shipbuilding. While they were under him they were sent to various schools for preliminary training, particularly in anti-submarine warfare and things of that nature. They all went to school somewhere in the specialty that they were primarily interested in.

We went into commission in September of 1942. Our shakedown cruise consisted primarily of running outside of Boston, trying to see that everything worked and becoming acquainted with the ship and so forth, and hopefully not to see a submarine at this stage.

Mason: What sort of a complement did she have?

Admiral Melson: I think it was 315, I may be a little short on that.

Mason: Were there any changes to be effected in the ship before her commissioning which you saw to? You were there and knew what was going on and what they were putting into her --

Admiral Melson: During the period in which they were still building after I reported, the officers who were assigned with me and myself made a daily inspection and checks of the ship to see that the plans were being carried out and to see that everything was right and that everything worked. We went around and watched all the equipment operate.

This not only had the advantage of checking it's operation, but it also gave us a certain amount of education in the equipment that we were going to have to use later. There was a lot of new equipment.

For instance one of the new pieces of equipment was the Sugar George radar, usually called the S. G. This was a new surface search radar which very few ships were getting at that time. It was a completely new piece of equipment. Very few people knew much about it, including ourselves.

It turned out to be one of the most valuable radars we had during the war, as far as surface action is concerned. I might say that occasionally it did pick up low flying airplanes, too, but it was primarily surface search.

Mason: This was a highly secret bit of equipment, was it not? How was it handled - it's installation?

Admiral Melson: Very highly secret at that time.

I don't remember any particular security precaution in it's installation. Of course, at that time the shipyard was under very strict security control and visiting was not allowed on ships. It was not under lock and key, but it was not open to the general public by a long shot.

Mason: I recall an account of the radar equipment that was installed on the WASHINGTON before she went over to Scapa Flow and the fact that some of it was not actually put on, the visible part, until after they put to sea.

Admiral Melson: That wasn't true in our case.

When I say the Sugar George radar was new, it was new equipment aboard ship. It had been developed up to that time, so I'm sure people knew about it, but very few ships had received it up to this time. It was very new in that respect.

I don't remember any special security precautions other than the normal precautions that were in effect during the war.

Operating outside of Boston a few days, going back and forth into the Navy Yard, we were finally ordered to report to Commander Destroyers Atlantic in Casco Bay.

Mason: There obviously were no bugs that showed up that had to be corrected then?

Admiral Melson: No serious bugs, we had lots of them, though. At that time I might say a lot of bugs were overlooked in order to get the ships to sea, but we had no serious difficulties.

The CHAMPLIN was a well built ship, and well put together.

The tonnage was 1630, not a big ship, but big to me at that time. It was my first destroyer command and to me she looked like the NEW JERSEY did in later years. She was a very good ship and very capable.

I might put in here that during the time I was in command of her, which was about two years, I never found any real serious deficiency in the ship itself. I don't mean that every thing operated all right a hundred percent of the time, but she was always ready and always performed. I only know of one time that she really let me down, and that was when we lost all power, but we were short on fuel oil to begin with.

We had our training period in Casco Bay. We performed little routine escort jobs, like escorting the INDIANA and the cruiser COLUMBIA from Casco Bay to the Canal Zone. They were on their way west. We also escorted the USS BOISE on our way back from the Canal Zone, she was coming back having been so severely damaged in the South Pacific, she was in very bad shape. We were glad to get her into New York. This was the first escort duty we had.

Mason: In this first escort duty were there any encounters with German submarines?

Admiral Melson: There was no encounter at all. This was on the coast, escorting from New York to Panama, and from Panama back to New York. There were no encounters at this particular time.

Of course, I must say I think we had pretty good information on submarines in the area. They kept us pretty well informed, and they kept us routed out of submarines areas.

At that time every ship that sailed on the coast was routed by the Eastern Sea Frontier in New York. They were told exactly where to go and what speed and what points to pass through. They usually were routed around any suspected submarines, so the chance of encounter with combatant ships making pretty good speed was slim.

Mason: What were the sources of this good information on submarines in the area that came out of the Navy Department?

Admiral Melson: Office of Naval Intelligence I think is where it originated. They kept the submarine plot.

I don't know the inner workings, I only know what we got, but they were broadcast from Washington at least daily giving submarine summaries of sinkings, sightings, and suspected locations, and all the D.F. information that they had from the various D.F. stations on the Atlantic Coast.

This was all promulgated to all the friendly ships at

sea. The routing authorities in New York and in all the Sea Frontier - I speak of New York because we were operating in the Eastern Sea Frontier mostly - broadcast this information at regular intervals. They told you where to go, how fast to go, what points to pass through, and all of this information. So they tried to route you around danger areas.

They did the same thing with convoys a little later like they did during this period, but unfortunately the convoys were slow and unwieldy in maneuvering, and it was hard to route them around all the suspected submarines in the Atlantic at that time. So the submarines got in on the convoys.

In this case where three destroyers were escorting, in one case a battleship, and in another case a cruiser, they were easily maneuverable. They had high speed, they could maneuver around these spots with ease. That is why we didn't get any attack.

Mason: One officer told me that the reports from the Navy Department - forecasts of where the submarines would be at a certain time were actually uncanny in accuracy.

Admiral Melson: If I can jump ahead of myself - I had command of a destroyers division later when we escorted a group of tankers from New York to Belfast. It was called a fast convoy, our maximum speed was about fourteen knots, which was still a fast convoy. We went across without ever sighting a submarine or having a contact.

I was the escort commander at the time and we kept a daily plot of all information coming out from Washington. We thought we knew exactly where all the submarines were.

Cominch, which was the controlling authority on ocean convoys at that time, routed us and told us exactly what we were to follow. When they saw us heading to what they thought was a group of submarines, they'd change our course. We'd go around or up or change our speed. They really conned us all the way across the ocean. At one point we passed a wreckage between two wolf-packs, one to the north and one to the south, without making a single contact.

We got in with no trouble. So in spite of the statements they saved a lot of ships, too, I'm sure.

Mason: In the CHAMPLIN did you have any contact with the QUEENS?

Admiral Melson: Not directly. I think twice when we were down at the New York area we saw the QUEENS go through. They usually had a destroyer escort for the first twenty-four hours out of port, and they usually made such high speed after that that the destroyers couldn't keep up with them. In the second place the best protection they had was their speed, so they traveled at top speed. When you saw one come over the horizon it wasn't very long before he passed out of sight on the other side. They'd make about twenty-nine or thirty knots.

Looking back on all this - it was a very interesting period. I regret to this day, and regretted my whole career, that I didn't keep a diary. That was violating regulations then.

Mason: Did you get involved in escorting any convoys to mid-ocean point and the British take over?

Admiral Melson: No, the ones we escorted we took all the way.

We sailed across with our squadron in December of '42 to Casablanca. This was in connection with providing cover for the attack on Casablanca. We were not one of the invasion force, but we were part of the follow up force.

We were in Casablanca about three weeks, along with the JEAN BART, she was tied up there at that time. It was a very interesting period. This was a year later after the start of the war.

The landing at Casablanca had just taken place, and we were part of the follow up force. We stayed in there and furnished anti-aircraft protection inside the harbor for about three weeks. The Germans were bombing the area almost every night. We came out of it with clear skin.

There were two things of particular notice, as far as I was concerned at that time. Being tied up inside the breakwater we all got to go ashore occasionally. Things to drink were rather scarce at this period. One evening we went ashore and met up with the man who raised ships, the salvage officer, Sullivan. He had brought up some wine from a sunken ship so we had some very good drinks.

Also, on leaving Casablanca at this time there was a very strong swell coming in from the northwest which were casting immense breakers up against the breakwater. The breakwater at Casablanca is practically in open sea, with the big seawall built right out into the ocean. As we went out the harbor we went down parallel to the breakwater, and the minute we got outside these big breakers hit us. I don't think I've ever rolled so much in my life so far. They just laid us right over on our side. Finally we got squared away and headed out and where the swells didn't bother us.

That was rather, in a way, a frightening experience. I don't think we would have capsized. Of course if you go over far enough that you take water in, then you could. It was just a condition which was not very conducive to keeping the skipper in a good frame of mind.

We went back to New York. As at the end of every trip across the Atlantic, we went back to Casco Bay for a training period. We had a few days of leave in New York and then took off for Casco Bay, for training where it was freezing and snowy and icy.

Mason: Why was this training necessary when you were actually operational?

Admiral Melson: To keep us all in trim, I guess, and to keep us up on what we were doing. They developed new methods. This business of searching for submarines with sonar was not an easy job, and the operators would get cold on the job - they'd lose a little knack of picking out a ping returning and so forth.

And we always had new men. There was always our experienced people being taken away from us to put new ships in commission, and we were always being fed in new men. So we had to go back through these training periods, and I think they were good.

Then when we finished these training periods, we'd go in our case to New York most of the time. We'd spend about a day and a half in New York, and then off we went on another convoy. So we didn't spend much time in the United States.

My wife use to ride the train to New York when we came in, and spent a day or two with us. We had a hard time finding hotel reservations and things like that. She stood up on the train I think most of the time - the New York to Washington trains were so full. That part of it was not very pleasant, the traveling. We enjoyed being together in New York. Of course, we all went out and had big steaks and things like that. That was in between trips.

Mason: Roughly how many units of the fleet were tied up with this convoy work out of New York at that time? I'm just trying to get some idea of the extent of the operation.

Admiral Melson: I don't know if I would attempt to guess. I know every destroyer on the East Coast at that time was involved in it. All sorts of figures come to mind, but I can't substantiate any one of them particularly. I just know there were a lot of ships tied up with it. Not only were there destroyers, there were Coast Guard vessels. PCs, and EIs. Occasionally the battleships and cruisers were involved for a troop convoy. Everything we had in the Atlantic Ocean I guess was involved in it, unless they were in the navy yard. I just can't put a figure to it.

Mason: Did the Canadian navy participate as far south as New York, too?

Admiral Melson: Not very often. They ocasionally had a ship, and a British ship occasionally. They usually dropped off somewhere along the route - either joined up out of Halifax or went into Halifax coming back, or came out from England and joined up for a short distance and go back in, to build up the size of the escort in the worst waters off England and Iceland. On the southern convoy trips I don't remember Canadians and British being part of them, not the ones I was on.

Mason: Were you involved at all on the Icelanic route?

Admiral Melson: Only partially. What I mean by that is - we'd go up on the fast convoy going into Northern Ireland. We'd go up by Halifax, tankers and cruisers, and take the great circle across from there. We got into some of the same waters, but we didn't get quite as far north as the convoys that went to Murmansk and Iceland. I was thankful we never got ordered to Iceland.

Mason: So then you didn't really have any contact with Dan Gallery up there?

Admiral Melson: No, I didn't. As a matter of fact I didn't have any contact with any of our carriers, the few we had. We'd hear about them. They were under Cominch's direction entirely, and he ordered them to areas of submarine concentration. Unless you just happened to run into them you probably wouldn't see them.

In the case of some of the troop convoys that never happened when I was there. They had a carrier operating in the vicinity, but even then you'd never see them. Occasionally you'd see a plane from them.

Mason: When I mentioned Gallery - he was originally connected with the PBY base in Iceland, before he became involved in the carriers.

Admiral Melson: I had no contact with him.

On the convoys to Northern Ireland, about two days before we arrived in port or maybe three, long range aircraft would come out from England or bases in that area and scout ahead of the convoy and on the sides to keep in contact with us all the way in. Twice during these trips a German came out also, so they were keeping track of us, too.

Mason: Did their intelligence seem to be awfully good as pertaining to our convoys?

Admiral Melson: I think it was pretty good. Of course, they were getting it I guess from three sources. Their own submarines were, of course, getting contact reports. They had some aircraft contact. And, of course, directional finders would find us - that was used at that time for detecting convoys.

We were supposed to sail under radio silence, but quite frequently some reason came up that you had to communicate. We did it in various ways, like the spurt communications and things like that. The message was made up in abbreviated form and it was sent in abbreviated form by radio. So you only hit the key a couple of seconds, and it was all over.

On the fourth of March we sailed from New York, in '54. This was UCG-6, which was quite a well known convoy for this particular period. It was a slow convoy from New York to Casablanca.

During this particular trip we lost five ships, which was one of the worst ones that I was with, out of about fifty ships. It was a slow convoy, mixed, some LSTs and some merchant ships.

We averaged about nine knots. I went with one later that only averaged five, but these were a little faster groups of ships. The LST was only good for eleven knots at that time wide open.

One of the ships torpedoed in this trip was the WYOMING, a French ship. She was a rather large French vessel. She had on board a number of second Lieutenant Army aviators which we picked up and had on board and took them to Casablanca.

On this five were torpedoed and the rest of them got in. This was the convoy in which about a day out, because we had so many survivors on board, we were detached and sent ahead to go on into port, having been relieved by another destroyer.

This was the time we lost suction and lay dead in the water for a longer period than I like to remember in a submarine area. Finally we got suction back and went on in at high speed.

This was also the time we lost the teaspoons to the group of aviators, which I believe took our silverware.

We usually went into a port like Casablanca and had a turn around period for a few days. Then we escorted another convoy back to the United States.

Mason: What would you be bringing back in the convoy?

Admiral Melson: After the ships unloaded you had them sail back in a convoy.

Mason: What did they use as ballast?

Admiral Melson: Probably water. Most of them were light anyway at that time. I don't think they had any problems. Of course, tankers always took on water. I don't know, they may have taken something else, but I doubt it.

Mason: There wasn't anything in the way of materiel or produce that they could bring back?

Admiral Melson: No. Everything was going in, nothing was coming out.

Our next escort job was rather interesting. We escorted a convoy of LSTs and miscellaneous craft to Oran, that's inside the Bay this time, via Bermuda. This, incidentally, was taking ships and men and materiel over preparing for the next step which was the invasion of Sicily.

In this convoy we had six destroyers. Two of them, the CHAMPLIN and the PARKER, had S. G. radars. They were the only ones in the convoy that had it.

There were about seventy ships in this outfit consisting of LSTs, tugs, mine sweepers, small mine sweepers, submarine chasers, and all the various small craft that they'd need in the Mediterranean. It was a question of sailing and repairing ships all the way across. The small craft had to refuel almost every day, couldn't make much speed with that going on. It made them very vulnerable and very slow. We didn't have an attack and got away with it.

Incidentally, I missed one thing on the UGS-6 convoy which I shouldn't have missed. It was on this occasion that we picked up, while we were with UGS-6 near the Azores, a submarine coming to attack the convoy.

It was on the surface. The radar picked it up and finally we made sight contact with it - we could see this boat coming in. We opened fire on it and it submerged. We passed over it and dropped depth charges. We saw no more or heard no more of the submarine. We stayed in the area until morning with another destroyer. Finding nothing but a little oil on the surface, we finally went back and joined the convoy.

This was before the occasion of losing suction and being dead in the water.

We heard no more about this submarine, but finally it was listed by the Germans as being lost in this particular area so we received credit for that submarine. But we gave credit to the S. G. radar for the pickup.

Mason: There was a very odd convoy that attempted to cross the Atlantic, I've found very little on it. I recall from my personal experience references to it in dispatches at that time. Admiral Bernard Bieri said something about it. I wonder if you have any knowledge of it. That was a motley collections of ferry boats and so forth, which were attempting to go across - this was one of Churchill's schemes. According to Bieri the whole thing was wiped out because it was so slow and so vulnerable.

Admiral Melson: No, that one I don't know about.

After getting this convoy of tugs, LSTs, and so forth into the Med and at Oran we underwent a period of training at Oran, the destroyer forces being under the destroyer command in Oran. Whenever a ship went in like this in the convoy and had to lie around and wait for awhile they always attempted to keep you up and keep you sharp, and didn't have any let down period at all.

Then we escorted a British convoy during this period we were in Oran from Gibraltar into Oran. This was one of our contacts with the British. This was completely British escort and we just joined it for the short legged trip from Gibraltar.

Mason: What was the danger to a short legged convoy like that - largely planes, based where?

Admiral Melson: Air attack. The German planes at that time were based in Northern Italy and they also came from Germany. These were all long range planes. They were not fighters or anything like that, these were the long range aircraft. They attacked with bombs and aerial torpedoes.

I've forgotten the name of the torpedo, but they had a torpedo at that time that they launched and controlled from the plane after it launched. They had an aerial following of some form. They'd launch it, stay away from it out of the range of our guns, and then try to direct it into a ship.

In July of 1943 we took part in the invasion of Sicily, in which we acted as screen and fire support vessel. We were one of the lead destroyers going into the beach leading the convoy in. We didn't take much fire, but we took some. Then we stayed around and gave fire support for some time thereafter.

In September '43 we escorted a fast troop convoy across to Northern England, and then escorted a fast troop convoy from Northern Ireland (Belfast) to the Med. This was an interesting trip, we went down the English coast.

Mason: That took you, of course, past the very dangerous Bay of Biscay, didn't it?

Admiral Melson: Yes. We didn't have any contact, nothing really happened until after we got into the Med. Then there were a number of planes reported. Then, finally, the transport SANTA ELENA was torpedoed. We assisted in the pickup of survivors.

We made several voyages in early 1944 to Northern Ireland, New York, and South Wales - to show you the places we were going.

Mason: All this time you were under the convoy command?

Admiral Melson: That's correct.

Mason: And there was no rest, you just kept on -

Admiral Melson: There were short periods in port, but not very long. We kept going.

Out in the middle of the Atlantic rolling around you as the skipper lie up there in your bunk and think about a submarine. I used to once in a while get a sniff of fresh bread being cooked - the cabin is right up above the galley. I'd send down and they'd bring me a piece of fresh bread, half a loaf. I'd cut it open and put butter in it. It was the most delicious thing at three o'clock in the morning that I could remember - hot bread and butter. Incidentally, I wasn't gaining weight eating that.

Mason: Were there any close calls for you during this time?

Admiral Melson: No. Once or twice the sound people reported that they heard torpedoes which they said had been fired at us, but I never could verify the fact that a torpedo was fired. We were never, that I know of, in any great danger of any sort. Except while we were in the Med there was always the danger of torpedo attack by the German planes. Of course, I guess you might say there was always the danger of submarine attack, but we never had any really close calls. I'm thankful for that.

Then about this time I became Commander of Destroyer Division 32, which included the CHAMPLIN - that was in January of 1944. I stayed on the CHAMPLIN and flew my pennant from the CHAMPLIN. We did the usual routine things - around the coast and up and down.

Then in February of 1944 I was relieved by Commander Jack Shaffer. He'd been Admiral Russell Wilson's, who was then Chief of Staff to Admiral King, personal aide. He said he wanted to come and relieve me of the CHAMPLIN and Admiral Wilson arranged that he did.

During the early part of this period in 1944 we were training in Casco Bay. While there a report came in of a submarine operating down off Nantucket. Two divisions of destroyers were ordered down to try and locate the submarine, and my division was one of those divisions.

Before this period I had transferred from the CHAMPLIN to the BOYLE, which was in that same division, but it was the regularly designated flag ship. I got orders to transfer to the regular flag ship rather than stay on my old ship, so I had to transfer.

I was a Commander at this time. I should have said back on 16 July 1943 I was promoted to Commander temporary service.

Back to this submarine hunt down off Nantucket - the CHAMPLIN with Commander Shaffer as the skipper made contact with the submarine and engaged in a more or less running battle on the surface with the submarine using it's guns and attempting to ram. During one of these runs on the submarine a fifty caliber bullet ricocheted off an ammunition storage on the bridge of the CHAMPLIN and hit Commander Shaffer where he was at the con of the ship in the bridge of the CHAMPLIN.

In the meantime the CHAMPLIN had dropped depth charges on the submarine and forced it to the surface. The submarine crew promptly abandoned ship, and other destroyers in my division went in and picked up most of the crew of the submarine.

Then the primary thing on my mind was to see what we could do for Commander Shaffer, who was reported to be in very bad shape and probably dying. We transferred a doctor to the CHAMPLIN, although the weather was quite rough and headed for New York to try to get him into a hospital. He didn't last very long and died enroute.

Lieutenant Baughan, now Rear Admiral Baughan, took over command of the CHAMPLIN.

On the way in word came from Admiral that Commander Shaffer's widow desired that he be buried at sea. We lined up the ships. They prepared the body and did the necessary things on the CHAMPLIN, and we buried him at sea just south of Ambrose Light at the end of New York.

The CHAMPLIN had been damaged a little bit in this particular action and she had to go to the navy yard.

Mason: What did you do with the German prisoners?

Admiral Melson: They were taken in and received by ONI I might add. They took them off very promptly. They had people standing by to take them off. My ship didn't have any, but two others had them.

Mason: Once they were aboard ship there was no attempt to question them there?

Admiral Melson: No, it was purely a question of security and taking care of them. I wanted very much to have the skipper of the submarine with me, but the weather was such that we just couldn't transfer him. So he went in another one of the ships. Of course, everybody says the Germans were arrogant, and apparently this fellow was quite arrogant about the whole thing. They were taken off of the ships under guard just the minute the ships hit the dock, which is the way it should be.

The CHAMPLIN continued to do routine escort work in the Atlantic until May of 1944 when we went to the Med as part of the build up for the invasion of Southern France.

Prior to the actual invasion my division and another division were assigned patrol duty off the Italian coast, and we patrolled the coast alternating with each other about ten days at a time for each group. We went to Palermo, Civitavecchi, Naples, Piombino, Elba, Leghorn, during the following months.

I had, in addition to the two destroyers that were with me, a group of British mine sweepers which were assigned to me for this escort duty. They swept and kept the channels cleared so that we could get in close to the coast.

Mason: For this operation you were under Admiral Hewitt?

Admiral Melson: Yes, the whole time that we were in the Med we were under Admiral Hewitt.

We also fired a great number of fire support missions for the troops along the coast. Actually, what we were doing was assisting in the protection of the left flank of our troops as they advanced from Rome and went north.

I found it a very interesting period, particularly working with this group of British mine sweepers. There were a number of small SCs. All this group was under my command and I was responsible for them. It was quite a variation from what we'd done before. All these Italian towns I'd never seen before and have never seen since, as we went up the coast. Later on, I have been back.

On the 13th of August 1944 we were drawn back from this duty and joined the convoys proceeding to Southern France.

Here again, on the BOYLE, we led one group of the invasion force into the southern coast of France. We were the advance ship to guide the others to their anchorages.

It was quite disturbing - we went in, of course, to be in the off loading spot just before daybreak, so all the approach all the night before was made in complete darkness without any lights. It was a dark night incidentally. It was a peculiar feeling to sail in on something like that ahead of a large group, all in complete darkness, knowing there were thousands of men behind you and ships all around you that you couldn't see, and just know that this whole group was going in.

Looking at the coast you could just barely make out the outline of the coast. Occasionally, big searchlights would zoom across the horizon. I think the Germans knew that we were on the way in, but they never spotted us by searchlight.

So we navigated in by radar and took stations in a geographical position that we were supposed to take about six miles off the beach, expecting at any time we would be spotted and fired upon, but we were not.

Then the other ships started coming in around us and the worry was - which one was going to hit us where we were stationed. They all went up and no one hit us, and they got in their assigned places.

Of course, at daybreak the invasion started, and we took part in the fire support of the landing.

Mason: Was there a softning up of the beaches first?

Admiral Melson: That had been done several days before without any indication to presume that we were landing.

My recollection is that there wasn't too much resistance. There weren't any big guns. There was firing from small artillery pieces and field pieces - tanks and things like that, but there wasn't any big gun action. There might have been further down the coast in places like Marseilles and big towns. It was really quite peaceful.

Mason: That is the story as I got it from Mort Deyo. I expect the fire had gone out of the Germans.

Admiral Melson: I was with Mort Deyo, I was under him.
The landing had already taken place in Normandy.

Mason: You had no real close connection with the Normandy buildup?

Admiral Melson: No.

After D-Day we furnished fire support for the ships as they required and operated in and out of the local support areas.

I forgot to mention that during this patrol duty along the coast of Italy our period of relaxation, which came every ten days for about four days, was spent at Capri. That was very pleasant.

On one occasion Admiral Deyo, who was the commander of my area, ordered my ship and two others to go into the Gulf of de Napoali to make a sweep in the Bay and try and raise fire from the German batteries on shore, so that he sitting off in the cruiser could spot the flashes and fire upon them. We did and we not only were faced with the gunfire from the batteries ashore, but there was the concern always of getting too close to a mine field. So the gunfire which we tried to avoid, and also the mine fields, made an interesting hour or so in the Gulf of de Napoali.

Mason: Then you were kind of a decoy.

Admiral Melson: We were a decoy. It didn't last very long, but an awful lot of shells landed in our area. Some fragments hit the ship, but nobody was hurt and we weren't damanged to amount to anything. Mort Deyo made a decoy of us that day.

Mason: Did you get ashore?

Admiral Melson: I went ashore one day just to the beach. I just saw the damage and wreckage on the beach where the landing party had had difficulty and ran into opposition, but I saw nothing of the Germans. They'd all gone well in by that time.

Of course, during this whole period we were subjected to gunfire and bombs both, more bombs from aircraft than anything, but not very many.

After spending a little time on the coast of Southern France providing fire support and whatnot we sailed for home, escorting the TEXAS, the ARKANSAS, and the NEVADA coming back from Normandy. The trip was very uneventful, except we had to fuel from the TEXAS, which was a rugged experience because of the way the ship was built. She was not designed to fuel destroyers at sea. It was a rather touch and go thing, but it came off all right.

Mason: By that time the German submarine menace was virtually nil.

Admiral Melson: We weren't worried about it at that time.

In November of 1944 shortly after returning to the United States I was ordered to the staff of Commander Destroyers Atlantic Fleet, then based in Casco Bay, the flag ship being the USS DENEBOLA. I reported to the staff as operations officer and remained there until August of 1945, when I accompanied Admiral Reed to the Pacific when he was ordered out to command Battleship Division Five.

Mason: You reported to the DENEBOLA - I wonder if you'd tell me something about that period of service which was nine or ten months.

Admiral Melson: Rear Admiral O. M. Reed was Commander Destroyers Atlantic during this period that I was attached to that staff in Casco Bay. The primary duty of ComDesLant at that time was to train destroyers and destroyer escorts for duty in the Atlantic Fleet. It really was a special training command for destroyer types on the East Coast.

All new ships, destroyers and destroyer escorts, reported to Commander Destroyers Atlantic in Casco Bay for their initial training period. He had teams of officers which went aboard each ship when it arrived and inspected it, checked out the crew, and then went to sea with the ship every day during their training period and supervised their training in gunnery, anti-submarine warfare, communications, and other things of that nature.

A new ship spent anywhere from six weeks to two months on this initial training period - the length of time depending entirely on how great the demand was for the ship at sea.

Mason: And all of these ships were destined for the Pacific?

Admiral Melson: No. Some of these ships were destined for the Pacific and a number of them were destined for the Atlantic.

In the early part of the war nearly all on this coast, except for a few, went to the Atlantic. As the war progressed and the war at sea built up in the Pacific, some destroyers went to the West Coast and some stayed in the Atlantic.

Later in the war, such as the period which I'm talking about now, when the war was close to an end and the submarine activity had died down, more ships were sent to the Pacific.

Of course, in the training command in the Pacific, there were destroyers built on the West Coast, which also were under the command of the West Coast.

It's hard to pin it down to either one or the other.

Mason: But the Casco Bay area for training was a relatively safe area at this point.

Admiral Melson: It was a safe period. As far as I know, at least during my time, I never heard of a submarine being in the operating area.

Although it was cold, there was a lot of ice and snow, it really was a good training ground, if you could stand the cold. It was isolated. It was inside of all the shipping lanes. All the convoys passed there well out at sea. So, you might say, it was a comparatively safe place. The weather, inspite of the coldness, was clear most of the time. We had lots of fog at times too, but the area was favorable for training.

Of course, a better training area would have been Guantanamo Bay, but the time spent in transit just couldn't be put into the training period.

Like in the case of my own ship - we went up there and had our training period and we went right out on a convoy run. We didn't take time to go south for the spring or have a training period down south.

Of course, ComDesLant also had other responsibilities in connection with yard overhauls of ships and the building of new ships. He had inspectors who went around to see that all the repairs were properly made, and he kept track of and supervised all new installations that went into ships, and things of that nature. What he was really was the type command of the Atlantic for destroyers, which is not much different from what it is today - the responsibilities are about the same.

Mason: Were we at that time accomodating any of our Allies

in repair facilities along the Atlantic Coast?

Admiral Melson: I'm not too closely associated with that.

There were a number of British ships in all the yards up and down the Coast undergoing repair, large and small.

Mason: And when that happened - our equipment was freely put on then?

Admiral Melson: Yes. They usually came out of the yard with our radar and our guns and our fire control equipment and so on, and other things, too, I guess, but those were the primary ones.

It seems that we developed these things, like guns and radar, and worked on them and produced them faster and better than the British. I guess that's simply because we were not a country under attack from day to day and had an opportunity to do those things.

Every ship of theirs that went into a yard, went out with a lot of American equipment on board. Of course, they had to be trained with this new equipment. So some of their light ships of destroyer classes came to Casco for training.

My job as operations officer was to arrange the schedules of sailing and so forth of ships of the destroyer force, particularly the operating area of Casco Bay - to see they obeyed the operating schedule, and keep track of where the ships were, and what they were doing, and who they were assigned to, and when they were coming to us, and when they were leaving, and things of that nature.

As a side issue - my family were up there. We lived in the Country Club at Falmouth Foreside. Later we moved in a little cottage just outside of Falmouth, where we were comfortable but cold most of the time.

The only really uncomfortable experience I had was getting back and forth to the ship from day to day. The DENEBOLA was anchored out in a stream and we had to go back and forth by motor launch. The boats were usually iced over, they stayed that way most of the time.

Mason: You make Maine sound like a very formidable place.

Admiral Melson: Well, it was at that time. Actually, we liked Maine, we enjoyed our time at Falmouth Foreside. The trouble was we were there right smack in the middle of winter the whole time, except when we first arrived.

When I left Casco Bay I had air transportation and flew west, stopping for briefings in Honolulu and Guam.

Mason: You said Admiral Reed also went?

Admiral Melson: He had already gone ahead of me. We didn't travel together.

I had the opportunity of meeting Admiral Nimitz in Guam on the way through. It was a very brief and short meeting and I had the opportunity to see what they'd done on Guam since the war had started, because I had been in Guam in 1930.

I arrived in Naha in Okinawa on the wrong side of the island. I wanted to be on the other side near Buckner Bay. I got transportation across the island by jeep and landed up on the waterfront where Buckner Bay was just one vast armada of ships of all sorts - not the whole Pacific Fleet, but a large portion of it was there at anchor.

I asked a beach guard where the TEXAS was, the TEXAS then being the flag ship of ComBatDev Five. He pointed to something way over the horizon and said, "She's about six miles that way."

After a lot of asking me questions and so forth, I finally got in a landing craft, an LCM, which said he was going out by the TEXAS and he would take me. I got in and had a very rough, wet ride.

The TEXAS was anchored at the far side of Buckner Bay. I arrived aboard and Admiral Reed was aboard ahead of me. I boarded as his Chief of Staff.

One little side note on this - I was assigned the Chief of Staff's cabin on the TEXAS. The TEXAS had been flag ship of the Pacific Fleet and flag ship of the United States Fleet over the years and they'd made a lot of changes in her living conditions. I had the Chief of Staff's cabin. The thing that attracted me, other than being a very spacious cabin, it was bigger than anything I'd ever had before, it had a bathroom with a bath tub with four legs on it - a regular land side type of tub.

I didn't have another tub aboard ship until later on the NEW JERSEY.

The first duty on the ComBatDev Five was to organize and sail for the West Coast. We were assigned this operation to return the short timers back to the United States. The war at this period in the Pacific was just over. Three battleships and four cruisers and I've forgotten how many destroyers were set up as a Task Force under Admiral Reed as ComBatDev Five to return to the West Coast with these people.

We sailed for the West Coast, stopping in Honolulu on the way back for a short stop for fuel. It was a very interesting trip back I might say, because the ships were packed with men, literally packed - soldiers, sailors, marines, everything that we had in WesPac. We were just serving as a transport. All they did was lie around the decks, sleep and eat - that's the way they came home. It probably wasn't very pleasant, but most of them either slept on the deck or in hammocks. They were so happy to get home that it didn't make any difference.

We arrived in Long Beach and went in and tied up to

the piers in San Pedro and discharged our passengers.

In November of '45 while we were still at the dock in San Pedro Admiral Reed was ordered to command the Sixteenth Fleet, which meant coming back to New York, and I was ordered back as his Chief of Staff. I was with him for three different tours of duty.

I went back to New York as operations officer on the staff of the Sixteenth Fleet, which then was the fleet which received all the vessels going out of commission being laid up in reserve in various ports up and down the coast. It was mostly a ship tending job.

I was there from November of '45 until June of '47, then I went over to the Naval War College.

Mason: This period was comparable to the demobilization of the troops, wasn't it?

Admiral Melson: Nothing happened except it was sort of a happy period for everybody, people were getting home.

#3 Melson - 100

Vice Admiral Charles L. Melson, USN   by John T. Mason, Jr.
Annapolis, Maryland   March 19, 1971

Mr. Mason: Mighty good to see you, Admiral.

Last time when we broke off you said you'd like to add a brief account of something that took place during the invasion of Sicily in the Mediterranean. It was an incident that you thought would be worth attaching to your story of the invasion of Sicily. So would you tell me that now, sir?

Admiral Melson: I'm sure this incident was well covered in many official reports. I know as a matter of fact that it's written up in several histories of the war of the Mediterranean.

My information is based on where I served from my own ship. At the time my ship and other ships of my division were on patrol off the coast of Southern Sicily when a large group of aircraft came across our patrol line coming in from the southeast. A great many of the ships on patrol, lacking proper identification of aircraft, opened up and fired on them.

A number of the aircraft were shot down, the exact number not known to me, but it's understood and reported that they contained paratroopers on their way in to a landing behind the German lines in Sicily.

It was the case of mistaken identity, and also of mis-routing aircraft through the landing areas.

Mr. Mason: Was the visibility poor at that time?

Admiral Melson: It was in early morning, it was still dark. They were headed in for a dawn landing, a dawn parachute jump.

That's about all I know of it. Of course, we'd have many cases of mistaken identity of aircraft in which friends have been shot down as well as foe, and this is another one of those particular instances.

Mr. Mason: Last time you were talking about the Sixteenth Fleet, the Atlantic Reserve Fleet, and you were Operations and Plans Officer on that Fleet. You told me something about it, and I believe you had something more to add.

Admiral Melson: Yes, I would like to add something to what I've already said in regard to the Atlantic Reserve Fleet.

The Atlantic Reserve Fleet was also under the Commander Eastern Sea Frontier, who was at that time Admiral Kinkaid. Under Admiral Kinkaid Rear Admiral O. M. Reed acted as the Commander of the Reserve Fleet.

The duties of the Reserve Fleet were to place the many ships coming back from the war zone in commission in reserve and mothball them for future use. To do this a number of Reserve Fleet berthing areas were established. There was one in Boston, another in New York, Philadelphia, Norfolk, Charleston, Green Cove Springs, and Orange, Texas.

The ships reported to these areas, discharged their crews, and the ship was turned over to the representatives of the Atlantic Reserve Fleet there at that time. They were then inspected, painted, and mothballed for future use.

In some areas it was rather difficult setting up these Reserve Fleet storages, if you wanted to call them that, because it involved building piers, and getting housing for the people to live there. One of the worse of course was Orange, Texas, which was pretty far back from the sea to get ships into and place out of commission.

Mr. Mason: The whole operation was fairly scientifically conducted, wasn't it?

Admiral Melson: Yes, it was.

Mr. Mason: And how this contrasted with what they did with ships in so-called mothballs after World War I.

Admiral Melson: The ships after World War I, as far as I know, had very little done to them, except a little oil and grease wiped on the working parts of guns and machinery.

But in this particular case it involved putting critical or sensitive elements of machinery and gunnery in cocoons which were humidified to keep out rust and dampness and to keep a constant temperature, and thereby preserve the equipment.

I might say that it has proved to be a very good system, as a number of these ships have been re-commissioned and gone back into service. They have been found to be in very good condition.

While in New York the headquarters of the Reserve Fleet aboard a hotel ship which was berthed in the Hudson River. Admiral Read lived aboard, and his staff spent time there as necessary when they had the duty and things like that.

Mr. Mason: You had quarters there, too?

Admiral Melson: No, I did not, I lived at home.

The people who were in New York without families lived on board. Of course, all the ballistic staff more or less lived there..

Mr. Mason: Why the great advance in the greater care exercised

#3 Melson - 104

with these ships? Whose foresight was that?

Admiral Melson: I'm afraid I can't answer your question directly. Presumably it came up in the Navy Department in previous plans they had made for laying up ships. They found, I'm sure, at the end of World War I that the preservation processes that they had taken were not really adequate.

Mr. Mason: They truly had an example of that in the fifty destroyers they handed over to Britain, didn't they?

Your tour of duty there came to an end in June of 1947?

Admiral Melson: In June of 1947 I was ordered as a student at the Naval War College, which I had previously requested. I reported there around the first of July.

I spent the first part of my stay at the War College correcting general signal books, which were used at the College and gotten out of date.

Mr. Mason: Why did this lot fall to you?

Admiral Melson: I reported in early, I was there with nothing to do, so they put me to work.

#3 Melson - 105

Mr. Mason: How many were there in the incoming class?

Admiral Melson: I find it difficult to answer that question because I never knew the exact figure. Of course, we had two courses at that time, we had the senior course and the junior course. There was developed the following year the logistic course. So really there were three separate groups of people reporting in, and I'm not sure I know the exact number.

Mr. Mason: What group were you with?

Admiral Melson: I was with the senior course. At that time I was a Captain, and the senior course consisted almost entirely of Captains with a few very senior Commanders.

The junior course was mostly Lieutenant Commanders and Lieutenants.

The logistic course, which was established by Rear Admiral Eccles at the War College, and was housed in Simms Hall, consisted of Captains and Commanders and a few Lieutenant Commanders.

The exact number in each of these groups at this time I must plead ignorance to.

Mr. Mason: Was there any difference in the course of study

between that pursued by the seniors and that by the juniors?

Admiral Melson: Not very much.

The senior course was on a little higher level, you might say, than the junior course. The senior course more or less trained officers for senior staff officers for fleets at sea and war plans officers, et cetera.

The junior course was just an echelon below that for officers on the various staffs who had junior positions. They, of course, had much more detail work than the senior course.

To put it briefly I think the senior course was a broad course compared to the junior course which was much more detail.

Mr. Mason: Tell me a little about that course of study. How much time did it engage you in? How much of it was exchanging ideas with the men informally?

Admiral Melson: The course took a great deal of time. In addition to working out various battle problems pertaining to that era of naval warfare, writing up operation orders, and then playing them out on the game floor- this took a lot of time, preparation, and study.

Also, while we were there we each had to write a thesis. In preparation for this thesis we had a long reading list which we had to go through - that took a lot of time.

Mr. Mason: Did you have some special officer to whom you were assigned as a consultant and tutor, so to speak?

Admiral Melson: The War College staff was broken down into various groups, each of which handled some phase of the operation. They didn't act as instructors in the sense of having classrooms and sitting around and asking questions and so forth.

You usually were given a problem to work out and you did most of it on your own or in consultation with a small group. On a big war problem which we had to work out we'd usually divided into groups of four or five with one officer more or less in charge. And they drew up the war plan or the operation order which they were working on to be played on the game board at a later date. It was not really classroom work as such.

The one requirement that caused more trouble and more difficulty than anything else was the writing of the thesis, which had to be a certain length, so many pages, and required a great deal of reading and preparation - like any thesis in a university. It seemed to be the load that most of them objected to - writing the thesis.

Mr. Mason: Was that because maybe they weren't quite as

accustomed to writing things, writing articles, and so forth?

Admiral Melson: Very few of them were writers to begin with. They'd all had about the same education and background that I'd had and were graduates of the Naval Academy. They had been at sea for a number of years without being involved in school work. It just came hard.

Mr. Mason: I recall Admiral Arleigh Burke telling me once that, I think it was in the sixties, at least it was when he was CNO, he was interested in seeing that a school for naval officers for writers was set up at the Naval War College sponsored jointly by the Naval Institute, largely a summer project I think, to encourage naval officers to pursue writing as an avocation.

Do you know anything about that, and what could you say about it?

Admiral Melson: I don't know. I just know that it was established, but it was before I got there. It was a summer course, and I was not involved in it at all.

Mr. Mason: Would you comment on its merits.

Admiral Melson: I think it would be very desirable myself.

I know that I'm one who could have benefited by such a course. But I've never been a writer, or a speaker for that matter. Any training that I could have gotten would have been very helpful.

Mr. Mason: During this time what was the nature of the war problem which you were working on?

Admiral Melson: During the course of the year you usually had two or three problems, depending on the size of a particular problem, and how long it took us to develop and how long it took to put it on.

You usually had one war problem during the year which was centered in the Mediterranean, and you had another war problem which was centered in the Pacific. That had the advantage of giving you some experience in both areas by examining charts, reading up on the background of the countries involved, and studying the resources and capabilities of other fleets that you might encounter. We just studied the whole area.

Occasionally there was a third problem which usually was in the arctic area around Iceland.

Mr. Mason: You hadn't progressed at that time of having a problem in the Indian Ocean?

Admiral Melson: No, I don't remember that we had one in the Indian Ocean. The Mediterranean, the Arctic, and the Pacific were the three that I remember.

Of course, they had the advantage of having an individual becoming acquainted with the area and the background and what goes on.

One of the particular items that came up in the problem of the Mediterranean was the question of the oil in the Middle East - the oil fields and how it was gotten out and the route of the tankers. I think it proved very beneficial in years later to some of us.

Mr. Mason: That was a question I wanted to ask. These theoretical problems that you dealt with - did they have influence on your thinking in future years? Did they provide insight that you actually could put to use?

Admiral Melson: For certain ones of us who became involved in those areas in later years they were invaluable. But of course a number of us never had much to do with those areas.

Like in my case - I spent very little time in the Pacific, but I spent a lot of time in the Mediterranean and the Atlantic. So the problems in the Atlantic and the Mediterranean were very helpful to me in understanding what was there and what could be done.

Mr. Mason: Of course, most of the men going to the War College were men who had been carefully chosen were they not? Your potential had been recognized and there was some probability that you would go on to higher command.

Admiral Melson: Yes. Of course, at that time anyone who wanted to go to the War College could put in for it, apply for it, but that didn't mean that you got it. You were selected out of a large number of applicants. As far as I know if you didn't apply you didn't go - that was one thing. But they were well selected and very carefully selected.

I'll speak more about that later when I come to the time when I was at the War College when we were selecting students for the War College.

Mr. Mason: One of the values of the War College experience for a student is his association with other men of ability in the Navy. Do you want to say something about that?

Admiral Melson: Yes, I'd like to say something about the students as a group.

The Navy personnel that were there were line and aviation, men of varied experience. They'd operated in various parts of the world and had good backgrounds. In addition to those we had representatives of the Air Force and the Army. True they were few in numbers compared to the size of the overall group, but they did a lot to help broaden the views of the naval officers who were involved in these operations.

I consider that it led to a better understanding between the services, too, both officially in the War College and in the unofficial approach to life outside the College.

Mr. Mason: This period that you were there almost coincided with when the National War College was set up. Why the need for the National War College when the Naval War College, and I presume the Army also, had representatives from the different services?

Admiral Melson: That was a question that was raised more than once while I was there as a student, and later on the staff - why they had a National War College?

Of course, there was the Army War College and the Naval War College. I'm not sure whether it had been set up yet, but there was an Air Force school being established.

There was also the Industrial College. Of course, this was a horse of a different color in a way. They are involved mostly in industrial affairs of the country, and how the military relates to it in what they need.

But the Army War College in Pennsylvania and the Naval War College were very close, except that they followed the line that meant the most to their own service.

The National War College was supposed to be on a little higher level than these two colleges, and to cover the overall picture. Frankly I must say, at this time, I've often wondered where the difference was because I couldn't really see it.

One thing I forgot before in talking about students - we had students from the State Department and from various other civilian organizations in Washington.

Mr. Mason: This also was true of the National War College.

Admiral Melson: That's true. As I say the two schools were very much alike, there was very little difference. The students were of the same caliber just about.

They would say that the Students for the National War College were selected because they thought that these individuals showed promise of going to staff positions and perhaps command later. They didn't say that they didn't at the Naval War College, but they picked them out as being individually specially selected. It's hard to reconcile this with our own selection board.

But that is an argument that's been going on for some

time, and I don't know that I'm fully qualified to answer all parts of it.

Mr. Mason: What was the faculty like back in 1948 at the Naval War College?

Admiral Melson: The faculty at the Naval War College were all naval officers, Army section and Air Force section officers about the same time and rank as the students. Most of them had been to the War College one year, and then were kept on the second year as instructors. Really and truthfully I think all of us were in about the same level of education, and the same background. There really wasn't much difference between students and instructors.

Mr. Mason: Therein, I would say that it did differ from the National War College, because the faculty there was selected from the ranking universities of the country.

Admiral Melson: I'm not sure of this, but I think there were a number of military people there as instructors too at that time.

Mr. Mason: Tell me about some of the contacts you made in that period at the Naval War College that proved beneficial.

Admiral Melson: Not necessarily to answer your question, but there are two things I'd like to put in here.

The logistic course was set up at the Naval War College during this year by Admiral Eccles, who, of course has since retired.

Admiral Spruance, the President, I believe had a great influence over all of us at the War College. As we all know he is a very quiet and retiring individual. He did not speak very often to the student body, but when he did everybody was very attentive and very appreciative of everything that he had to say because he was a man with quite a background of the war which had just completed two years before that.

As far as contacts among the students are concerned I don't believe that I established any close contacts with individuals which have been lasting to any extent.

I'm sure that most of my classmates there have all done pretty well, but I can't think of any that I've had any close contact with.

I've always remembered this period at the War College. It was a very fine year. And I felt that every officer would benefit by going to the War College at some period of his career, preferably along about the time I went, shortly after I made Captain, because it offered an opportunity to relax a little bit from the rigors of every day life aboard ship and the little things which took up so much of your time. It gave you an opportunity to read and study and relax a little bit. I feel that it was very beneficial to everyone.

Mr. Mason: Can you give me any personal recollections of Admiral Spruance in that time?

Admiral Melson: I'm afraid I can't directly. As I said before he was very quiet and very reserved. It wasn't very often that you had the opportunity to engage in any private conversation. We used to see him around the halls at the War College quite frequently, and we met him at his annual reception for the students. I really can't recollect any particular conversation that I had with him.

Mr. Mason: You not only spent a year there as a student in the senior group, but then you remained on for a duty on the staff. Do you want to tell me something about that? Who requested that you stay?

Admiral Melson: In May of 1948 word came out that Admiral Spruance was retiring that June. Admiral Allen E. Smith, the then Chief of Staff at the War College, asked me if I would like to be the Secretary of the War College.

After some consideration I decided I would, and I

#3 Melson - 117.

reported and served for about two weeks directly under Admiral Spruance as Secretary of the War College. Then when Admiral Spruance retired, Admiral Smith became the temporary President of the War College.

This lasted through the summer of '48, and then Vice Admiral Donald B. Beary was ordered in as President of the War College. Admiral Beary was supposed to be red-headed and a fire eater. I thought I'd better have some second thoughts about being Secretary, but I found that after I knew him he was one of the most pleasant and finest individuals that I'd ever met. He was President of the War College during the following year while I was the Secretary.

Mr. Mason: Tell me about the duties of Secretary.

Admiral Melson: The Secretary of the War College is the business administrator of the school. He handles all the funds and allocates funds. He takes care of the Civil Service personnel at the War College, the enlisted personnel, and has all the responsibility for all the housekeeping chores of running the school. Occasionally, you become involved in some of the academic side, but not very often.

During this period the War College REVIEW was conceived and the first issues were published.

Mr. Mason: Whose idea was that, sir?

Admiral Melson: That was Admiral Beary's, I imagine. It probably came from a member of the staff, but I'm not sure just whose idea it was.

The REVIEW consisted of a limited number of articles, at that time it was five or six, the articles being reprints of speeches made at the War College by prominent people. While we could have published many more than five, money was a factor because we had to keep the size of the book down.

I remember if was five times a year that we put out the REVIEW at that time, in a small phamplet, which was sent to all former students, foreign schools, and any officer who so desired to get it by merely asking for it and to be put on the mailing list. It was free of charge.

We thought it was a very fine publication.

My interest in it was primarily because I had the responsibility of getting it out and finding the money to pay for the printing and the paper and so forth. Since then it has developed into a much more sophisticated publication. Where we used very cheap paper and so forth, the present one is a hard back magazine of color.

Mr. Mason: In your time there did you have a special editor for this magazine?

Admiral Melson: Yes.

The War College at this time handled correspondence courses in strategy and tactics and international law. There were a group of officers on the staff, which was a section of the staff, which handled this. They put out the REVIEW. The editor of it was the officer in charge of the correspondence course of strategy and tactics.

Mr. Mason: Tell me a little about these correspondence courses. How effective were they, and how widespread and popular were they with the Navy personnel?

Admiral Melson: At the time that I was at the War College and knew a little about how they were handled and how they were done, we found that the correspondence courses were very popular.

Credit was allowed on certain examinations that you took for promotion in those days. If you remember at that time every officer had to take a written examination for promotion, and one of these was usually in the field of strategy and tactics and, completing it successfully, you were excused from this particular examination. Therefore, it became very popular for all the officers to take it. It probably was a good thing.

I've forgotten how many assignments there were in each course. You got around twelve assignments, and you usually had to work these up on your own aboard ship in the hours that you were off duty, using the few books that the War College sent you for reference plus such as you could find aboard ship.

I think they were very useful in training young officers to have some knowledge of how operational orders were issued and written, and all the things that went into an operation order and why it was there. It gave you some experience in order writing.

Mr. Mason: It was largely the younger officers who participated?

Admiral Melson: Yes. By younger officers I mean up through the grade of Lieutenant Commander. I'm not sure, but it seems to me that it was restricted to officers below the grade of Lieutenant Commander.

Mr. Mason: Was there a fee attached?

Admiral Melson: No fee.

Mr. Mason: This meant that you had added personnel there on the staff at the College, didn't it?

Admiral Melson: Yes. That had to be absorbed in the War College budget. It was very worthwhile, and it carried on for some time. It's still functioning, but I think at a very much reduced rate than it was before.

Mr. Mason: In your job as chief administrator of the College did you have any particular problems - with space, with buildings, with housing?

Admiral Melson: Space and housing was always a problem at the War College. In this particular job my concern was primarily with the assignment of space and the assignment of housing. There were no quarters for officers, except quarters assigned to the President, the Chief of Staff, and a house was available for the Secretary, which I wouldn't live in because it was too small. I still lived in a house in town.

Since then there's been considerable change, which I'll cover as we go along. When I went back as President I found things were quite different.

Space within the College was at a premium. I mean office space and space for the students to work and so forth. As a matter of fact they took over Simms Hall, which before had been a building of the Naval Station. I'm not sure of its use now. It was an old brick building with steam lines exposed all over the building, a heating plant. I believe it had been a barracks. That became the headquarters of the logistic department.

One interesting thing which occurred while I was there - I might add before I say this that I did have the opportunity to meet a great many of the speakers who came to speak at the War College. A lot of them were military, and a lot of them were professors from various institutions. I found that part very interesting. I had no direct contact other than meeting them, and I might add handing them their check as they left.

Mr. Mason: They came as part of the teaching program?

Admiral Melson: A lecture. We had a system of outside lecturers who came in and talked to the entire student body.

Mr. Mason: How generous was your budget in those days?

Admiral Melson: Very small. We really had to struggle for funds. I'm afraid Washington (the Navy Department)) wasn't very liberal with allocation of funds for the War College at that time. Funds were hard to come by for routine operations, and almost impossible to come by for any new development.

Of course, you can't blame the Navy Department entirely

because they were operating under a restricted budget, too.

At graduation at the War College in 1949 the Secretary of the Navy Dan Kimball was the speaker. Mr. Kimball's speech had been written up for him before he left Washington, but had not been cleared by the various authorities in Washington before he left for the War College. So he arrived in Newport without his speech. It arrived about two hours before he was due to go to the platform, and he barely had time to scan it. He had a little difficulty giving this particular talk in view of the fact that he was not very familiar with it.

It was the source of some discussion with me, the Secretary, and Mrs. Melson whenever we met thereafter. We did know him, and met him a number of times thereafter, and he always brought up the subject of his speech at the War College.

Mr. Mason: I meant to ask you - what was the subject of your special paper, your special dissertation, when you were there as a student.

Admiral Melson: I was afraid you would. I would have to research to get the title of the thing. My memory isn't what it use to be.

Mr. Mason: Would it have been something that you selected yourself, because of your primary interest?

Admiral Melson: They gave you a list of topics to choose from, all based on your course at the War College. I regret to say it's slipped my mind. I did look it up when I was back there as President, I didn't really want to see it, but it's on file.

Mr. Mason: In that time what were the facilities for relaxation at the Naval War College? I know now they have a lovely club, an officers club.

Admiral Melson: The club that they have today was in existance at that time, although it was much smaller. It was not as well fitted out as it is today, but there was a small club in the same location. They had their Saturday night dances, and usual small parties during the week.

They had a package goods store there, which we were all quite happy to have because it was much cheaper than in town.

Outside of that there were a few tennis courts, and there was a bowling alley. That was about all, except for a few softball games which the students got up among themselves.

Mr. Mason: You were in fact a part of the town, too, weren't you, at least the naval element in the town?

Admiral Melson: Yes, although there was very little association at that time between the students and the town. Not because there was any objection in either case, but they just didn't have the same interests. The students were kept pretty busy, as a matter of fact, and they had very little time for social activity.

The city did give a reception once each year for all these students and the staff out at Newport, which we were all invited to. That was just a big affair, nothing very personal about it.

Mr. Mason: And what about the relationships with the summer colony, the wealthy contingent?

Admiral Melson: As far as the students were concerned there was very little contact. You probably realize there are many social affairs in Newport, and students were very seldom invited to any of them unless they had some personal contact of their own, except the charity affairs. When they had a charity affair we usually always received an invitation with a price tag on it.

Mr. Mason: Did the War College, as such, take part in the

Cup Races?

Admiral Melson: Not while I was there, no. The Navy did, but not the War College itself.

The Navy furnished a destroyer to start the race and to go along with them for safety purposes. But the War College directly had no connection with the Cup Races.

That about covers it for the particular period at the War College.

In July of 1949 I was detached from the War College and sent as Commander Destroyer Squadron Twenty, a command that I wanted very, very much.

Mr. Mason: Why? Where was this command located?

Admiral Melson: The squadron number had no particular significance, it was the fact that it was a destroyer squadron, which was something that I had to have in my career pattern, if you want to call it, to have some success in the Navy.

Those 'black shoe' officers who were not in submarines all had to get a command of some kind, and a destroyer squadron was an outstanding command.

After a few days leave I proceeded to join the squadron. As I had to report to the squadron in Guantanamo the question arose as how to get to Guantanamo. Airplane flights to Guantanamo were not as plentiful at that time as they are today, so after some investigation I found that a submarine was leaving Key West.

I forgot to mention here that I went to Key West to attend the Sonar School as part of my training before going as a destroyer squadron commander, thus my presence in Key West.

Mr. Mason: Tell me about that. How long a course was that?

Admiral Melson: The course there was only two weeks. It was a squadron commander's course. It involved a very broad course in sonar - how it operated, how you detect a submarine, the tactics for forcing submarines to the surface, and things of that nature. It was a very abbreviated course, nowhere near the detail it is for the younger officer to go there to actually operate the equipment.

Mr. Mason: Was this under the aegis of BuOrd?

Admiral Melson: I think it was at that time.

I asked for transportation aboard this submarine, which was going from Key West to Guantanamo, and it was granted. I then had my first trip to sea in a submarine, and I enjoyed it immensely because I had no duty aboard the submarine, I was just a passenger. The feeling that you got, that came over you when you first realized that you were under water, is very difficult to describe.

In my case - after we put out to sea from Key West nothing was going on and I went down below in the submarine with the thought of maybe catching a short nap, which I did, but I woke up with the most peculiar sensation. There was no noise, everything was absolutely quiet, and I couldn't quite figure out where I was. Then I realized that we had submerged. We made most of the trip submerged and arrived safely in Guantanamo. It was a very pleasant trip.

In Guantanamo I reported to the USS BARTON, the flag ship of DesRon 20, and I relieved Captain Dash as squadron commander.

Mr. Mason: This destroyer squadron was part of the Atlantic Fleet?

Admiral Melson: This destroyer squadron was part of the Atlantic. It had been in the Pacific, and had just come around from the Pacific reporting to the Atlantic Fleet.

The duty as Commander Destroyer Squadron Twenty was very interesting assignment. Having served most of my time in destroyers up to that point I felt very pleased to have command of a squadron.

At this time the squadron was considered among the more modern ships, most of them being of the Sumner class, having been built during the war.

We operated in the Atlantic during the following year, carrying on routine exercises and taking part in fleet problems. There was very little of unusual interest.

The squadron took part in a fleet exercise in the Northern Atlantic off of Labrador in the fall of 1949. The operations in this area are found to be quite difficult due mostly to weather, but it was a good experience for all of us who had operated mostly in southern waters in the past.

The flag ship of Admiral Speck, then Captain Speck, who had another squadron in the same problem, became disabled during the problem and was adrift with no power off Labrador coast for some twelve hours, during which time the BARTON stood by to assist as it required. The weather was such that we were very fearful that she might possibly be blown ashore. Fortunately, she retrieved power and everything worked out all right.

Another thing which is of very special interest to me - during this time that Admiral Speck's flag ship was having problems I spent most of my time in the CIC of the BARTON. And I must say that I smoked almost continuously during that particular time - I think it was a matter of nerves and worry about the other ship, and whether it would get out all right.

In the morning when things were cleared up and everything seemed to be all right again I went down into my cabin for breakfast, and I found that I didn't have a cigarette.

I asked the mess boy to get me a package of cigarettes out of my cabin. He came back and said, "Captain, there're no more cigarettes. You smoked them all last night."

The reason I tell this story is that simply I've never smoked since. That's of interest in regard to me.

Another event of interest that occurred while I had the destroyer squadron was the MISSOURI grounding in Norfolk channel. As most of you probably know the MISSOURI ran aground on the way out of Norfolk in the spring of 1950, and remained a monument for a considerable time.

My squadron was operating in and out of Norfolk at the Naval Base at that time, and every time we went in and out we passed the MISSOURI, which was a good reminder to all of us that it didn't pay to get outside of the line of buoys. I can assure you we always stayed inside. It was a shocking sight to see this big ship aground.

In May of 1950 I was ordered detached from the desroyer squadron, and ordered as Administrative Aide and Chief of Staff to Vice Admiral Hill, then Superintendent of the Naval Academy. Admiral Hill had formerly been head of the National War College before coming to the Naval Academy.

#4 Melson - 131

Vice Admiral Charles L. Melson, USN   by John T. Mason, Jr.
Annapolis, Maryland   April 20, 1971

Mr. Mason: Admiral, it's good to see you again this afternoon.

When you broke off last time you were about to tell me about your tour of duty as Administrative Aide to Admiral Hill during the time he served as Superintendent of the Naval Academy.

Tell me about the nature of your job, what did you do?

Admiral Melson: The Administrative Aide and Chief of Staff at that time had many varied duties, mostly of care and upkeep of the Naval Academy and administration of the Severn River Naval Command.

The Administrative Aide, as such, was just what the title implies. He was Administrative Aide to the Superintendent of the Naval Academy charged with the administration of the Academy other than academic. The Chief of Staff was a title that went with the Severn River Naval Command.

Admiral Hill had the dual title of Superintendent of the United States Naval Academy, and Commander of the Severn River Naval Command. It was in the capacity of Chief of Staff that I served at this time.

As Administrative Aide to the Superintendent of the Naval Academy the duties were primarily concerned with supervising the operation of the physical side of the Academy.

Mr. Mason: How much money did you have to work with?

Admiral Melson: We never had enough. I don't remember any exact figure these days, but we not only had the problem of trying to keep up financially but we also made many trips to Washington to ask for a little more, which was rarely forthcoming.

Mr. Mason: Was this request lodged with the Navy Department, or did you go directly to the Congress?

Admiral Melson: No, we went directly to the Bureau of Personnel, which had the management of the Naval Academy affairs and provided the money at that time.

There just never seemed to be enough money to go around. It appears that this has changed considerably in these days from the evidence of the building that's going on there.

I was fortunate in having a public works officer, Hebe Jones, who was most efficient and did a wonderful job at keeping up the Naval Academy with the small amount of funds that were available.

As I remember there was no major construction project during the period. It was a question of keeping the place clean and running, providing the necessary logistic support to the Commandant of Midshipmen in Bancroft Hall and to the heads of departments at the Naval Academy.

Mr. Mason: How many boys did you have to accomodate at that time, how many students were there?

Admiral Melson: At that time there were, I believe, around 3300.

They were accomodated in what you might call old Bancroft Hall, which consisted primarily of the first, second, third, fourth, fifth, and sixth wings. The seventh and eighth wings were added at a later date.

There was very little new construction and building at this time, except in the nature of upkeep of what we had.

Mr. Mason: Was that extensive with some of the older buildings?

Admiral Melson: We felt at the time that it would cost almost as much to keep the old buildings operating as it would have to try and build new additions or new buildings.

The condition of the buildings was such that they needed renovation very badly, and the ordinary routine repair was quite an expensive item.

Mr. Mason: Was this the point of view that was imparted to the Board of Visitors?

Admiral Melson: Oh yes, this was all presented to the Board of Visitors. The Board the Visitors were aware of it. But as I say money was not very plentiful for anything at that time. It just wasn't worth counting on.

Mr. Mason: Tell me about the complexion of the Board of Visitors. Is this made up of members of Congress or what?

Admiral Melson: No. The Board of Visitors is made up of prominent civilians and a few members of Congress. But the people who were very active on the Board of Visitors were usually a group of four or five top civilians who came to the Naval Academy to the meetings, and took a very active interest in what was going on. They are the ones who guided the course of the meetings. Usually the members of Congress that were members sat in rather infrequently. We hoped that they would carry the messages back to Congress itself, but whether they did or not we don't know.

Mr. Mason: Were they usually members of Congress who were influential in appropriations and this kind of thing?

Admiral Melson: No, not necessarily. At the moment I don't remember the names of the members of the Board, but they were all presidential appointees as you probably know. I wouldn't say they were unduly influential in their particular area.

Mr. Mason: Your jurisdiction also covered the various boats and so forth --

Admiral Melson: At that time there was a Naval Station which was located partially across the river on the north shore of the Severn, and partially based at the Naval Academy on the Academy side.

The REINA MERCEDES was at that time the station ship and it housed the mess attendents that took care of the mess hall in Bancroft Hall, and housed part of the various enlisted men that were attached to the Naval Academy for various assignments, mostly in the department of seamanship and ordnance and gunnery.

The sailboats and motor craft that were attached to the Naval Academy were normally berthed across the river at the Naval Station.

The Naval Station was a separarate command, Commanding

Officer Naval Station as such, and it operated under the Naval Academy and furnished services that were required for instruction of the Midshipmen - such as yawls for sailing, and YPs for ship handling and boat handling drills and such.

Mr. Mason: So your cognizance did include that?

Admiral Melson: It included all that. That came primarily under me as Chief of Staff. In other words I had a direct interest in that.

Mr. Mason: In that time was the Naval Academy the recipent of gifts of yachts and so forth?

Admiral Melson: It was indeed. I don't remember at the moment which one came during that period, but almost every other year or so we received a new yacht from some wealthy man who wanted to get if off his record so he didn't have to pay taxes and support the craft. They're quite expensive too, to keep up.

Mr. Mason: That's an interesting development, isn't it, that such vessels are turned over to the Naval Academy?

Admiral Melson: That continued even until this day. Almost

all of the large yachts now at the Naval Academy were gifts to the Naval Academy, and also a number of smaller ones.

Of course, at one time a sizable number of small sailing craft were built for the Naval Academy under government appropriation, but eventually they began to wear out and had to be replaced, and they were replaced with government funds.

In addition to that having these larger sailing craft gave the Midshipmen more experience in handling the boats.

The question of upkeep was always a problem because very rarely did the donor give funds to take care of the craft or to help upkeep them. So there was the problem of always finding funds and getting additional funds from BuPers to keep these boats running.

Mr. Mason: So this acceptance wasn't just an automatic thing on the part of the Naval Academy.

Admiral Melson: No. You had to determine how you were going to keep these boats functioning, keep them up, keep them ship-shape. And they cost a lot of money to keep going.

So that's one reason every once in a while some of these gift yachts are passed on by the Navy to take one that's in better shape and place it with the fleet at the Naval Academy.

Mr. Mason: What sort of an official act coes it require to accept a gift of a yacht?

Admiral Melson: It requires the authority of the Secretary of the Navy if I remember correctly. It always had to be cleared with him. I think that's a more or less standard practice. The government takes over ownership actually.

Mr. Mason: As Administrative Aide did you also get involved with the purchase of supplies and food and so forth?

Admiral Melson: No, not directly. That was all handled separately by the Commissary and the commissary officer.

I was involved to the extent that they were all responsible to the Superintendent, and I was in the middle with no responsibility particularly except to administer to all and see that everything went along smoothly and without any difficulty. I don't remember any serious difficulty.

It's like any other organization where various members of the staff are responsible for their own little bailiwick, and through the chain of command to the man in charge.

#4 Melson - 139

I think I should cover the Chief of Staff's functions here before I get too involved in the Naval Station.

The Severn River Naval Command at that time took in all the naval activities in this area of the Severn River, in the administration and military command. There was no responsibility for the interior functioning of the command in the sense of directing their daily operations and things like that, but it was part of the basic command.

There was the Naval Experiment Station at that time. The Naval Station was one, the Naval Hospital was one, the Naval Air Facility was one. I think that covers them all. They were under the direct military administration of the Superintendent of the Naval Academy.

Mr. Mason: Were there any scientific labs or anything of that sort?

Admiral Melson: At the Naval Experiment Station. Everything of that nature was under the Experiment Station at that time. That has since changed as you probably realize.

Mr. Mason: And your duties as Chief of Staff in connection with his command were what?

Admiral Melson: I was the representative of the command of the Severn River Naval Command and functioning as these various commands. I had to arrange for things like annual inspection of each of the activities and take part in them as a rule along with the command of the Severn River Naval Command, which I will again state was also the Superintendent of the Naval Academy.

The job as Administrative Aide was primarily to take the load off the Commandant of the Severn River Naval Command for the daily administration of these activities. It was not an overwhelming load, I can assure you, but it was something that had to be done.

It's comparable to a squadron commander who has a squadron of ships under him, each one of these being an individual ship.

It was a very interesting assignment, I must say, all the way through.

Mr. Mason: In addition to the Board of Visitors, what about the VIPs who came? Did they fall within your purview? Did you have to arrange for their entertainment and the like?

Admiral Melson: No. They came in and as a rule were handled directly by the Superintendent through his personal aides. I came into it occasionally when some logistic support was needed in one way or another, like automobiles or boating or anything of that nature. But usually it was handled by the Superintendent's personal staff.

I might say at this point that I was part of that personal staff. I was a personal aide in addition to these other assignments. So I usually attended all the social and official functions involving VIPs.

Mr. Mason: That becomes somewhat burdensome at times, doesn't it?

Admiral Melson: Very. It wasn't so very bad with Admiral and Mrs. Hill. They were very good hosts. It was a pleasure to go to the affairs that they supervised and had, because they were good hosts. They had nice parties, and I enjoyed them as much as anybody else. Also it gave me the opportunity to meet many people whom I would not have met otherwise.

I don't have a list, and I've forgotten just who was here during this period of time, but there were a lot of very distinguished people. The ones that stand out in my mind, of course, are the ones that came while I was Superintendent. My memory doesn't go back quite that far on that.

Mr. Mason: What about the hoards of ordinary tourists? What sort of policy did you have to govern control of them?

Admiral Melson: Tours could be arranged for any group of tourists that came in, guided tours, and they would be escorted by one of the yard police or by a Midshipman in some cases and in some cases by officers.

For the ordinary tourists who just came down by bus to see the Naval Academy they were all given brochures about the Naval Academy and directions about getting around, but other than some general guidance by yard police nothing was done.

All the areas that we could were kept open to visitors all the time - like the rotunda of Bancroft Hall, Dahlgren Hall when drills were not in progress, and the other areas where it didn't interfere with the daily routine of the Midshipmen.

One place that the visitors were normally not allowed was the mess hall. Occasionally special tours would be set up there.

I don't remember the tourists being any great problem, except we had a lot of them all the time. The way you see the buses lined up along the wall - that hasn't changed any in the last twenty years. It used to be that way then, too. They come in droves. At the beginning of spring the visitors start, and they are always here for the parades.

Mr. Mason: The Naval Museum there on the grounds - it is officially under the Naval History office, isn't it, under the Director of Naval History? How did his control and your control function jointly?

Admiral Melson: I don't remember the Naval History office having any direct control over the Museum.

Mr. Mason: Maybe there wasn't. However, I do understand that he wears that hat in connection with all naval museums.

Admiral Melson: He may have some overseeing control, but as far as I know the Naval Academy Museum is right under the Superintendent of the Naval Academy.

If you go back in the history of the Museum, Captain Harry A. Baldridge, later Rear Admiral Baldridge, was the curator of the Museum at the time that I was here then. He was a rather strong-willed gentleman, and no one did much overseeing of that Museum except Mr. Baldridge.

As far as I know the only control is invested directly in the Superintendent. Undoubtedly, there was a liaison between them, but that I'm not sure of. I may be wrong on the control, but I don't think so.

Mr. Mason: Tell me about Admiral Hill as Superintendent.

Admiral Melson: Admiral Hill was a very enthusiastic gentleman, as you well know. He was very active. He was very much sports oriented. He attended football practice daily. He went to all the other events. I don't mean the games, he went out to watch the Midshipmen practice, and to all the other various sports.

His aide at that time was Commander William F. Bringle, who now is on his way as Admiral Bringle to London. (Bush Bringle).

This is diverging a little bit from the immediate thing, but I think it's of interest. Bush Bringle was the flag Lieutenant at the time I was Chief of Staff. He has just recently left command of the Seventh Fleet, which he had for almost three years. He is now Commander Air Force Pacific, and has just been selected four-stars and will go to London to command Naval Forces Europe.

Coming back to Admiral Hill again - for a man of his age he certainly was active. I never saw him walk up a flight of steps, he always went two steps at a time. I think we all admired him very, very much. He kept us going.

Mr. Mason: Was his interest not only in sports, but was it primarily in the educational process?

Admiral Melson: Yes, I think he was interested in the whole activity. Of course, the Naval Academy is a little different now from what it was twenty years ago, but that's to be expected.

Mr. Mason: In what way?

Admiral Melson: In the educational side.

At that time, and I must say that I speak partly from ignorance because I was not involved in the academic side, I'm under the impression that while the Superintendent was interested in the academic side there was not the pressure there is today to improve and change the courses, which has been going on for some time.

At that time the academic courses were more or less stereotype, and had been for some years. And I might say that they were that way when I got back as Superintendent, too. It was only then that we made the change.

I know he was extremely interested in the educational side, but I can't personally speak of any great knowledge on that.

I was not a member of the Academic Board at this time, but the Academic Board used to meet twice a year to discuss the Midshipmen who were 'unsat'. That involved, in some cases, dismissal. He took it very seriously. It was not a routine thing - the meeting of the Board to consider the future of these young men in their academic subjects.

I think that Admiral Hill did a fine all around job. Of course, you must remember that I speak a little bit from the outside, as far as the academic side of the Naval Academy was concerned at that time.

Mr. Mason: As Administrative Aide did you and Mrs. Melson have to do your fair share of entertaining? Did you have quarters on the grounds?

Admiral Melson: I had quarters on the grounds. I lived at 30 Upshur Road, a beautiful big set of quarters, but no help. We didn't have to do any social entertaining. Admiral Hill did it all, and we helped him. So we didn't have to do any ourselves. Of course, we had our own personal entertaining, but that was something entirely different.

Mr. Mason: This job continued for what - a period of two years?

Admiral Melson: I was there from May of 1950 until October of 1952, a little bit over two years. It was a very enjoyable job, it was a busy job, and both my wife and I loved every minute of it.

Mr. Mason: What about the summer period when so many Midshipmen were away?

Admiral Melson: The summer period was usually a busy time, because the Midshipmen left around the first part of June to go on cruises and the Plebes started coming in before the end of June. So there was only a three week period in which there was any real break in routine.

During that time we were always very busy, as far as I was concerned, renovating Bancroft Hall and doing clean up work for the coming year. There seemed to be always plenty to do. That was the time we took any leave if we could.

Mr. Mason: How did you handle requests that inevitably came from the teaching staff for improved facilities and that sort of thing? Did you have a screening committee or —

Admiral Melson: This all came up through the head of the individual departments - requests for changes. They all came across my desk.

I sat down and made out the budget each year, based on what was requested. Then between Admiral Hill and the Academic Board and myself we allotted what money was available to do what we could. Everybody didn't get everything they wanted. There never was enough money for what everybody wanted, but we seemed to make out. Maybe not as well as we would like to, but we did make out.

Mr. Mason: There must have been contingents of visitors who

came as representatives of foreign navies.

Admiral Melson: There were continually visitors from foreign navies, some times large groups and some times small.

An occasional training ship came into the Naval Academy. The Italian training ship came in and the Spanish training ship came in. But they didn't involve much more than a reception aboard ship, a reception at the Naval Academy, and some sight seeing tours for the members of the crew. They usually had lots of midshipmen aboard so they were interested in touring the Naval Academy.

It wasn't any great chore. When you do it year in and year out it becomes a routine thing.

Mr. Mason: Did you have to have overall supervision of the transportation of Midshipmen when they went various places to attend games?

Admiral Melson: No, that was usually handled by the Commandant of Midshipmen.

There's a very peculiar relationship at the Naval Academy in the command set up between the Commandant of Midshipmen and the Superintendent. The Commandant of Midshipmen is a Commanding Officer in his own right. It's like Bancroft Hall is a ship, and the Commandant is the Captain of the Ship and he runs it, but he runs it under the supervision of the Superintendent.

#4 Melson - 149

Mr. Mason: His rank is usually that of Captain?

Admiral Melson: Captain, occasionally it's a Rear Admiral. Right now it's a Rear Admiral. The Commandant is usually a very senior Captain and they are quite frequently selected for flag rank while in the billet of Commandant.

Mr. Mason: Isn't that in a sense a bit redundant - to have a command within a command like that?

Admiral Melson: Yes and no, that's not a very good answer to your question but -

In one case you're concerned with a group of Midshipmen, at this time roughly 3300, and they're the most important part of the Naval Academy. Their welfare and benefit is what the Commandant of Midshipmen is responsible for.

Mr. Mason: But so is the Superintendent, is he not?

Admiral Melson: Indirectly, it's an overseeing job.

All the material part of the Naval Academy is a great responsibility, too. That is under the various heads of the departments and it is under the Superintendent.

The thing about the Midshipmen is the matter of discipline is the dividing line between them, because when a Midshipman gets in difficulty or he had to be investigated and passed on up the line somebody has to make the decision on the different kind of punishment he gets or what should happen to him.

It's just the commanding officer of a ship with various departments under him.

The only real difference is that the Commandant of Midshipmen has more responsibility and authority in his particular niche than any heads of departments at the Naval Academy.

As I say it's a very peculiar relationship, but I think it's a very good one.

Instead of each head of department having something to do directly with the control of the Midshipmen, it's all invested in the Commandant. Another head of a department cannot take disciplinary action over a Midshipman. He can report him to the Commandant, who then can investigate him and take him over for disciplinary action.

There are thousands of little details that come up day in and day out with four thousand young men around, and you need one man to keep that under control.

Mr. Mason: I suppose comparable in certain schools to the dean of men, who has the immediate supervision of the male contingent.

Admiral Melson: You might put it another way, too — the Naval Academy is Bancroft Hall and the brigade of Midshipmen.

All these other activities and heads of departments are really supporting activities.

Mr. Mason: Since you mentioned the REINA MERCEDES - why was it discontinued as part of the Academy picture?

Admiral Melson: I wasn't here at the time it was discontinued, but I think this came about under a general reorganization throughout the whole Navy in which they disestablished the Potomac River Command, they disestablished the Severn River Naval Command, and a couple other commands of that nature were discontinued.

I'm not quite sure of the present set up as of today, but the Superintendent has a supervising authority over the other commands here in the area, but no direct control.

Mr. Mason: The counterpart of the Severn River Command continues, but the Superintendent doesn't have the same control that he once had?

Admiral Melson: No, there is no counterpart to the Severn River Command as such. The command was abolished, and all the things that contributed to it. Each one of these are individual commands now, and they operate more or less under the Washington Naval District which corresponds to a naval district.

#4 Melson - 152

Mr. Mason: Was this because of growth?

Admiral Melson: I really don't know. It was a reorganization of the Navy Department in general, and they recommended and carried out the disestablishment of certain commands - such as the Potomac River Naval Command the Severn River Naval Command.

Mr. Mason: Admiral, you'll enter a really exciting period in your career now. When you left the Naval Academy your next command was of the magnificent battleship, the NEW JERSEY.

Admiral Melson: If I may go back for a minute to your statement that I left what you infer to be a quiet period - I'd like to repeat that being at the Naval Academy as Chief of Staff was an exciting period and interesting period, and a very busy period. I just repeat that to give emphasis to the fact that it was a busy period.

In October of 1952 I was detached from the Naval Academy and was ordered to command the USS NEW JERSEY.

Mr. Mason: Did this come as a surprise to you?

Admiral Melson: Not really. I'd been very hopeful that I would get a command of a major ship when I left the Naval

Academy, because I was at that stage in my career where it was the thing I had to do as things were going at that time.

It came as a bit of a surprise when I actually got command of a battleship, because there were many other ships I could have gotten. Of course, not being an aviator I hadn't thought about a carrier or anything like that, and I was satisfied with any big ship that I could get.

It wasn't a great surprise, but it was certainly a wonderful feeling to be ordered to command a ship like the NEW JERSEY, of which there are not many in this world. Actually, there are a total of four, including the NEW JERSEY.

Here I come to what I think is perhaps one of the most enjoyable periods of my naval career. There was more personal satisfaction in commanding this big ship than any other assignment I had. I don't mean to down grade any other assignments I had, but this was a big ship which you went to sea in which obeyed your slightest command. You had a large crew. Actually, the crew on the NEW JERSEY got up as high as 3800 when I had flag aboard.

There's a great deal of personal satisfaction in controlling a piece of machinery this size at sea. There was a lot of satisfaction in later assignments, but I don't know quite how to put it down, except it wasn't the physical satisfaction in these other assignments that you got out of taking a big ship to sea. This was a big ship.

Mr. Mason: And she was relatively new at that point, was she?

Admiral Melson: No. The NEW JERSEY was built during World War II, and she was one of Halsey's flag ships. She was Halsey's flag ship in the Third Fleet back around 1944, and she operated all during the war. Then she was placed out of commission and recommissioned again later. You might say she was about ten years old. Whether that's old or young in the age of ships it's hard to tell. In a sense she was comparatively new, I guess.

Mr. Mason: And she carried all the finest electronic equipment.

Admiral Melson: She had the most modern equipment of that era. If she were to go to sea today they'd tear all that off and put something else more fancy on her, I'm sure.

She did have a very competent installation which could do many, many things, some of which I might touch on as we go along.

Mr. Mason: That raises an interesting point. Stepping out of a shore assignment, did you have to do a little brushing up in order to master all the installations on

#4 Melson - 155

the NEW JERSEY or did you comprehend them?

Admiral Melson: I went to a couple of schools on my way to the NEW JERSEY, short courses.

Mr. Mason: Tell me about that.

Admiral Melson: I went to fire control school at Dam's Neck for a short period of time for a very abbreviated course. I went to a short ship control school in Norfolk. That's about all there was to it.

Of course, I had commanded ships before. While it was a big ship there wasn't much difference in the overall principles applied to it as a destroyer. All you needed was more water and more room.

I reported aboard the NEW JERSEY in Norfolk in late October and we operated from then until Christmas time in the Norfolk area. I might relate my first experience.

I went to sea with the old Commanding Officer, Captain McCorkle, now Admiral McCorkle. I made a training trip to sea with him. We were out a couple of days and came back. He left and there I was swinging around the hook in Hampton Roads. It was all mine.

The first time we got underway everything went along nicely. We started down the channel. The only trouble was the channel didn't seem to be wide enough. It looked to me like we were wider than the channel. These were all first impressions.

We went to sea and operated for about a week, came back in, and again that channel didn't look big enough, particularly when something else was coming down channel coming out when you were headed in.

Mr. Mason: I suppose you were mindful also of the MISSOURI.

Admiral Melson: I remembered the MISSOURI every time we went past that spot.

When we came in to anchor the first time - Captain McCorkle had given me lots of information about anchoring, how far the ship had to run to stop, and how far it had to run before the propellers would take hold when you backed down, and so forth - I followed all these instructions very carefully, I thought. We got in this spot and I gave the order to drop anchor. The anchor went off and I just thought that chain would never stop going out, and I thought that ship would never stop. And I was as sure as could be that we were going to end up in the Newport News shipbuilding yard. But everything seemed to work out all right with no trouble.

Actually, I guess all these impressions were exaggerated because it was my first time that it was my sole responsibility. I'd seen the same thing happen under McCorkle, but it didn't impress me the way it did when I was the one that had to give the orders.

We operated in and out of Norfolk until Christmas. We spent Christmas time in Norfolk. I remember the Christmas decorations on the NEW JERSEY in particular. The ship was completely outlined with electric lights, and each gun had its own string of electric lights. So when you got off you had a profile of the ship all in lights. It was an impressive sight. I'm sure the peace loving people wouldn't exactly approve of that illustration.

Then after Christmas we continued to operate off Hampton Roads for a while. He made a trip to Guantanamo Bay with the other three battleships. The division of battleships actually made the trip down to Guantanamo Bay for a few days of operating and then returned.

These were all just training exercises, and nothing of any great note occurred except it was then and would be now, I think, quite a sight to see these four big ships steaming along in formation.

Mason: What were the others?

Admiral Melson: The WISCONSIN, the IOWA, and the MISSOURI. It was quite something.

Mr. Mason: I suppose by that time you'd achieved a great

degree of confidence as skipper?

Admiral Melson: Oh no, I never had a great degree of confidence, I don't believe, but I had some, anyway. I had no difficulty.

Mr. Mason: Did you ever experience a feeling of - here you were in charge of an almost invincible power, in terms of the battle wagon, the gun power?

Admiral Melson: It wasn't so much the gun power. We had nine sixteen-inch guns and lots of five-inch guns, but that didn't impress me quite as much as one particular thing did.

During these operations off the Virginia Capes we were in some very rough weather, and what impressed me was the way that big ship behaved in heavy seas. There just wasn't anything that bothered that ship, she just steamed through as steady as could be.

You'd stand on the bridge and look at the bow, and you could see the bow quiver as it hit the seas and it would swing back and forth, but that was because it was built with a flexible bow. There was a certain amount of movement built into that part of the ship.

The main part of the ship was really a very heavy steel box. The bow was built of lighter weight material up ahead, the stern was light weight, and it surrounded this box which contained all your ammunition and the handling wheels for the sixteen-inch guns and all that. It was just a tremendous steel box with a shaped bow and stern. When you hit these heavy seas the bow would just quiver back and forth as you'd stand up there and watch it.

Some time before that we heard the story of the PITTSBURGH, a heavy cruiser, which had lost her bow in the Pacific.

I use to stand up there and watch this bow shake like that and wonder if it was going to stay on. But it did through a lot of rough weather with no problem.

They were wonderful ships at sea. They were wet in that waves just sort of washed over them and went on by, but they were just grand to handle.

I had a great deal of enthusiasm for battleships. I was probably one of the last battleship sailors.

Mr. Mason: Do you think their passing is an irreparable loss to us?

Admiral Melson: No, not the way things have developed in this day and age. I do think, however, that it would be a great mistake to scrap these four ships, because they'd still serve a very useful purpose if needed.

#4 Melson - 160

Mr. Mason: I suppose an illustration - the recommissioning of the NEW JERSEY for Vietnam.

Admiral Melson: That's not too good an illustration, although she went out and did some service, but I don't think she really did very much. It wasn't the ship's fault, it just wasn't their type thing. Korea was a little different. Apparently she did do some useful bombarding down in Vietnam.

Mr. Mason: There's nothing really like the fire power of sixteen-inch guns, is there?

Admiral Melson: No, there's nothing that you can compare to it. There isn't a bomb that you can compare to it.

When I get over here I'll try to give an example of how these sixteen-inch guns really operate.

Mr. Mason: Why then are the battleships considered obsolete in our time?

Admiral Melson: There's nothing afloat for the battleships to fight, for instance. About all they do these days is bombard a shore, which they are very good at.

These particular ships, if converted, would make wonderful command ships. But the way the war at sea is progressing these days the tendency is towards smaller craft. Whether that will last or not I don't know.

Mr. Mason: You mean - the size makes them vulnerable?

Admiral Melson: No. I think the present CNO has expressed himself by saying that he wants lots of smaller ships that can be lots of places. If you have one bit ship you don't have the diversity. And if you don't have another battleship to fight really the reason for their existance is about gone.

There isn't any other big ships in the world. All the British have been scrapped. The French have two or three old ships. The Russians have no battleships.

I just hate to see them pass, because they're just such wonderful seagoing ships. Expense was the big problem.

On the NEW JERSEY to operate that ship fully took about 3400 men - that is to man all the guns, the engine room, and so forth. Of course, that is a war time condition really. You could put a small crew aboard to steam around, I guess.

We did reduce the crew a couple of times to bare minimum, but they're costly. There's no question about that. They cost a lot to build, and they cost a lot to keep up. They cost a lot to move around and go places.

Mr. Mason: Could they be converted into atomic type ships, atomic powered ships?

Admiral Melson: I doubt it, because I think it would be too expensive. It's probably cheaper to start from scratch to build these ships, at least that's what the naval constructors always tell you. It's easier and cheaper to build a new ship than it is to convert an old one, that is a navy conversion.

I think the battleship days are just about washed out, because there's not enough pressure to bring them back to active duty.

The war at sea has changed so much. It seems to have changed a great deal.

It's latest career was operating task force carriers at sea, with battleships and cruisers in support. They were all working on the coast of Korea and all functioning very well.

Today there doesn't seem to be quite that demand for that type operation. It's changing times, I guess.

Mr. Mason: Was there any sentimental attachment to the NEW JERSEY on the part of citizens in the state of New Jersey when you were there?

Admiral Melson: Very much so. The people of New Jersey

were very proud of the ship, and they did little nice things for the ship, and kept it publicized in New Jersey.

The Commanding Officer of a ship has no funds other than special personal funds which he can use with his discretion in operating the ship. He has allotments and various funds for operating the different departments and things like that. But if you to into some port and have to give a dinner party, it's very difficult occasionally to ask for special funds for it.

People of New Jersey gave the Commanding Officer a slush fund, which they kept filled up all the time, it ran around five hundred dollars, which he could use for things like that without accounting to anybody. He could do things with that that he couldn't do with government funds. And that was a nice little gesture on their part.

Mr. Mason: There must have been some sort of organization within the state of New Jersey that did this.

Admiral Melson: I think it's the Society of the USS NEW JERSEY.

Mr. Mason: Did you have to pay your obeisance by calling in a port ever?

Admiral Melson: No, I never was in the New Jersey.

They gave the NEW JERSEY a beautiful silver service. It's back in the state of New Jersey now.

Mr. Mason: Where is she in mothballs?

Admiral Melson: She's in mothballs in Bremerton, I believe. She came back from the Far East to a West Coast yard.

They always had a great deal of interest in the ship, and were constantly corresponding with the Commanding Officer about different things. They showed a lot of personal interest.

After Christmas we went down to Guantanamo on this trip for various operations along the East Coast.

Mr. Mason: All this was a prelude to Korea?

Admiral Melson: We knew we were going to Korea. Part of our job at Guantanamo was shore bombardment, in training preparation for our trip to Korea.

On 5 March 1953 we left Norfolk bound for Korea, just the one battleship, the NEW JERSEY. At that time the MISSOURI was already out there.

We left for Korea by way of the Canal. Transiting the Canal was an interesting operation in itself with a ship this size. We had just inches to spare on both sides, and just inches under the bottom all the way through, but we went through without any great todo and made it.

Mr. Mason: What speed did you go through under those circumstances?

Admiral Melson: You're towed through, that is in the locks you're towed, about two or three miles an hour. When you get out in the lakes, in between the locks, maybe fifteen or sixteen knots.

From Panama we went to Long Beach where we spent several days, taking on provisions, and fueling.

We then headed out into the Western Pacific via Honolulu. We had our wartime complement aboard. The whole time I was on board we had that.

We spent a few days at Honolulu, and were briefed by CinCPac's people on the operations in Korea and of what was going on.

At that time CinCPac was Admiral Radford. We had a very nice reception at his quarters while we were there, not for me but it was one he was giving.

Then we headed out of Pearl Harbor for WestPac.

The reason I am going into this part in such detail was the next thing that came up. After we had passed the C buoy off Pearl Harbor the executive officer came to the bridge and said he had a dispatch which had come in just before we had left the dock, and he held it without showing it to me until we were clear of the harbor.

It was a dispatch saying that Captain Warner Edsall, the Commanding Officer of the MISSOURI, had had a heart attack on the bridge of the MISSOURI while passing through the net in Sasebo going into the harbor. As I understand it he died almost instantly.

The reason why they withheld it from me, I guess, was they didn't want me to have a heart attack going out from Pearl Harbor.

Mr. Mason: Was it a tense time when you were departing?

Admiral Melson: It always is going in and out of a harbor in a big ship. You've got a pilot you've got to worry about. You've got boats around you. It's a busy period.

Normally it's better not to have interference at that time. In this case it wouldn't help it in any way if I knew it. If they had told me before I left the dock it wouldn't have made any difference. For some reason or other he thought it would be better to wait until I got out.

We started that trip across the Pacific from Pearl Harbor at eighteen knots headed for Yokosuka. As I remember it was a very pleasant cruise. We were alone.

En route we passed the heavy cruiser, ROCHESTER, returning from Korea on the way back to the States. She was commanded at that time by Captain Richard Phillips, who was a classmate of mine. (He's of course retired now and lives in Washington). We exchanged the usual greetings when passing in the night.

We finally arrived in Yokosuka. I found that we were supposed to go into the harbor behind the breakwater and go alongside the MISSOURI, which by then was in Yokosuka for the shifting of the flag of Commander Seventh Fleet to the NEW JERSEY.

Mr. Mason: You were becoming a unit of the Seventh Fleet?

Admiral Melson: Yes.

It was sort of a touchy problem putting two ships like that alongside each other at a buoy. I didn't like it one bit, but they sent a pilot out with tugs who knew his business pretty well. We eased in alongside the MISSOURI without doing any damage to either one.

Shortly after we got alongside we had the usual visit from the various staff members of the Commander Seventh Fleet, all dashing over to see what the staterooms were like and where they were going to stow their files and all that sort of business.

Two days later Admiral Jocko Clark and his staff moved aboard, and we became officially flag ship of the Commander Seventh Fleet.

I'd heard many stories about Jocko Clark. Some of them

made me wonder what kind of life I'd live as flag Captain, but I say here and now I never dealt with a more pleasant individual. The whole time he was on board the NEW JERSEY he never once corrected me or told me how to do anything. He said, "Do this or do that," and that was it.

I saw a lot of him and I found him a very interesting individual and a very competent officer. I say at the beginning - I enjoyed very much my time with him.

Shortly thereafter we took off for Sasebo, which was the base of the battleships operating out there. I might say the reason was - most of the ships in the Seventh Fleet replenished from replenishment ships - ammunition, oil, food, and so forth - but the sixteen inch shells for the battleships presented a different problem. While it could be done, they didn't care for it.

So the battleships, after being up in the firing line for a while, went down to Sasebo to load up again, take on ammunition. It seems to me we did that about every two weeks.

Mr. Mason: What's the weight of a sixteen inch shell?

Admiral Melson: A little over a ton.

Mr. Mason: Hadn't Sasebo also been the base for the Japanese battleships?

Admiral Melson: Sasebo had been a base for the Japanese battleships. I think a battleship was built in Sasebo, not one of the mighty big ones. It had some facilities for taking care of big ships.

After a short visit to Sasebo this time we took off to go up to what they called 'bomb line' which was an imaginary line just north of Wonsan to join Task Force 77. Task Force 77 was the fighting and operating force of the Seventh Fleet. We went up to join them, and I got my initiation joining up with a fast carrier task force.

We first contacted them by voice radio and arranged a rendevouz. Or rather they told me where they were to join up. I finally located them. They were launching aircraft making about twenty-eight knots when I came in over the horizon.

Fortunately, I came in ahead of them, so I didn't have to chase them. It was quite interesting going in, yourself at twnety-seven knots to join a task force making twenty-seven knots, surrounded by destroyers. You just sort of thread your way through until you find your slot and you stay there.

No sooner had we gotten our slot when Admiral Clark did something which he was doing all the time from then on, I think. He wanted to go over to visit the flag ship of Task Force 77, which was a carrier. So off went our helicopter for its initial try at landing on the fast moving task force.

I might say that it was sort of routine operation for the NEW JERSEY to go off on various little errands for Admiral Clark, not personal, but official, then dash madly back and join the Task Force for a day or two.

Then you'd take off and go over to the bomb line and bombard for a couple of days. Then you'd go down and pick up Admiral Clark at Pusan or some place where he was on his way back to the ship.

To explain a little more fully the operation - the Task Force operated constantly in this area just to the east of Wonsan, some times a little bit north, but in general, in that area. They launched flights day and night to bomb North Korea. They'd launch a flight, turn and pick up another flight coming back, this went on constantly.

Occasionally, when the bombs were getting short and ammunition was short and fuel was short the replenishment force would join up for a day to replenish them. Then away they'd go again to continue this round and round of bombing.

Tied in with this - Admiral Clark to administer his duties as Commander Seventh Fleet had to go ashore and confer with the Army and Air Force people ashore in Korea. So one of our duties would be to run down the coast to a small airfield, send him ashore by helicopter, then when the helicopter returned we'd turn around and go back to the bomb line and bombard some more. Then a couple of of days later we'd go down to another place along the coast and send a helicopter in. We'd pick up Admiral Clark and away we'd go to join Task Force 77.

It's not a very good explanation of the operation, but we were just constantly on the go all the time.

Mr. Mason: It was General Mark Clark, was it not, who was in command?

Admiral Melson: Yes. He was aboard. I'll mention him a little later.

Admiral Briscoe was ComNavFE at that time and he quite frequently came out to the Fleet for a visit.

Mr. Mason: I understand that the waters in that area, the coastal waters, were heavily mined, were they not?

Admiral Melson: In close to shore. We had pretty good intelligence as to where the mine fields were, and stayed clear of them. That was one of the many advantages of having the battleship - we could stay outside of these shallow coastal waters and shoot pretty far in.

Mr. Mason: What were your targets - the railroads and - ?

Admiral Melson: The railroads, the guns mounted in caves,

and things of that nature.

The harbor at Wonsan was ringed with guns. Yodo is a little island that sets right in the entrance of the harbor at Wonsan. On Yodo we kept, I mean the United States did, a small detachment of naval intelligence people who operated there all the time. They had radio communications to ships and whatnot.

Mr. Mason: Did they operate as commandos or something?

Admiral Melson: No, as far as I know they made no forays. It was sort of a look-out station.

Across from Yodo about two to three miles of water was the shore of Korea. Occasionally, small vessels, like destroyers and cruisers, would go into Wonsan harbor, circle around, bombard the shore stations, and come out again. All this area had been mined. We kept mine sweepers in there all the time which kept channels cleared so the ships could operate inside.

I only went inside the harbor once while I was out there. I went up to the entrance several times, but I went in once to bombard. To me it was sort of touch and go because it was very narrow quarters in a swept channel, and we were being fired on all the time. We never actually got hit, but we did get splinters aboard from shells.

One time we went in we had the Assistant Secretary of the Navy, Mr. Floberg, aboard. I think it was rather interesting to him because he was standing up on the flying bridge above the coning tower and there were several close misses. I think he got quite a kick out of that.

Mr. Mason: What sort of mines did the Koreans use? Were they influence mines?

Admiral Melson: Contact, as far as I know.

We would occasionally see a mine that had broken loose float by and try to sink it, but the ship never hit one, thank goodness.

We saw one sort of pick up in the bow wake. It washed down the side. The wake of the ship sort of pushed it away, and it never got in close enough to hit us.

One time we went down to pick up Admiral Clark at an airfield down the coast. We were in a very heavy fog and couldn't see a thing. You couldn't see the bow of the ship most of the time. On our surface search radar we picked up all these small 'pips' which were fishing vessels off the coast of South Korea. We sailed right into the middle of them because we had to to get in close to the shore. As far as I know we didn't hit any. The boys in CIC had them all plotted in, and they did a wonderful job of guiding us into this place.

Mr. Mason: The native fishermen were unperturbed by the war.

Admiral Melson: They had to eat, I guess.

Then Admiral Clark left a small harbor in a small Coast Guard cutter and came out through all this mess to meet us. Our CIC coached the boat right up to the gangway, and he came aboard. That was one time he put his foot on deck and said, "Thank God, I'm back aboard again," because he was nervous about it, too.

There were trains that ran almost every night up and down the coast taking supplies into the city of Wonsan. One night we sent a whale boat with four volunteer officers in close to the shore to give us warning of an approaching train so we could try and block the tunnel, which they were supposed to pass through. The idea being to catch them in the tunnel, and block both ends.

They went in and things got a little taut there for a while, because we were afraid they were going to end up on the shore instead of coming back to the ship. About that time they reported a train and we fired a prearranged slavo into the tunnel. We never did find out whether we blocked the tunnel or not, but we were very happy to get that four back aboard ship. This is something the staff had dreamed up, it wasn't my doing.

Mr. Mason: I understand those trains were rather remarkable in that during daylight the tracks just disappeared, and were reassembled at night.

Admiral Melson: That may be true in some areas. I can't vouch for that.

I do know this - that coast line was very rugged and there were many, many tunnels. We were sure that trains came down and when it got daylight and they could be spotted they just went in the tunnels and stayed until everything was clear and then they continued their journey. There was just one tunnel after another all along the coast.

You could see where trains had been hit by bombs or shells. You could see them with binoculars, we were in that close.

Mr. Mason: Were you ever subjected to air attack?

Admiral Melson: No. There were two or three scares while we were with the Task Force 77.

They apparently had one small plane that used to go out occasionally on scouting missions at night. We'd pick him up on radar and he'd sort of circle formation. By the time our planes got there to chase him, he had long gone. He stayed close to the water, and I guess once the planes got up they couldn't see him. He used to come out once in a while and sort of circle us on, I guess, a scouting mission.

We never had an air attack as such.

Mr. Mason: Did you use planes, helicopters, or what for spotting?

Admiral Melson: Helicopters.

We used to use Army planes to scout quite frequently - small planes, spotting planes. We'd contact them by radio and they would act as fire control for us. That was particularly true when we were firing well inland. Quite frequently they'd call for us to fire over the hills into the valley beyond which we couldn't see, even by helicopter. They would spot on those for us.

You'd see these little planes flying around over there and you'd wonder how they ever stayed up. They'd disappear behind a mountain and you thought they'd never come out again. Then they'd zoom up and pretty soon there they'd be.

We had very good liaison with the Army on these spotting missions.

Mr. Mason: Tell me about General Mark Clark. You said he came onboard the NEW JERSEY -

Admiral Melson: He came on board while we were up in

Yokosuka.

Mr. Mason: Then you had to go back for your shells, too.

Admiral Melson: We'd usually pick up our shells in Sasebo, but when we could we'd go back to Yokosuka. It wasn't too much of a run. We'd spend a couple of days there and give some liberty to the men, and load up there.

General Clark was aboard once for dinner with Admiral Clark and I had the pleasure of meeting him. There wasn't more to it than that, except that I met him.

I've got to touch on some of the visitors here -

We made a special trip, which I think is of interest. We left Wonsan with Admiral Clark on board, and went to the west coast of Korea off of Inchon. We anchored in the harbor at Inchon, in which there was a very big conference held, including a lot of the Army people down on that.

At that time President Syngman Rhee and his wife, Francesca, came aboard with Admiral Briscoe and several other ranking people.

After we finished the conference we went up to Chinanapo, Korea in company with the British cruiser, HMS NEWCASTLE, and did some bombarding in that area. This time the British planes from the cruiser spotted for us. That was a rather interesting trip.

We had Syngman Rhee and his wife aboard several times for visits. They were aboard at Pusan, and at Inchon. They were aboard in Yokosuka. They always came out in a helicopter.

As I've said, Mark Clark was there, and at one time or another Admiral Briscoe came out. Ambassador William C. Bullitt visited us for a few days. Admiral Felix Stump, of course, was out to see us. And I've already mentioned Assistant Secretary Floberg.

We had innumerable Korean officers out. The thing that interested me particularly about these senior Korean officers that we saw was how much they reminded me of the Japanese officers. They dressed, carried themselves with a swagger, and acted just like you'd expect a Japanese officer to act, particularly the ones we heard about during the war.

Mr. Mason: They had been trained where and by whom - the Korean navy?

Admiral Melson: I think any training the navy had was from us.

Mr. Mason: Although you were Seventh Fleet, you were also United Nations, weren't you?

Admiral Menson: Yes, United Nations Force.

We were operating under the United Nations, but except for this one British cruiser I didn't see any other units around - the United States Navy and one British cruiser as far as the sea forces were concerned.

Mr. Mason: You were in a class by yourself with the battleship.

Admiral Melson: When I say us, I mean the Task Force 77.

In addition to the carriers and destroyers in Task Force 77 there were quite a number of small patrol craft and mine sweepers operating.

Mr. Mason: This was where the other navies were involved I believe.

Admiral Melson: There were some, but I can't say much because I didn't see them.

Mr. Mason: Thailand, Canadian navy, Australia.

Admiral Melson: They were there I know, but my contact with them was nil.

Mr. Mason: Were the discussions going on at that time?

Admiral Melson: I must say I don't know too much about it because I was too far away, but I'll tell you what I observed.

Discussions were going on at that time, and Lieutenant General Harrison was our senior negotiator. They met on truce negotiations during July.

Among other visitors Max Taylor was out several times.

While we were at anchor in Inchon waiting for this conference to go on, it was the tenth anniversary of the NEW JERSEY. So the bake shop built a cake like the NEW JERSEY and I had the pleasure of cutting it on the quarterdeck.

In July 1953 the truce negotiators were meeting more or less seriously during that time, and it ended up by the signing of the truce.

The last day we did any active firing was on the 26th of July. I think the truce was signed the next day. That's when we had word that Lieutenant General W. K. Harrison had sent out a message that the truce had been signed and the war was over.

Mr. Mason: Prior to that, when you first went out, did you feel any repercussions from the negotiations or the sense of frustration which our people endured?

Admiral Melson: I didn't, and I don't think the ship did.

If any of the crew did I wasn't aware of it.

We were all very active in our own little daily routine and we didn't have a daily newspaper with headlines to inform us how things were going. We were just sort of in our own little world very, very busy.

I think that might be true for a lot of people who are actively engaged in a war as compared to those of us who sit back here and listen to the radio and television every day.

News was kind of scarce aboard ship. We got press news which we put out every day. I think press news at best was very skimpy, and doesn't go into all the pros and cons of the situation.

I had no particular feeling of frustration. Maybe I was enjoying my ship too much.

Mr. Mason: Did Admiral Clark get involved?

Admiral Melson: He was present at the signing of the truce. I don't believe he signed it, I don't think he was a signer. But he was present along with Admiral Briscoe. General Harrison was the man who did the signing, as far as I know.

Mr. Mason: You arrived after President Dwight Eisenhower had been there, did you not?

Admiral Melson: Yes.

The commanding officer of a ship, even a big ship like the NEW JERSEY, and being a flag ship operating very actively in a war of this nature your days are full. At night you get what rest you can. And you just don't get the feel of these daily frustrations, if you want to call it that, going on in the world. You're just too busy with what you're doing day in and day out.

Mr. Mason: That's in a sense, a blessing.

Admiral Melson: It is.

Our days were busy days. Our nights, when I could sleep, I slept pretty soundly.

A lot of the time I think it was boring to the crew. I don't think they had this great interest in the war, but nevertheless they all had enough to keep them pretty busy.

Mr. Mason: Were the activities so intense that you didn't have any opportunity to have any kind of an educational program underway on board? Did you have anything of that sort?

Admiral Melson: We had the normal training courses and things like that going, but the crew were at battle stations a good percentage of the time, particularly the A. A. batteries. We hadn't had an air attack, but you never knew when you might have one.

When we were on the bomb line, for instance, all the gun stations were manned almost twelve hours a day while it was daylight, and occasionally at night.

You might say we were just engaged in doing our part in fighting the war.

I'm sure that a lot more went on down the bow of that ship than I know about, because I was up on the bridge and I very rarely ever left it at sea. I got my reports from the executive officer. How much they kept from me I don't know.

Mr. Mason: Who was your exec?

Admiral Melson: I had two execs.

The first one, a Captain, on the way out there got detached and went back to Chicago. He was an artist, he painted. He was knifed on the street and was killed in Chicago.

The second exec, Commander Freddie Chenault, was a very fine officer and — but did make flag rank as far as I know. He did a very fine job.

On the 28th of July 1953, having left Norfolk on March 5th, 1953, we had logged 37,519 miles, and we fired over 4,000 rounds of sixteen-inch shells. That's a lot.

They finally decided we'd go to Hong Kong for rest and relaxation. So away we went to Hong Kong. We could not get into the inner harbor at Hong Kong -

Mr. Mason: Why - because of her draft?

Admiral Melson: Yes, Pirates' Bay, I think they called it. We couldn't go inside because of our draft. Some of the carriers could get inside, but they didn't have quite the same draft we did.

We dropped anchor, and within fifteen minutes we were completely surrounded by sampans. They were six and eight deep tied up all around the ship, all selling something or other.

You might say we all had a delightful time in Hong Kong.

Mr. Mason: By that time Admiral Clark was not with you?

Admiral Melson: Yes, he went with us, the war was over then, for rest and relaxation.

Then on the way back to Japan after our ten days stay there we stopped off the coast of Formosa and took on board the midshipmen of the Nationalist Chinese Naval Academy, and what must have been all the officers of their navy. I'd never seen so many.

They came out in destroyers alongside and boarded. We made a short trip up and down the coast during the day and fired some guns for their benefit, and then sent them home. I didn't know then that some day I'd be in Taiwan.

Then we went on back to Yokosuka. En route we stopped at Pusan and President Rhee came aboard and presented the Presidential Unit Citation to the Seventh Fleet. On that day General Maxwell Taylor, Ambassador Ellis, and General Pak of the Korean army were aboard.

Leaving Pusan we went on to Yokosuka. By that time the WISCONSIN had arrived to relieve us and we doubled up our buoy the same as before - the same as we did with the MISSOURI when we arrived. We transferred the flag to the WISCONSIN. When that was completed we were released from the Seventh Fleet and set sail.

I had one thrill as we were going out of Tokyo Bay. A submarine net was stretched across the entrance to the Bay and there was a comparatively narrow entrance between the entrance buoys that held the net. The current, which ran rather strongly, sat directly across the opening. The pilot still had the Connas we passed through the net.

I was standing in the wing of the bridge watching this and I could just see us being set down on this net. I had visions right then and there of snagging one of those nets around the propeller and being anchored at

Tokyo Bay for a while. For fortunately we put the helm over and swung the stern out and passed through safely.

Then we had a very uneventful trip to Honolulu, where I was relieved by Captain Atkeson.

Mr. Mason: She must have been due for a refitting at that point, was she not?

Admiral Melson: Yes.

I flew back to the States and had a few days leave with orders to report to ComBatCru as his Chief of Staff in Norfolk.

Interview No. 5 with Vice Admiral Charles L. Melson, U.S. Navy
At his residence in Annapolis, Maryland
May 3, 1971   by John T. Mason, Jr.

Mr. Mason: Admiral, we're about to begin chapter five today, and this is your duty in the Atlantic, which was an interesting and manifold type duty. You had been with the NEW JERSEY last time, you returned from the Far East, now you want to resume your story.

Admiral Melson: When I was detached from the NEW JERSEY in October of 1953, I proceeded to Norfolk, Virginia, and reported to Commander Battleships-Cruisers Atlantic Fleet as his Chief of Staff.

Mr. Mason: And who was he?

Admiral Melson: Rear Admiral E. T. Wooldridge was then Commander Battleships-Cruisers Atlantic Fleet, and during my tour he was later relieved by Rear Admiral R. E. Libby.

During this period I served on various ships with the Commander, among them being the MISSOURI, the IOWA, and the ALBANY. As is so often the case the flag and staff shift from ship to ship depending on what the individual ships are doing and where the staff has to go to carry out their own duties. In this case we managed to be on three different ships - two of them being the battleships which I was acquainted with before.

Mr. Mason: I take it sometimes a cruiser is more feasible for the command ship.

Admiral Melson: In this particular case, while the battleships were more roomy and better for a large staff, the ALBANY, which is a heavy cruiser, really suited our purpose better when we went to the Med, although while we were in the Med we were on the IOWA part of the time.

During the period shortly after I reported to the Battleships-Cruisers outfit, we spent most of the Spring of '54 on the East Coast of the United States carrying out various training exercises and visiting various ports.

In the Spring of 1954, this is repeating a little bit, Rear Admiral Wooldridge was detached from duty as ComBatCruLant and ordered as President of the National War College. He was relieved as ComBatCruLant by Rear Admiral R. E. Libby.

Mr. Mason: Would you pause for a moment and tell me something about Admiral Wooldridge. You had a chance to observe him, you served with him. Since he went on to the War College I'd like to have a bit about him.

Admiral Melson: Admiral Wooldridge was a very fine man in all respects - professionally, socially, and just an all around fine naval officer. I had known Admiral Wooldridge before when he was Commander of Destroyers Atlantic Fleet, based in Newport. It was as a result of this acquaintance that I was finally ordered later to be his Chief of Staff in this other assignment. He was a very quiet individual, very easy to get along with, he very rarely lost his temper or became excited. And he was very easy to serve and be with. He was also very considerate of all of his subordinates and the people who were on his staff. On top of this he was an intellectual. While he had the normal naval background, he seemed to have the ability to foresee events, he was a wonderful planner, and he was just a very outstanding senior naval officer.

Mr. Mason: I suppose those last attributes you mention were ones that were taken into consideration when he was named to be President of the War College.

Admiral Melson: I think they were. And I might say that, while I did not attend the National War College, I did on occasion visit him there and I only heard the very best.

He was not the first - Harry Hill was the first - but I think he did a very fine job from what I know.

It's very interesting, which will come out later, that

I heard of one of my very best assignments in his living room at a cocktail party at the National War College, which I'll cover later.

Admiral Libby was an entirely different type individual. He was very quick, very active, and he too was quite intellectual. He liked to write, he was good at planning, and he had held some very excellent assignments prior to this. I had known him for several years before this.

Both of them in their assignment, ComBatCruLant, gave me almost full authority in my particular job, and it was rarely if ever, that I had to refer anything to them before taking action. They were willing to let you go ahead and do what you were supposed to do. I'll admit if you didn't do right, you'd probably get your knuckles cracked, but we didn't do too badly.

They both remained close friends of mine throughout the years since this particular assignment. Admiral Wooldridge had lived here in Annapolis for some time until he died here a year ago.

Admiral Libby went on to become Commander of the First Fleet and was made a Vice Admiral in that command. Through some difficulties, which I would rather not go into, with the administration, he decided he could do better outside. Admiral Libby is now with the Copley Press in San Diego, and does a great deal of writing.

In the Fall of 1954 ComBatCruLant and his staff was ordered to the Mediterranean for duty with the Sixth Fleet, Admiral Libby being the Force Commander.

During this period we visited numerous ports in the Med and a few on the Atlantic side of Europe, and participated in Fleet maneuvers. Nothing of any great consequence took place.

Mr. Mason: There was no real challenge on the horizon.

Admiral Melson: There wasn't anything going on, it was just daily routine.

During this period I did have a chance to make a quick trip to Paris and to London with Admiral Libby and back to the ship.

Mr. Mason: Was this in connection with NATO?

Admiral Melson: In connection with NATO. And incidentally, it was my only trip to London. I was only there twenty-four hours.

Really my tour of duty with BatCruLant, other than being in contact with certain individuals which we've mentioned, and a little traveling - was rather unexciting, it was interesting, routine naval type operations.

Mr. Mason: In the Mediterranean the Royal Navy had practically withdrawn, had it not, by that time?

Admiral Melson: No, there were units of the British Navy in the Med at that time. This was 1954 and '55. They were still there. As a matter of fact, we were in Gibraltar and we went by Malta several times, and there were units of their fleet there at that time. It was not strong, but they were in evidence.

Mr. Mason: Did you have joint exercises with some of the NATO navies?

Admiral Melson: Not on this particular cruise we didn't. It was confined entirely to operations with the Sixth Fleet itself. There were no foreign units involved.

Mr. Mason: And what was the stated mission of the Sixth Fleet in the Mediterranean in that time?

Admiral Melson: I'm not sure I can state the mission as such, but primarily to show the flag and to be on station in the event that anything occurred in that area in which we were interested.

I might cite as an example the affair in Lebanon when we sent Marines ashore to bring our people out. And there's various occasions when you might have to have a small landing party to help in some particular instance.

I might add - I think this is now general knowledge - that the primary reason that the Sixth Fleet is there, other than showing the flag, is to have the aircraft carriers with aircraft and the equipment to counter-attack in case of a surprise attack. Now the thinking on that has changed a lot as years have gone by, but that's the reason they're sent over there and that's the reason they've been maintained, and it's still a very important part of our defense. You might compare it in a sense to nuclear submarines we have on station in the Atlantic, except that the Sixth Fleet has been on station a lot longer than nuclear submarines in the Atlantic. They're basically there for the same purpose - to deliver nuclear weapons at the proper time if called upon. I think that's general knowledge now; at one time it was quite secret that they carried nuclear weapons and so forth.

I became quite involved in that planning on my next duty as I'll mention as I go along.

On the 6th of February, 1955, I was detached from duty as Chief of Staff, ComBatCruLant, and ordered to the staff of CinCLant in Norfolk, Virginia as Assistant Chief of Staff for Plans. At the time I received my orders we were anchored off of Genoa, Italy in very bad weather, and the only prospect of my getting ashore in a reasonable time was by helicopter, which I did, and from there to Rome by train, and by plane on back to New York and then to Norfolk.

Mr. Mason: Did this come as a surprise to you - this assignment?

Admiral Melson: No, it did not come as a surprise because there had been some preliminary exchange of dispatches between the Commanders concerned as to my availability - the usual things that they talk about when they're looking for somebody to handle their staff.

I welcomed this change of duty because it was going to a larger staff. Furthermore, I'd be based in Norfolk and would be with my family for a while. Most of the time I'd been on the go, so I was willing to settle down for a while.

I reported to Admiral Jerauld Wright, who was then CinCLant, for duty in the latter part of February, 1955. My family and I settled in a very small set of quarters, known as Quarters "D", at CinCLant headquarters in Norfolk, Virginia.

My orders, which ordered me to this staff as Assistant Chief of Staff for Plans, further gave me additional duty on the staff of Commander of the Atlantic Area, which in a sense put me on the staff of the Commander, Supreme Allied

Commander Atlantic - they were all tied together.

The assignment as Plans Officer, Assistant Chief of Staff for Plans, involved the development of implementing plans for the various war plans, which basically originated in the Office of Chief of Naval Operations and from the Joint Chiefs of Staff. The problem of keeping these plans up to date, changing them as the forces changed for one reason or another, or as he put it the situation changed, and have them ready to implement in case of an attack and so forth. Involved in this planning - perhaps the most secret part at that time - was the nuclear aspect of these plans. Basically, they provided for hitting various enemy targets, which I will not name, when the time came with nuclear bombs to destroy the enemy. These plans were quite involved and in quite detail, and it took a tremendous amount of time and planning to write these plans. And they were constantly changing - to the availability of weapons, ships, airplanes. Occasionally, changes in government which changed our basic plan ...

Mr. Mason: Friendly or not so friendly ...

Admiral Melson: Sometimes they were friendly and sometimes they were not so friendly.

That's about as far as I can go into that particular phase because at this moment I'm so far away from it that I'm not sure what is ...

Mr. Mason: Would you say something about it? This was the era when the Eisenhower Administration was stressing massive retaliation as a defense or offense for atomic threat from Russia, and the whole reliance was on this type of thing, wasn't it, rather than the more conventional?

Admiral Melson: Everyone in those days was talking about, as you say, massive retaliation which involved putting as many planes as you could in the air and hitting the other guy with all you had the first time around. The question of whether you had anything to go back with the second time wasn't of great concern at that time. You were supposed to dump your full load the first time, and if you had anything left over you'd just use it to the best advantage after that.

Mr. Mason: I suppose it wasn't of very great concern because there wasn't anybody else with equal atomic power at that point.

Admiral Melson: No. And the other problem was that maybe the enemy would hit you, he may not have quite the power we did, but depending on where he happened to hit it could have damaged us a great deal and reduced our readiness a great deal, particularly if he hit first.

We tried to provide for all these various contingencies in the plans. I sometimes thought we had so many contingencies I wasn't sure of what we would do, there were so many ways to go about it.

I might further point out that at this time the area of CinCLant's responsibility was quite large - all the North Atlantic, the South Atlantic, the Med, and all the tributaries through these various bodies of water, and it involved the land areas which bordered these bodies of water. The Navy's responsibility in this case in it's planning did not stop at the shore line.

In the nuclear planning our plans had to jibe with the Air Force and such plans as the Army had along the same lines, because if this type of massive retaliation was to be successful it couldn't be any one particular group to do this, we all had to do this together at the same time. So targets were allotted in various areas.

Mr. Mason: This meant then naturally that you had to be, as a planning officer, intouch with the Army and the Air Force.

Admiral Melson: I had them on my staff; I had a representive, let's put it that way. I had an Army officer, an Air Force officer - who was a liaison between their planning, and we all worked together.

It was very interesting work and I enjoyed it very much. In spite of the fact that it was planning and nothing might happen, for some reason we worked long hours every day.

Mr. Mason: And how much was this revealed to NATO allies? How much were they cognizant of?

Admiral Melson: I'm not sure I can say at the moment. Our plans were usually stamped "Top Secret NATO," "Top Secret U.S.," and so forth. In certain cases items were left out of one plan and not transferred to another. In other words, we didn't tell completely everything.

Mrs. Melson: There wasn't full exchange ...

Admiral Melson: There had to be some hold back. But planning was pretty good between the two, it had to be coordinated.

Mr. Mason: You were using British bases, too.

Admiral Melson: Absolutely.

It's difficult to say what was held back; it wasn't very much I can tell you that. We had certain little items from time to time that didn't get in all plans.

I'd like to say one thing here - this may have something to do with why I was ordered to this particular job. To me the training I had at the War College as a student was invaluable to me in helping to prepare these various plans. The technique involved, the format, the way you go about planning - all this was very useful to me at this time.

Mr. Mason: Is it possible to give a specific illustration of the application of your knowledge?

Admiral Melson: I don't think so, except as I was ordered there as Plans Officer having been to the War College. It's hard to put it down in black and white, but it's just a certain amount of training that's built into you - how to make plans, how to write them up, there's a way of doing all these things - an orderly way I'd better say, and we all did them in an orderly way then we understood what the other fellow was doing.

The SacLant plans followed our format very closely; they were very much the same.

I know we could have developed written plans without the War College training, but there again, I think you need something like that to do the orderly manner in which you should proceed and put the stuff down on paper. You learn a lot of other things in War College, too. A lot of the areas which we are talking about in this planning we had developed similar plans at the War College, purely as a drill, but we had studied the area. We studied the railroads, the water connections, how many lakes and things like that we had to contend with - we had all this background in our heads fortunately. At least I think we did; I know it was helpful. We were not approaching any particular part of the world without some knowledge of that part of the world.

If you're going to write a plan of what to do in case Russia attacks us, and you're going to retaliate, you like to know where the cities are, where the rivers are, where the factories are, where they do these various things that might be possible points where you would want to attack. And that is something that you pick up at the War College.

Mr. Mason: So it's not only techniques, but it's factual knowledge.

Admiral Melson: It's factual knowledge that you acquire also. That's one of the reasons that I've always supported the war games at the College. There's been some talk of abandoning them. But the war games that you do up there makes you get down and study these other countries, study what they can do and what they have and where they're vulnerable. I think the war gaming is a very useful tool.

might say, in preparing for war. We're not going to have any more wars now, so it doesn't make any difference.

Mr. Mason: What is the rationale back of the suggestion that they drop the war planning?

Admiral Melson: I think there's a tendency of a lot of people to think that you should gain general knowledge by reading and studying, but not the sitting down and writing out actual plans and doing things like that.

Actually in the war planning at the College, you sit down and write up the operation, you write all the annexes, you write all the little details, and figure out your forces.

What some people like to do - is all book learning, if I may put it that way, and I don't think it will be as useful in the long run as the war planning.

Mr. Mason: Or perhaps not make as permanent an impression on a man.

Admiral Melson: That's right. That's purely a matter of opinion.

I think times are changing now - we're not sending big fleets to sea to fight other big fleets, which is the way the war gaming originally started, with one fleet against the other.

Now in planning something you plan maybe a group of ships here that's sending airplanes to attack a target way inland, which is a little different proposition. Of course, the way things are developing now maybe we won't have any more wars - we'll see - I doubt it.

In the Spring of 1955, which was very shortly after I had reported to duty on CinCLant Fleet staff I was selected for promotion to Rear Admiral. In June I took my physical exam for promotion and failed to pass because of a cyst on the thyroid gland. I went to the hospital in Portsmouth, Virginia where they operated and removed this cyst. And they sent me back to active duty. I took my physical promotion exam again and passed satisfactorily. I received my commission as a Rear Admiral in September of 1955, but the date of it was 1 June 1955. In other words, there was no loss of precedence due to this hospitalization.

A month after I was promoted to Rear Admiral I got new orders from the Bureau of Personnel ordering me to report to CinCLant as the Deputy Chief of Staff. So, in effect, I fleeted up one number.

Mr. Mason: That was commensurate with your new rank.

Admiral Melson: My new rank. And I became the Deputy

Chief of Staff for Plans and Operations and relieved Vice Admiral R. B. Pirie in that particular assignment.

When I reported to CinCLant initially Vice Admiral Stewart Ingersoll was Chief of Staff. He was relieved by Vice Admiral Pirie at the time I relieved him as the Deputy Chief of Staff. Later Pirie was relieved by Vice Admiral Cat Brown. I quote these names to show who I was with at that time.

The job of Deputy Chief of Staff was a broader job; I had many more responsibilities.

Mr. Mason: This covered by the term 'operations'?

Admiral Melson: Operations, yes.

And I had more authority in the sense that I was authorized to release operational dispatches and things of that nature. Also, I became involved a great deal more with the SacLant people - foreign officers who were associated with the SacLant there in Norfolk, which made life considerably more interesting.

Mr. Mason: Tell me a little about SacLant, will you?

Admiral Melson: SacLant stands for the Supreme Allied Commander Atlantic, which at this time the individual concerned was Admiral Jerauld Wright. He had a staff which functioned parallel to the CincLant staff, except that the staff was made up of not only U.S. officers but officers of other allied military services, mostly naval.

SacLant is merely an organization under NATO to control military operations in the Atlantic area. It very closely parallels CinCLant's duties and authority, except it operated under NATO rather than just a straight U.S. command.

In case of a combined operation of any kind then they operate under the SacLant rather than under the Commander-in-Chief Atlantic.

Mr. Mason: There's always a U.S. admiral in command?

Admiral Melson: It has been at all times, as far as I know. The Deputy Commander of SacLant is usually a British officer, a Vice Admiral of the British Navy. And other officers down the line hold corresponding positions.

The Deputy Chief of Staff of SacLant was an American officer - opposite of mine on CinCLant - and the Operations and Plans officer was a British officer as I remember. I've forgotten the make-up of the staff exactly, but there were French and Italian officers on the staff.

One of the side issues of this particular arrangement of SacLant which has no bearing on the strategy that they were implemented in - but they had a liquor mess.

The liquor mess was operated under the SacLant hat. They were all imported liquors mostly - things were hard to get for us normally. Prices were very cheap. But in order to be a member of that mess you had to be a SacLant officer, so a number of U.S. officers wore a second hat as a SacLant officer.

Mr. Mason: I'd say that was rank discrimination.

Admiral Melson: In this day and age.

Mr. Mason: Could the fruits of this privilege be enjoyed on a U.S. naval vessel?

Admiral Melson: No, this was just at headquarters in Norfolk. Of course, the mess was primarily for foreign officers there, but in order to keep that duty free signal they had to limit the people who were actually assigned duty on SacLant. A limited number of the U.S. side were assigned additional duty on SacLant. For instance, I was assigned to the Western Atlantic, which is also a NATO command. So I had the privilege of that liquor mess. It was always in hot water, I might add.

Mr. Mason: Did CinCLant get concerned with Latin American navies?

Admiral Melson: Yes, I don't remember any particular involvement. They were part of NATO too, not all of them, but some. I've forgotten which of these were involved in NATO. They took part in the NATO exercises.

Mr. Mason: They would be under SacLant then.

Admiral Melson: Yes.

Each year at that time there was usually two sets of exercises. One was an Atlantic exercise under Commander-in-Chief Atlantic, which was purely U.S. And another exercise under SacLant, which involved all the foreign navies that could send ships, and that operated under Admiral Wright as Supreme Allied Commander Atlantic - that was the combined training between the navies that were operating together. Of course, the U.S. forces were in all cases numerically far superior to any of these other participating nations, but that's because they had more ships.

Mr. Mason: Was there any obvious contrast to be made between CinCLant exercises and SacLant exercises - one being a conglomerate navy and the other being our Navy?

Admiral Melson: No, I can't think of any off hand, except on the SacLant side we all operated together - we had the language barrier and this becomes quite a problem when you're trying to maneuver ships at sea by voice radio.

Mr. Mason: How do you deal with a problem like that?

Admiral Melson: Normally you have interpreters with you. But even then, when you have to go to somebody else to transmit your orders you never know how it's going to come out. It's not as speedy, there is a delay. And I think you know, it's hard to put your expression into some other foreign language the way another American would understand it. What I'm trying to say is - it's hard to make a foreign individual think the way you think when you give an order. He may understnad it, but he doesn't quite have the insight into what you're trying to do. And sometimes that could be critical in some areas. I don't think there was any great difficulty in that respect.

Mr. Mason: Does this then in theory at least make a SacLant battle force potentially less effective than a fleet force of our own?

Admiral Melson: It would in a sense that - if you take the Navy football team and put it up against another football team made up of individual players in other schools not as well drilled as the Navy team because they hadn't been together as long - you'd have that difference. I would say in that case the Navy football team would probably be superior - of course, a lot depends on what kind of talent they have, too.

Without a question, if we eliminate the British for a minute, I think that our ships and men are all superior to most of the other nations. And when you put them together trying to operate as a unit then you have trouble.

The best way to operate, in my opinion, would be when you have an organization that tight to try and divide your forces up a little bit into national forces and let each one have it's own specific job to perform.

Mr. Mason: Sort of a task group principle?

Admiral Melson: Yes.

Unfortunately, in most cases like this there are not enough of the foreign navies to produce a large enough task force to do much of a job - it always falls to the United States, who has the greatest number of ships.

For instance, if you take one of these small South American countries which is under NATO, and they always like to be represented in these exercises - they have one or two ships, they don't give you much to work with. So you do have to use them.

It produces problems operating forces of this type,

but we seem to have gotten along all right, although we've never really been involved in a conflict together as a combined unit. There may be isolated incidents where they've operated, but there's never been any large action involvement.

Mr. Mason: Yes, you can cite the incident in Korea when the United Nations force was something more than U.S.

Admiral Melson: I think that most of the SacLant exercises that I knew anything about at the time were rather successful and worked out very well. There were problems, but I think they were overcome - most of them, one way or another.

Mr. Mason: Now what role did the Supreme NATO Commander play in the development of your plans and exercises?

Admiral Melson: Normally a plan would be developed by SacLant. The Atlantic command had their own plans. The SacLant would develop a NATO plan and they would take into consideration all the forces which were assigned to NATO. After a plan was worked up and developed, they sent their plan to the other Allies. And each Ally, each including ourself, would make up a similar plan based on carrying out our part of the plan with the forces we had. So actually CinCLant took SacLant's plan and developed a plan from that. In addition he usually had his own plan which was not much different, but you had to have it in case NATO broke up - you'd have to have your own plan. I must say we had about half a dozen plans for everything on different sides. We had a SacLant plan, from that we had a CinCWestLant plan, we had a Commander Atlantic plan, and then all the national plans which developed from those.

Mr. Mason: I was wondering what role General Norstad would have, or what cognizance he had of your plans as they developed. He was then the Supreme Allied Commander.

Admiral Melson: He received copies, and of course there was a certain amount of coordination that had to be with his staff, but I don't know if he was directly involved in details. We all were complying with whatever the overall plan was.

Mr. Mason: You've been talking about the various plans necessary to be developed by the different commands and their tie-in with the Supreme Allied Commander in Paris.

Admiral Melson: I think that covers that pretty well.
 The Commander-in-Chief Atlantic - one thing I failed to mention before - was also the Commander-in-Chief of the

Atlantic Fleet, which was the hat he wore as the U.S. representative commanding the ships of the Atlantic Fleet. And as that he had certain routine training duties, deployments, and things like that. For instance, ships that would train in the Norfolk area, be dispatched to the Med to relieve the ships in the Med, the ships in the Med would come back for logistics and for yard overhaul and then go into a training period. So there were many duties to be taken care of like training, upkeep, logistics, and so forth, that also came within the cognizance of this same staff.

Mr. Mason: Did you have anything to do with exercises - amphibious?

Admiral Melson: That was all part of the whole exercise plans. Of course, the amphibious base was practically next door to our headquarters in Norfolk. We were very close to their operations. They were like any other force; they were just one force of a number - the submarine force up in New London, the destroyer force in Newport, the amphibious force in the Little Creek area. Of course, the Air Force was scattered in various air stations up and down the coast. These were routine fleet duties which all fleets have, which are about the same.

That just about covers my duties with CinCLant, unless you have some further questions.

#6 Melson - 212

Interview No. 6 with Vice Admiral Charles Melson, U.S. Navy
At his residence in Annapolis, Maryland
January 28, 1972   by John T. Mason, Jr.

Mr. Mason: Admiral, I'm just delighted that we're resuming this series after a hiatus of some eight or nine months. Last time you told me about your tour of duty on the staff of CinCLant and talked about the ramifications of those duties and what have you. Now I think you're about ready to talk about your assignment in command of Cruiser Division Four; the actual date is March 17th, 1957.

Admiral Melson: On March 17th, 1957 I assumed command of Cruiser Division Four and broke my flag as a Rear Admiral in the ALBANY at Guantanamo Bay. The division was composed of the cruiser MACON commanded by Captain Ray Malpass, the ALBANY commanded by Captain Sieglaff, and the CANBERRA commanded by Captain Mauro.

From the time that I took over our operations composed mostly of training in the Guantanamo area, then on the East Coast on up the Coast to Boston, where we went into the Yard for a short period of upkeep and recreation.

Mr. Mason: This was a part of the Second Fleet, was it?

Admiral Melson: This was part of the Second Fleet, that

is correct, a cruiser division.

In May I shifted my flag from the ALBANY to the MACON, as the ALBANY was going to the Yard for a considerable period of overhaul. Then from 8 to 12 June, 1957 we loaded Midshipmen off the Naval Academy and proceeded to an anchorage in Hampton Roads area, where we participated in an international naval review - NATO review. The ships concerned were a number of members of the Second Fleet with quite a number of foreign war vessels which came to Hampton Roads for the purpose of this particular review. The ships were reviewed by the President of the United States - from one of the ships of the fleet.

Upon completion of the review the MACON proceeded to sea with the ships of the Midshipmen's cruise force. In this force was one battleship, four cruiser, and about twelve destroyers.

Mr. Mason: How many classes were represented by this?

Admiral Melson: Three class of midshipmen.

I was the second in command of the task force; Rear Admiral McManus was in command.

From 12 June to 2 July we were at sea conducting training exercises mostly for the benefit of the Midshipmen. They were elementary type as required for the first few days at sea with any task force, particularly with a lot of young Midshipmen who hadn't been to sea in a long time. This was all preliminary training for gunnery exercises to be held later on the cruise.

Mr. Mason: The Midshipmen were actively employed in duties aboard, weren't they?

Admiral Melson: The Midshipmen were actively employed in all the various operations going on in the fleet. Depending on their class and seniority they held various jobs - from duties of the fireman in the fireroom up to acting as navigator and conning the ship from time to time. We tried to give them the maximum amount of training that we could in the short time that we had them at sea.

Mr. Mason: I suppose being present at the NATO exercise was also part of their training, was it?

Admiral Melson: Being present was very incidental - it wasn't by design. It just happened to fall into the plan.

Mr. Mason: On that occasion was there some interpretation of the NATO exercise for them? Were there lessons to be learned by the Midshipmen from the assembly of naval vessels?

Admiral Melson: Not very much, except to see the foreign warships and know what they looked like and be with them. There was no liberty ashore, no mixing of the crews with the Midshipmen ashore, or anything of that nature. This was purely an exercise held in Hampton Roads. When we left Hampton Roads the NATO ships departed and went on their way. On this trip south we were just a United States task force conducting a Midshipmen training exercise.

The Midshipmen, while on board ship, were assigned various duties and as time went on they rotated in these duties to get the maximum experience they could while on the cruise. From my own past experience as a Midshipman I think that this training is most useful, most beneficial, because in order to command ships and do things you have to realize what the men under you have to do and how they have to go about doing it, even if it's just scrubbing a deck. You have to know a few of these things - where you get the water and where you get the scrub brush - so you can really do it all.

Mr. Mason: In addition to the officers normally assigned to a cruiser like that, were the Midshipmen also accompanied by some of the instructors from the Academy?

Admiral Melson: They were accompanied by a small number of instructors from the Academy who went along for disciplinary purposes, to keep track of them, call the roll, and so forth. They also had to attend a certain number of classes on subjects that the Naval Academy prescribed - like navigation conducted by Naval Academy instructors, and ship board instruction conducted by shipboard officers. There were certain areas where the Naval Academy officers did the instructing. Of course, they all helped together in the overall training of the Midshipmen.

Mr. Mason: What role did you, as skipper of this cruiser outfit, play in their instruction?

Admiral Melson: To oversee the overall training of the crews, to arrange for our passage through these various waters in South America, to control the ships at sea to see that they didn't have accidents.

Mr. Mason: I mean in relation to the Midshipmen - did you have any actual contact with them as a body of students?

Admiral Melson: Yes, I was going to say that we saw the Midshipmen daily on the bridge and in various parts of the ship. And I made it a policy to have a certain number of Midshipmen in every day for lunch in my cabin with myself and two or three of my staff. That way we had a chance to talk with them and find out what they were thinking about and how they were getting along and see if they had any comments to make upon the cruise. That was perhaps one of the most interesting parts of the cruise to me as an individual - the feedback from the Midshipmen. We heard what terrible ports we were going to, why didn't we pick better ports, how much liberty were they going to get, and occasionally we had a comment on life aboard ship - some of which was complementary and lot of which was not, because you realize they were living there just about the same way a seaman does and that's a bit crowded, as you know - at least it was in those days. Now they're getting much more comfortable quarters.

About the first of July the force split into two task groups. My task group consisting of the MACON and the CANBERRA and eight destroyers proceeded to Santos, Brazil, while the other ships of the task force consisting of the IOWA and the other destroyers and cruiser went to Rio for a visit. Unfortunately, it couldn't be arranged so that the two groups could interchange ports, so we had to be satisfied with where we were going. At first there was a certain amount of disappointment when we heard we were not going to Rio, but after all our visit to Santos proved to be a very good visit. Everybody enjoyed it immensely.

As you know, Santos is one of the centers of the

production of Brazilian coffee. I think we all got our fill of good Brazilian coffee there. Also we could visit San Paulo, which is one of the up and coming cities of Brazil. It was very modern in many respects with a number of skyscrapers - I think it's second in size. Some of their facilities, as I understand it, left something to be desired in that they built these very beautiful buildings - they were beautiful above ground - but the sanitary facilities and drainage and so forth on the ground underneath left a little bit to be desired. But we had a very nice visit. The Brazilians were very pleasant, very cordial, and we couldn't have asked for a better time.

Mr. Mason: Was there any contact with the Brazilian navy during a visit of this sort?

Admiral Melson: None, except that Brazilian liaison officers were assigned each ship, and one was assigned to me. A Commander Cunha was assigned as my personal liaison officer. He and his wife were most attentive - took me to see things, recommended places to go, and were very nice. As a matter of fact, we corresponded for quite a time after I returned from the cruise. I think that all the ships had that same experience, as far as a liaison officer was concerned.

There were no unpleasant episodes, and it made a very good visit for the Midshipmen. Although I was not in Rio with the other group, I understand that they had somewhat similar experience.

On the 10th of July we sailed from Santos and met the other group off of Rio on the 12th of July, and then proceeded to San Juan, Puerto Rico, holding training exercises in route. We were in San Juan, Puerto Rico from the 22nd to the 25th of July to give the Midshipmen a chance to have liberty in that city. I think we all enjoyed our stay there.

Mr. Mason: When they had liberty like that, did they use their ship as their home base or ...

Admiral Melson: They lived aboard ship. Of course, Midshipmen that asked for it could be granted leave to visit other parts of the island - like any other person in the Navy. If they wanted to they could just live aboard ship and go on liberty each day, and come back and have their meals aboard ship.

On the 25th we sailed from San Juan for Culebra Island. If you remember, Culebra Island has been in the news considerably just recently because that is the island the Navy has used for many years as a target for gunfire and bombing practices.

We arrived off the island and spent two days there off the area, staying underway all the time. There was no liberty or anything like that. We conducted firing exercises on the island with the Midshipmen taking a direct part in the firing. They're the ones that actually loaded and fired the guns and controlled their gunfire.

I meant to say that all the ships of the task force were not together and were all off Culebra for this firing. Then when we sailed on the 27th of July we sailed as the whole task force for Guantanamo Bay, Cuba.

Mr. Mason: And you want to comment on the value of an island like Culebra as a place where the Navy can actually use live ammunition.

Admiral Melson: Of course, the real benefit that you get out of conducting target practice is to see the result of your firing. Unless you have an actual target that you can fire shells into, you never really know whether you are hitting or not, or what damage you've done. So you need something at the point of aim that you can actually shoot at, otherwise it's like shooting target practice with a 22 rifle and not having the target - you never know where your bullet goes. So I consider it vital to have some type of target that you actually shoot at and hit - and not do any damage, of course.

As you know, people do live on Culebra, but they live in a section which is not used for target practice. And they are in no danger as long as they do not wander into the firing area, which is very well marked.

So I would think the Navy would try it's best to retain their rights in Culebra.

Mr. Mason: Did I not see a statement to the effect from the Navy that they could get along without it?

Admiral Melson: I didn't see that, it may be though. Of course, to get along without it means they have to find some other place.

And it's always possible to fire at moving targets at sea where there is no population, but there is a difference in firing shore bombardment where you fire at a fixed target and firing at a moving target like a ship. And we really need the training in both.

Not too long ago when I was in Korea with the NEW JERSEY, our whole job consisted of firing at unseen targets on the beach - railroad trains, etc. And you need training along those lines.

In firing at targets at sea you normally have computers and other equipment to keep track of your target for you and predict it's movement. In the land area, if you can see your target it's usually a fixed target. The only relative motion you have is that made by your ship. But it's a little different problem to work out than the other. Of course, we're used to firing at moving targets at sea - that's our business. Shore bombardment's a little bit different problem, and you do need to train at it once in a while. It is good to have a good point of aim to shoot at.

Mr. Mason: And in World War II in the Pacific shore bombardments came to be the real effort of the heavier ships.

Admiral Melson: I think that we should hang on to Culebra if we can. If we can't, I'm sure that we can probably find some other little spot of land that could be used for the same purpose. But Culebra has certain natural advantages that are desirable - it has a good anchorage where you can anchor at night when you're not shooting, and it's close, and there're other advantages that go along with this. I'm sure there are some isolated pinnacles in the ocean that we could go out and shoot at, but there are a lot of otherproblems that go along with that, too, in the way of logistics.

As I said, on the 27th of July - this incidentally is all 1957 - the task force gathered together and sailed for Guantanamo. En route three days there we again had exercises underway, which is all training for the Midshipmen.

We were in Guantanamo a very short time - from 30 July to 1 August. Here the Midshipmen had an opportunity to see Guantanamo which is one of our largest naval bases. And particularly being on foreign soil - Cuba - they had an opportunity to visit a few of the local islands and to purchase a few tax-free items at the exchanges before they headed back home.

On 1 August the task force headed north for the Hampton Roads area, where upon arrival we discharged Midshipmen. And my flagship, the MACON, proceeded to Boston, which was home port.

Mr. Mason: Why didn't you transport the Midshipmen right up to Annapolis?

Admiral Melson: We picked up the Midshipmen in Annapolis. In sending them back ships of the amphibious force picked them up and ferried them to Annapolis so that we could proceed on our way, so we wouldn't be delayed. It's good training too for the amphibious force, I guess, to have to carry a large group like this. Another thing - on the unloading the LSTs and so forth could get right into the dock at Annapolis to discharge the Midshipmen. If you come on other ships you'd have to unload and ferry them in by small boats which is quite an operation, particularly if the weather is bad.

Upon arrival in Boston I transferred my flag back to the ALBANY, which was the assigned flagship for that division. And we spent the rest of August in the Boston Shipyard getting ready to deploy to Europe.

Mr. Mason: Was she being refitted, and were new pieces of ordnance being put on?

Admiral Melson: No, she was just having a routine upkeep period prior to deployment. Later she did go in for a complete revamp, but this was not the time. By complete revamp - I mean she went in and the whole topside was cleared and they put all this new gear and equipment and made a missile cruiser out of her, which she was not before - she was a gun cruiser.

Mr. Mason: Would that be a part of what they call the FRAM program?

Admiral Melson: I've never heard FRAM used in relation to these changes in cruiser. FRAM has been used primarily in relation to the destroyer, but it is the same thing. You take an old hull and completely refit it with new equipment.

Then on 3 September with the normal ship's complement on board we sailed for northern European waters for NATO exercises. The three ships of the division - the ALBANY, the MACON, and the CANBERRA made this trip.

From the 14th to the 17th of September we were anchored in the Firth of Clyde off of Largs, Scotland, Mrs. Melson was fortunate to be able to come to Europe at that time and met me at Largs, and we spent three or four days there together. Then she went on south and we joined up later in the Med.

We spent the time 14 to 17 September in Largs getting the various operation orders, and there were loads of them. There were stacks of paper we had to collect and read and find out what each individual ship had to do, and this was no small job I can assure you.

Mr. Mason: What was the overall purpose of the exercise that was forthcoming?

Admiral Melson: The overall purpose was the NATO exercise involving various - I won't say all the forces, because they didn't all participate - units of the NATO fleet. The United States, of course, had a very heavy commitment to furnish a large number of these ships.

The exercise was to be an exercise up off the coast of Norway in early winter. It was to stop a deployment of presumably Russian ships from the north down through the straits off the Norwegian coast to the Atlantic.

I've forgotten which ships were involved, but certain ships of our fleet were the enemy, but I was not with them, I was on the friendly side.

Mr. Mason: Would there be foreign observers to an exercise of that sort?

Admiral Melson: Members of NATO had observers on all the ships, but nothing other than those foreign ...

Mr. Mason: How could you exclude the Russians from observing from the air or some other way?

Admiral Melson: You couldn't and they were up there. There were Russian trawlers in the area.

Mr. Mason: Electronic ones?

Admiral Melson: I presume they were. And there were also their aircraft, which I think they do in all these exercises. This is just one of a number of exercises we've held in this particular area.

Mr. Mason: Would the Norwegians on an occasion like that be sensitive to the fact that the exercises were being held off their coast?

Admiral Melson: As far as I know they were not.

I was about to say that we were right in on the coast of Norway. You could see the coast without the aid of glasses, and it was a very rugged looking coast I must say. The days were very clear, and the visibility was wonderful. You could just see the whole stretch of the west coast of Norway without any difficulty at all. If they were sensitive, I was not aware of it.

The balance of the month of September was spent with these exercises. Then upon completion of the exercise I proceeded with the ALBANY, the MACON, and the CANBERRA through the English Channel - I might say incidentally that was the first time, and also the last time that I've ever been through the English Channel - on to the Med going by Gibraltar en route. We headed straight for Suda Bay in Crete.

In Suda Bay there was an interesting event which didn't seem very unusual at the time, but to me now it does, in that the Captain of the ALBANY - Captain Sieglaff - was relieved by one Captain Jack McCain. There was no indication at that time that my new flag Captain would one day be the Commander-in-Chief of the Pacific. I found him to be a very fine officer and I admired him very much, and we became very close friends.

About the 9th of October we left the area of Suda Bay and paid a visit to Athens and Salonica in Greece and to

Izmir in Turkey.

Mr. Mason: On this occasion did you become a part of the Sixth Fleet?

Admiral Melson: Yes, we became part of the Sixth Fleet when we passed Gibraltar - we reported to the Sixth Fleet for duty on passing Gilbraltar.

Mr. Mason: You were kind of itinerant cruisers, weren't you, going from one command to the other?

Admiral Melson: We got around. Actually, we spent about six months in the Med in the Sixth Fleet, and in that job I was the second in command and usually controlled the Fleet for various logistic type exercises - such as refueling and supplying and so forth.

The Fleet itself was usually maneuvered by the flag officer in the carriers. Admiral Cat Brown, who was Commander of the Sixth Fleet at that time, was on his own cruiser flagship.

In Izmir I met General Gursel of the Turkish Army, who later became the President of Turkey and died not too long ago.

We spent Christmas 1957 moored in Genoa. Mrs. Melson met me there and we had the opportunity to travel a little in northern Italy going by train to see Florence and to some of the smaller towns in the vicinity of Genoa. I couldn't get too far away from the ship.

Mr. Mason: Why?

Admiral Melson: You never got very far away from your ships when you're out like that. When you're in the United States it's different - if you have some sudden emergency and they want to get you back to your ships, you can get back quickly.

Mr. Mason: But you're not likely to be dispatched somewhere?

Admiral Melson: Oh no, not just like that, but you like to keep within reasonable call of the ships.

Our stay in Genoa was very pleasant. We met a number of Italians that we are very fond of, and there were a number of Americans living in the small coastal towns that were very interesting. There's one small village - an art colony just down the coast from Genoa.

We departed Genoa on the 7th of January 1958 en route to Bacelona, Spain, where we arrived on the 11th of January. We remained in Barcelona until the 21st, and then went to Palma, Mallorca. This visit to Palma was used to gather the whole Sixth Fleet together to get the commanding officers together for a conference with Cat Brown - one of his conferences while we were over there.

Mr. Mason: During this period when you were with the Sixth Fleet - it was not long after the disturbances in the Eastern Mediterranean - Lebanon, Suez, and so forth. Was there any semi-alert because of these events which had transpired?

Let me ask you about this conference at Palma that Admiral Brown called. Was there any specific purpose for that?

Admiral Melson: No, he usually tried once or twice during a tour of a group of ships in the Med to have a fleet conference which all the commanding officers and the flag officers would attend so they could become acquainted with him and he could become acquainted with them and to talk about the exercises which they were either going to do or had just completed. It was a customary thing. I forgot to to mention that we had one shortly after we arrived.

Mr. Mason: What kind of a commander was he?

Admiral Melson: Cat Brown was fine.

Mr. Mason: He was tough, wasn't he?

Admiral Melson: He was tough, but I'd known him before. I'd served with him at the War College, I knew what to expect, and I got along well with him. Too bad he's so badly crippled now. Cat was a good commander to be at sea with.

I remember particularly one incident off Norfolk some years before when I had the NEW JERSEY. He had a CarDiv at that time. This would have been about 1953. We were exercising off of Norfolk, Hampton Roads area, and he had his planes all in the air from the carriers and a sudden fog set in and caught him with his airplanes in the air. Then we started chasing around trying to find an open hole in the sky that we could bring the planes back to the carriers with. We were making our maximum speed on the NEW JERSEY practically the whole time - 27 knots - and we got in very close to the coast in shallow water and the geyser at the stern was higher than my bridge. I became a little concerned, because of the shallow water. But he turned away and brought us out and we got all the planes back. So it was worth what little risk we took. Cat's a _fine_ officer.

Mr. Mason: If you had gone aground under those circumstances the blame would have fallen on you, however, would it not?

Admiral Melson: Yes, but really and truthfully while the danger of going aground was very small unless we did something foolish because while we were in shallow water we still had water under the keel. When you get in shallow water like that at high speed it just pulls the water from your stern up and it comes up like a geyser behind and you get this high. As I said the one on the NEW JERSEY was as high as my bridge. Running around in the fog at high speed is all part of the business. There was just as much danger of running into each other if we lost track of each other on our radar, but there was no damage done. The main thing was to get all the fliers back aboard.

We left Palma and proceeded to Naples where we spent a few days prior to sailing. Then we left there on the 22nd of January and arrived in Gib on the 28th.

In Gibraltar we were relieved by another cruiser going into the Med. It took us about a day and a half to relieve each other. Then we sailed for Norfolk and arrived in Norfolk on the 11th of April.

Mr. Mason: Once you left Gibralter you became a part of what fleet?

Admiral Melson: Lant fleet. There's a CHOP line you cross shortly after you get outside of Gibraltar. Then you chop over to the fleet's area that you're in.

Upon arrival in Norfolk I received orders to report for duty to the Assistant Secretary of Defense for International Security Affairs for duty.

Mr. Mason: Was this a surprise assignment?

Admiral Melson: This was a complete surprise to me; I knew nothing about it.

As you know the International Security Affairs in this case happened to be the Far Eastern desk, which involved all the activity in Southeast Asia.

I must admit I was sort of flabbergasted because I had never been involved in the political side of activites anywhere and this would be that. I thought I would enjoy it and would like it. I didn't know it then, but a lot of things were going to happen.

My orders included a certain amount of leave, so Mrs. Melson and I decided it might be a good idea to use part of this leave to house hunt in Washington. While we were in Washington staying with Admiral Wooldridge, who was then Commandant of the National War College we attended a cocktail party that he gave on a Sunday afternoon at the War College at Fort McNair. It was a rather large party and there were a large number of naval people there, including the Chief of Naval Personnel, then Vice Admiral H. P. Smith. During the course of the party

Admiral Smith took me aside and told me not to sign any leases for a house in Washington.

I might say at this time I was just about to sign a lease with Admiral Smedberg for his house in the Bethesda area. I must say this left me a little at a loss to what he meant, because he didn't elaborate any on it other than to say not to sign up for a house. I consulted with Mrs. Melson and she was as flabbergasted about the whole thing as I was.

About ten minutes after the first conversation with Admiral Smith, he called me aside again and stated in substance that he didn't think it was fair to keep it all from me, but I was going to be ordered as Superintendent of the Naval Academy and it was to be kept secret until he told me I could release it, and that I needn't worry about quarters, that I would have a very good house at the place I was going.

So I informed Gypsy of that and we wondered what we would do when we'd get back to Norfolk. The people in Norfolk thought we were going to Washington to find a place to live and if we came back to Norfolk and said we didn't have a place to live but we're not worried they would wonder what was going on. That was not too material at the time.

Anyway, my orders did come out to report to the Superintendent of the Naval Academy as his relief reporting in late June.

Mr. Mason: Succeeding whom?

Admiral Melson: Succeeding Admiral Smedberg.

Mr. Mason: What happened to the assignment in the International Affairs?

Admiral Melson: I forgot now, I lost interest in it.

Mr. Mason: You never actually reported there?

Admiral Melson: No.
A few days after I returned back to Norfolk I received a change in orders, cancelling my orders to the International Security Agency and gave me five weeks temporary duty in BuPers with about three weeks leave. I took my leave and then reported in to the Bureau of Personnel for temporary duty, and during that time I found out all I could about the Naval Academy, what goes on down there, and all the background that I didn't know - where they got the money for running the place, and all the personnel problems, and so forth, the background, before my coming here for duty.

Mr. Mason: How did you actually react to an assignment like that? Did it seem like a formidable one?

Admiral Melson: No, it didn't seem formidable. I was just so surprised at it because the Superintendency of the Naval Academy is one of the prize plums in the Navy, I think. To be picked for it I think is quite an honor, at least it was for me. Not a great number of people have it, as you probably realize. There just isn't any better job in the Navy.

During the brief temporary duty I tried my best to findout all I could about the Naval Academy - the things which would be helpful to me when I came down here.

Mr. Mason: But you already knew a lot because you'd been ...

Admiral Melson: I had a good background, no question of that, but there's still a lot in Washington that I didn't know about.

I asked for and got temporary duty orders to visit the Air Force Academy. The Air Force Academy was the newest school of that type out, and they were conducting a lot of changes in their curriculum - trying to improve it. They were, perhaps, a little bit more advanced than West Point and Annapolis, which remained two rather staid schools. They were experiementing a bit in methods of teaching, different developments in courses of instruction. I thought it would be worth my while to find out what I could, so I spent several days at the Air Force Academy and received very fine treatment from all of their people, particularly General McDermitt, who was their dean at that time, retired Air Force.

After this visit I returned to Washington and prepared to report to Annapolis.

Mr. Mason: You had various concepts about curriculum anyway, didn't you?

Adm. Melson: I did. But when I was here before as Chief of Staff I was not directly involved in the curriculum; I was more involved in the logistics of supporting the Naval Academy where the Superintendent handled all the matters affecting the curriculum. I did come in contact with it, yes, and I did know something about it.

Then on the 27th of June I relieved Admiral W. R. Smedberg as Superintendent of the Academy. There were a number of VIPs in the audience, including the Secretary of the Navy naturally, Mr. Francke, who I became much better acquainted with as time went on, and he turned out to be one of my best friends.

After the ceremony Admiral Smedberg walked down the walk from Bancroft Hall — we held the relieving ceremony on the terrace of Bancroft Hall — and got into his red convertible and drove off. That was the last I saw of him for about a year.

We proceeded on over to the Superintendent's quarters for a luncheon which I was giving but had nothing to do with the planning of. The luncheon was for about in the neighborhood of eighty people, including the Secretary of the Navy and a few others. I found that the quarters had a very fine staff; everything went off very nicely. With a sigh of relief we sat down about four o'clock and we had a chance to talk about what went on.

We were both very pleased with the assignment. The question always lurked in the back of my mind at that time, and still does, as to whether I had the qualifications for the job. And I guess only time will tell.

Mr. Mason: Perhaps this would be an appropriate time to talk about it - as you entered this new assignment what were your ideas about it? Did you have any intentions of changing various directions or things of emphasis?

Admiral Melson: No, I did not, because one of the questions the Secretary asked me the first time I talked to him - incidentally I talked to the Secretary before I even came down to the job; I had been interviewed -

Mr. Mason: Does he nominate, does he make the appointment?

Admiral Melson: He approves it, let me put it that way. Smith actually put my name in front of him, and said this is who we recommend. Then he has a chance to look at my record which is produced. He has the final say.

The Secretary asked me, "What do you propose doing at the Naval Academy? Do you have anything in mind?" I told him, "No, I didn't," because I felt that I needed to know more about the place before I went down with any idea of changing things. True, I was a graduate of the Naval Academy; true, I'd been there as Chief of Staff, but I felt I had to get down and know about the present day at the time before I'd say, "Yes we wanted to make these changes."

Mr. Mason: That's a sensible approach. What was Mrs. Melson's idea of her role in the Superintendents' House?

Admiral Melson: She knew pretty well what her role would be because we'd been here, as you know, with Admiral and Mrs. Hill. Mrs. Melson was sort of the number one assistant for Margaret Hill, and she became pretty well indoctrinated as to about what was expected of her. We were there for a little over two years with them and we learned a lot.

And I think I learned a lot from Admiral Hill. As I said, the only thing with Admiral Hill he was primarily an active individual - interested in sports and things like that - and while he took an active part in academics he was not like Calvert. He was not an educator; I don't know whether you'd call Calvert an educator, or not. I think Calvert thinks he is, and is trying to be. Hill was an entirely different type man; I think you can appreciate that. He never (I'm talking of Admiral Hill now) missed an athletic event that he could possibly get to. He went to ffotball practice every day throughout the football season; he was that kind of an active individual. He played golf, and was much more of a field man I guess you'd call it than an office man. So, I say I didn't get much on the curriculum side from him. And my job didn't involve the curriculum.

I suppose you find all sorts of people become

Superintendent, and I don't mean that in a derogatory way at all. What I'm trying to say is that it depends on their interest as to what they will emphasize.

Mr. Mason: What did you ultimately come to emphasize after sizing up the situation?

Admiral Melson: That ought to come at the tail end of this.

My approach, and I don't know that I ever sat down and thought this out as such, looking back on it now, I was very much interested in all aspects of the Naval Academy whether it was academic, athletic, or logistics - such as keeping the place going properly. I tried, and I think I can safely say that, not to let any one particular thing take charge. I was interested in the whole picture. I am not an athlete; I only engaged in the athletic pursuits in so far as necessary for my health and Uncle Sam said I should. I've never considered myself an educator. I probably came nearer to being an engineer than anything else. Taking that part into consideration I tried to take everything more or less evenly so as to see that it ran properly. Whether that's right or wrong I don't know; time will tell.

Mr. Mason: It was a going concern that you stepped into.

Admiral Melson: And kept going. And we made changes as

time went on. We made changes in curriculum to keep up with the times. We changed football coaches when the necessity arose. We added more land to the Academy when we ran out; we didn't want to fight the City of Annapolis to get some more land. We just tried to keep everything running on an even keel and do as well as we could. That part of the discussion is really something that's going to come a little later.

I was tremendously interested in keeping this Academy a real going concern. It didn't make any difference to me whether it was in athletics or the debating team or what it was. It hurt when Navy couldn't come out on top; it really sincerely hurt. The whole objective was to try to keep competitive and keep on top when we could. We didn't win every time, as you probably know.

Mr. Mason: Did you maintain a close liaison with West Point and the Air Force?

Admiral Melson: Yes, we kept very close relations with them. We had a Superintendents' conference every year; depending on the year we met at one Academy or the other. We met at the Naval Academy once while I was here, and we met at West Point once. The Superintendents got together and discussed various aspects of academy life and our problems, which were very similar, I might add.

Mr. Mason: I would think this would be useful to all three of you.

Admiral Melson: Yes, extremely useful.

At these conferences, except at the Air Force Academy, at West Point I stayed in the Superintendent of West Point's house, and when they came here they stayed in the Superintendent's house. It sounds like a small point but it made for a getting closer together, if you understand what I mean. You had dinner together in a very informal atmosphere and you got to know these people quite well. At the Air Force Academy we stayed in one of the halls, I've forgotten what it was now. I found them very useful, and it took away the little bitterness that occasionally builds up between schools of this nature. You become so competitive you become bitter to each other; you can't lose a game to the other fellow without thinking that if you'd done something else you'd been better or he didn't play fair. I think we overcame a lot of that by these meetings, although it was at the top.

Mr. Mason: It was a meeting at the top, and yet in getting together you realize that you're all serving the same master.

Admiral Melson: And good will among the Superintendents fed down I think to the lower echelon.

Mr. Mason: Did you also maintain any kind of a relationship or liaison with universities and colleges, the associations there?

Admiral Melson: We were a member, and they still are members, of the various inter-collegiate organizations that have to do with schools and so forth. I can't think of the names of them right now, but we did keep a liaison with a number of schools. We had a number of the presidents and professors of other schools down here to speak to the Midshipmen. I personally didn't, but a number of our people also visited these other schools.

Mr. Mason: Is there something to be learned from their experience in private universities and state universities?

Admiral Melson: Oh, yes, I think so, because our problems are all very similar. There are only two real differences: one is we're a military school and they're not - that affects the students, not the running of the school particularly. The other is the source of income at the Naval Academy, West Point, and the Air Force Academy comes from the government, where these other schools have to depend to a certain extent on donations in a way to do the things that they want to do. Of course, they all have incomes from either state or trust funds or something like that, but they don't have the same type of income.

The Naval Academy hadn't until last year conducted fund raising drives to build buildings and things like that;

#6 Melson - 244

they got them from Uncle Sam. Now Admiral Calvert started this foundation businesssduring this last year with the idea of building certain additional recreation buildings for Midshipmen. So far as I know that's the only time we've ever done something of that nature. We might have done a simple thing like decorating certain parts of Mem Hall. We did for the stadium; I put the stadium in a different category from anything else - the stadium is not a necessity; it's a nice thing to have. Do you agree with me?

Mr. Mason: I think maybe it goes beyond being not a necessity, in that athletics play such an important part in the life of the Academy that the facilities are necessary for this.

Admiral Melson: When you start reasoning that way then you come back to my point of view - the government should provide it.

I haven't discussed this much with Calvert, but I'm not very much in sympathy with this drive because I think if it's a necessity then they should be provided like the rest of them. To attempt to raise money from an alumni, such as myself and others, which are not well paid in the sense you normally think of it - I don't mean we're starving but they're very few millionaires among naval officers who can make grants to schools or things like that, very few, and that's what these other schools have - they have alumni which have gone out and made a lot of money in the world and they can afford to invest in it. Where here when you start asking the Naval Academy graduates to contribute to something like this, he can't contribute very much. There are a few Naval Academy graduates who have done quite well, like Ross Perot, and there's the chairman of General Motors, a few people like that, but they're very few and far between. I think Ross Perot is careful with his money. Somebody said the other day when the market was going down - that he was a billionaire yesterday but he's only a millionaire today.

Mr. Mason: There are obvious differences certainly between the Academy and public and private schools of higher learning. You stress the military and this immediately makes a difference in the curriculum and the ways of controlling - discipline and all that.

Admiral Melson: But there're many other ways in which they're very much alike. It's hard to sit down and pick them out, but you can do it.

I think the Naval Academy has progressed in many ways over the years. As time goes on you make progress. One year you don't make any, the next year and the next year you make a lot more. Everything they have today has been developed by people who have been here in the past, and it's all added together to give you the Academy you have today. As time goes on, the contributions that are made by the people at the Academy today will give us a better Academy ten or fifteen years from now. No one person can do it all in a certain period of time.

One disadvantage in the past which has been corrected is the Superintendent's tour of duty was basically two years for a great number of years, including the time I was there - there are one or two exceptions to that. I am very happy to see Calvert get four years, because two years is not enough time for any one man. It takes you a year to find out what it's all about, the next year you make your mind up what you want to do, and then before you know it you're gone. Calvert has the advantage of being able to carry it out all the way.

Mr. Mason: What did you do in order to relate to the student body? What was your policy in this area? What was your concept of your relationship as Superintendent to the student body?

Admiral Melson: I'm not quite sure I know quite what you mean, but I'll attempt an answer first, then you can tell me.

I never believed in being buddy-buddy with the student body. I tried to maintain my place as Superintendent as someone for them to respect, and not be on the same plane with them in ordinary duties. I met frequently with them in groups; I had any number of them in the quarters from time to time. I had two sons here at one time so I felt I knew pretty well what went on at the academy. And I tried to be strict without being severe - to draw the line on that. Does that answer your question?

Mr. Mason: Yes, it does. I was thinking of the superintendent before Admiral Calvert who had, I think, a different idea of relating personally to the Midshipmen.

Admiral Melson: I think personally in order to maintain their respect, to keep their respect to you, that you have to be a little bit distant. The minute you start patting people on the back you get patted right back.

Mr. Mason: This being a military organization anyway ...

Admiral Melson: It's a peculiar thing to say, but being this close to the Academy the last four years I know very little about what goes on at the Academy today. I don't like to get into names or situations, but the man that is there now I think does a very good job of it. I mean I respect the way he does it. I think they're a fine couple and they're doing a very wonderful job, but that is observation - you might say - from a distance. There's a certain aversion to having ex-superintendents around.

When I first moved here - I won't mention any names - I had a superintendent tell me that ex-superintendents shouldn't come back and live in Annapolis. I didn't welcome this remark at all, and you probably know who said it. This is where I wanted to come to live, and that made no difference, so we came here. But at the same time I have stayed away from the Academy. I called on Calvert when he first came and told him in substance that I was here, if there was anything in any way that I could do to help him in any way to please call upon me, but otherwise he wouldn't hear anything from me. I've been over there to the house, but purely social; we've had no official contact.

When I came back as Superintendent I had an ex-superintendent who had been here when I was Chief of Staff who I knew very well living in town. Some people made the remark, "How are you going to get along - Harry Hill is going to be running the Naval Academy for you." I said, "Well, I don't think so. Let's wait and see." We got along fine, there never were any problems.

Melson #7 - 249

Interview No. 7 with Vice Admiral Charles Melson, U.S. Navy
(Retired)

Place: His residence in Providence, Annapolis, Maryland

Date: Thursday afternoon, 17 February 1972

Subject: Biography

By: John T. Mason, Jr.

Q: All right, Sir. It's good to see you up and well again after your bout with the 'flu'. Today, Chapter 7 is going to deal, I believe, primarily with your period of duty as superintendent of the U.S. Naval Academy. However, you want to discuss some of the preliminaries to that job, I believe.

Adm. M.: I reported to the chief of Naval Personnel in April 1958 for duty as the superintendent of the Naval Academy. During the period of temporary duty with the chief of Naval Personnel, who at that time was Vice Admiral H. P. Smith, I tried to prepare myself for my duties as superintendent.

Q: How do you prepare for that job?

Adm. M.: That is something that I had to find out for myself. I read everything I could find about the Academy, the things that had happened in the past, particularly the financial position, the academic situation, and other areas that might affect the administration of the Academy.

Q: Are there any extensive reports extant from former superintendents that you could draw upon?

Adm. M.: None, as such. There were a number of letters and documents written by former superintendents, but there's nothing like for instance, this particular piece of recording that I'm doing here. There was nothing at that time to look back on and read. As part of my preparation, I visited the Air Force Academy for about a three-day visit to study their organization, setup, administration, and curriculum. At that time, the Air Force Academy was brand new and had started in with many new ideas about how a military academy should be organized and run, and particularly new ideas regarding the curriculum. I say new ideas regarding the curriculum in the sense that they were new as far as the military academies were concerned. They tended to lean more to the present-day college curriculum than the other academies had before.

Q: You mean much broader?

Adm. M.: Broader. In the past, the academy curriculum, particularly at the Naval Academy and West Point, had been very narrow and very fixed, and the Air Force idea was to broaden its curriculum and allow people to choose electives and to validate courses that they'd taken elsewhere in a much more liberal manner than had ever been done before.

Q: What was the philosophy back of that approach?

Admiral M.: I'm not sure that I can answer that as far as the Air Force is concerned, but I think that with the development of many new weapons, many new methods of warfare, and all the changes that were going on, that the seniors in Washington felt that they needed a graduate with a broader educational background, and with this in mind, they decided to broaden the courses at the academies - at the Air Force Academy. I found out later that West Point was experimenting along these same lines but had not moved at that time.

I came to the Academy with the idea that my primary responsibility was to do something at the Academy to improve the curriculum. This was something which undoubtedly upset the old-timers in the Navy but something that I felt was coming. I will go into that in more detail in a minute.

Q: Let me ask - did you visit West Point Academy also prior to your assuming duty?

Adm. M.: No, I didn't. I went to the Air Force Academy and it was the only one I really had time to go to and it being what I considered to be the most advanced at that time.

I relieved Admiral Smedberg as superintendent on the 26th of June 1958. The relieving ceremony, which is of general interest, I think, was held on the steps of Bancroft Hall and was well attended by distinguished visitors from Washington, including the Secretary of the Navy, the Undersecretary, and a number of assistant secretaries of the Navy, as well as CNO and others.

Q: The CNO being?

Adm. M.: Admiral Burke. The Secretary of the Navy at the time was Mr. Franke. After the ceremony Admiral Smedberg got in his car and left the grounds immediately and I proceeded with Mrs. Melson and other guests to the superintendent's house for lunch. The lunch had been arranged in advance by Admiral Smedberg's people and I found myself entertaining some fifty-odd people for lunch with very little information on how it would be served or what would be served. But I found that the trained staff in the superintendent's house took care of all the details, and lunch went off in fine form.

Q: Was it a buffet lunch?

Adm. M.: A sit-down lunch.

Q: The dining room doesn't accommodate all those people does it?

Adm. M.: Yes. They put up extra tables. This is a quite frequent occurrence. It was not just on this one occasion that they serve large lunches, as I found out as time went on.

After all the guests had left, Mrs. Melson and I sat down and looked around to see just where we were and what we had, and we found we had a tremendous amount of things to be done to get settled and to start in carrying out my new duties.

Q: Did you feel comfortable and at home in the superintendent's house?

Adm. M.: Yes, I felt at home because I had spent a lot of time there as a guest when I was on the staff. I knew the house reasonably well and I knew the staff headed by Chief Reddick, who had been there for a number of years, and I had no qualms about how well the house would be run. Fortunately, relieving at the time of year I did, it was in the summer and the school was not really in active session, and we had a little bit more time to settle our thoughts before the academic year would start. Most of the upper class were away on midshipmen's cruises and the new plebes came in shortly after I relieved, but the machinery was so set up that they were no problem as far as getting them entered and settled down to a training program for the summer.

Q: Did they all come in as one group, or did they dribble in?

Adm. M.: At this particular time, the midshipmen dribbled in a few each day for a period of almost a month. That practice has since been discontinued.

Q: Was that a good practice?

Adm. M.: No, I think I prefer the present practice because you make up for a lot of lost time. It takes a lot of time to take these boys in a few at a time and outfit them and start them into the routine of the Academy. Whereas under the present system today they all come in two or three days, they're settled down and hard at work within a very short period, and there's no great problem of introducing new boys every few days.

Q: It avoids duplication, then?

Adm. M.: It avoids duplication. The present system is much better.

Melson #7 - 255

I intend covering my tour at the Naval Academy under several headings in order to take up each subject in its entirety and keep from duplicating and having to go back and redo this over again. The headings that I will cover are the curriculum, the entrance requirements, the athletic program, the maintenance and building program, and so forth.

The first one that I would like to cover is far the most important and it is the curriculum at the Naval Academy. In the past and even during that year, we were following the academic organization which had been in effect for a great number of years. I hesitate to say how many years it had been running without any great or major change. A copy of this organization is enclosed as Reference A. If you want it, I can copy the diagram.

Q: I would, indeed, yes.

Adm. M.: With this in mind, I set the staff to work studying the organization and to decide what we should do to not only improve the curriculum, but what type of an academic organization we needed to make it effective. In other words, we were going to modernize the Naval Academy curriculum and modernize the organization to carry it out.

Q: May I interrupt you and ask a question? What caused you to reorganize the curriculum? What in the past had convinced you that it was necessary to do at this point?

Adm. M.: It appeared that we had to broaden the curriculum from a very narrow base so that the youngsters could have the opportunity to spread out and take more advanced subjects and to take advantage of the time that they had to leave the Academy with the very best education they could. Many of the youngsters were much more capable of carrying a heavier academic load than the program that was in effect at that time permitted them to do. Some youngsters could barely keep their heads above water in the program, but others were backing water all the time and trying to fill in the time because academically they were better prepared to go ahead. Some boys were quicker and smarter and the program then in effect was just holding these youngsters back. So a new program had to be devised that would permit the youngsters to choose other subjects and classes in order to broaden their own education, and still at the same time we had to retain the old format so that we would not eliminate a great number of boys just because they were not quick educationally.

Q: I would imagine that your broad experience in the Navy was useful to you in inaugurating this change?

Adm. M.: It was, but I want it to be understood here and

now that I am not and have never stated that I was an educator. I merely had the idea of trying to do the best at the Academy that I could, and this was one of the things that it seemed to me had to be done.

Q: How much leeway did you have in reorganizing the whole thing? Are you accountable, as superintendent, to any higher authority in this area?

Adm. M.: Yes, I was going to come to that in a minute. I was accountable all the way up to the Secretary of the Navy, but as I go ahead here I'll show how the new program was approved. I might say, while on this point, that I had already consulted with Admiral Burke, the chief of naval operations, and Mr. Franke, the Secretary of the Navy, and had their blessing to go ahead with this new program. This was not their approval of the specific program but it did give me the backing to go ahead with what I wanted to do.

A program of this nature is not something that you can do overnight, so I visualized that, if during the year of 1958-1959 - the academic year 1958-1959, which was my first year - I would have to lay the groundwork for the organization and the curriculum which at the earliest could not be put into effect before 1 September 1959. With this as a target date, we got our organization set up, which I have mentioned already, and we sent it in and got the approval of the Secretary of the Navy and the chief of Naval Personnel for this change. The next thing was to work on the curriculum.

The old organization had consisted of the superintendent, with the secretary of the academic board underneath him, and twelve departments - twelve academic departments - under him on a horizontal line. Those departments were: the executive department under the commandant of midshipmen; the department of seamanship and navigation; the department of ordnance and gunnery; the department of aviation; the department of hygiene; the department of English, history, and government; the department of foreign languages; the department of electrical engineering; the department of marine engineering; the department of mathematics; and the physical education department. As you can see, this, in my way of thinking, was a very difficult organization to handle a number of fairly well related subjects. The academic board consisted of the heads of all these departments, which meant that I had to deal with twelve individuals as members of the academic board. It seemed to me that this could and should be streamlined. To this end, we reorganized into four divisions: one division, headed by the commandant of midshipmen; a second division, headed by the director of naval science; a third division, headed by the director of social sciences and humanities; and a fourth division, headed by the director of science and engineering. Underneath these four headings, we grouped the departments under the appropriate director. Under the commandant of midshipmen, we placed physical education. Then, under naval science, we placed the command departments, the weapons department, and the naval hygiene department. Under social sciences and humanities, we placed the English, history, and government department and the department of foreign languages. Under the director of science and engineering, we placed the science department, the engineering department, and the mathematics department.

Chart B shows this new organization. In this way we grouped related subject matters into four groupings, which meant that the academic board was reduced from twelve to five members, and I had to deal with only four individuals myself, which, to me, made a much better organization.

Q: Did you get any brickbats from the academic people?

Adm. M.: Strangely enough, the new organization plan was very well accepted. The heads of departments and the people in top positions all agreed, both the military and the civilian staff, that this was a good move and worked hard at it. I only had one individual who objected, and there was nothing left to do except to override him.

The two charts enclosed, when compared, will show very well

what the changes were and how they worked. The new organization was placed in effect in the summer of 1959. At the same time that the new academic plan was effective, it was decided to allow midshipmen who had the credits and could show that they had on entering the Academy to validate certain courses in certain areas. This, naturally, had to be very limited to fit into our own program.

Q: Who determined this, the academic board?

Adm. M.: The academic board, with the advice and consent of the professors. They've changed now. You see, the professors were not in what you might call, not command positions, but directive areas where they could direct what was to be done.

In addition, midshipmen were allowed to select electives to replace the courses which they had validated, so that they would have the appropriate number of hours in each year. The validation and the elective program were very well received by the midshipmen, and we had to limit the number of electives the midshipmen could take for several reasons. One is we didn't have the staff at that time to accommodate the midshipmen in all the various electives that they wanted. The scheduling of classes, getting midshipmen back and forth from one class to another, became quite complicated with this new arrangement. It involved a great deal of planning and was something we had to work out as we went along.

Prior to this time, the midshipmen had always marched back and forth to classes in sections, because the former organization was so cut and dried that it lent itself to organizing the boys in groups to go from one class to another and back and forth. Under this new academic arrangement, it became quite involved and, while we held on to the marching back and forth in sections, the sections had to split up upon arrival at another academic group, so the boys could go to the various rooms for their classes. This was not true under the old arrangement, where everybody in one section went right to the same classroom.

It was proposed at that time that we stop marching to class, but we elected not to stop at that time because we were still feeling our way ahead with this new organization and, being a military institution, we hated to do away with the military side of life at the Naval Academy. When the time came to abolish marching back and forth to classes, it meant that we were coming closer and closer to a large university where people went back and forth to classes when and if they pleased. However, this decision was delayed and was not effective during my time as superintendent but the following year. Under Admiral Davidson, they stopped marching back and forth to classes and walked back and forth to their individual classrooms.

Q: Would I be correct in imagining that this was an area where criticism would be leveled from the alumni more readily than perhaps in the course area?

Adm. M.: That's one reason I didn't do it, if you understand what I mean! I might say that there was a great deal of comment on these changes from the alumni. They were not at all unpleasant in their remarks and comments, but it was something new that had to be digested, and it takes time to persuade them that this was the right thing to do. I kept a report running in the <u>Shipmate</u> to try and keep all the alumni informed of what we were doing. I must say that we did not come up with a sophisticated organization and layout that ran smoothly, as I would have liked, but I think we have to remember that this was a major step at the Naval Academy, to break away from something which had been going on for fifty or more years into a more liberal way of running the Academy.

Q: You didn't truly expect perfection overnight, did you?

Adm. M.: No, but I was disappointed. I think you can see what I mean. Can we just talk this thing through?

Q: Surely.

Adm. M.: What we had, as I have already said several times,

was a very fixed academic routine and curriculum in effect for a number of years. To get away from that meant making a major breakaway from everything we had been doing over that time. A little thing like scheduling classes doesn't sound very big until you try to change if after it's been running for a long period of time and you find you run into a great many difficulties. And then, too, on the academic side, there was a great deal of feeling and discussion among members of the board. Although they were in sympathy with this program, when it came down to the details of what electives should be allowed and who could validate and all the little details, I found that they all had very different ideas, and it took a little time and effort to resolve all these and get them going.

Q: And the board was comprised of some naval officers and some civilians?

Adm. M.: The board was all naval officers. We had the advantage of civilian advisers. Professor Jeffries was one of them. Bill Shields, who's retiring in a few days, was one of them. All the professors were helpful when asked, and a great many of them volunteered their comments. And I might say at this moment that this brought forth, in a way, how little influence, or how lacking in influence, were many of the senior professors at the Naval Academy, to try and resolve this situation somewhat, and, at the suggestion of Professor Jeffries - senior Professor Jeffries - I set up the academic council composed of all the senior professors. The duty of the academic council was to advise the superintendent and his staff on academic matters.

Q: How many were there - senior?

Adm. M.: There were seven at that time.

Q: This is senior in terms of length of service?

Adm. M.: Yes. I understand now there are some thirty senior professors and that this academic council that I set up at that time has been considerably increased in number, and I'm not quite sure how it functions myself at the present time.

Q: Was there a great willingness from within the teaching staff to embrace these changes?

Adm. M.: Yes. I must say that I think the civilian staff were all for these changes. They saw something which might come of it for the benefit of the Academy in the education field, and for their own benefit, and I believe that has proven true since.

Well, in the academic year of 1959-1960 the new academic organization, the new curriculum, validation, and elective programs were all put into effect.

Q: This leads one into the area of text books for the new curriculum. How was this matter handled?

Adm. M.: This was all handled - I don't know that I can cover the details - but it was all handled in a normal routine way of ordering new books to stock in the Midshipmen's Store, were issued to the midshipmen, and when - that was one of the controlling factors, as I say, in the number of electives we allowed to begin with, because we couldn't - we didn't have the stock and we couldn't get stocks that quickly. It takes time to do these things, and that's what we had to have.

Q: I was more interested in the selection of the text books you used. Was there a text book committee to pass on them?

Adm. M.: Yes, there was, and that - I don't have the composition of it here - but it was usually headed by one of the heads of department plus the professors in all the departments concerned for that particular book. We had a regular book committee.

Q: Were some of the text books generated from within the teaching staff?

Adm. M.: Yes. I'm afraid I wasn't too much involved in the

details of this, although I approved all the list that was sent out to purchase books. You have to depend on the staff to do part of this for you.

Melson #8 - 266

Interview No. 8 with Vice Admiral Charles Melson, U.S. Navy
(Retired)

Place: His residence in Providence, Annapolis, Maryland
Date: Monday afternoon, 20 March 1972
Subject: Biography
By: John T. Mason, Jr.

Q: All right, Sir. I believe today is to be a continuation of your time as Superintendent of the Naval Academy.

Adm. M.: Last time we met I covered the curriculum. Today I would like to speak about some of the building projects and the work that is going on to increase the facilities of the Naval Academy, particularly during the period while I was here.

For years the Naval Academy had been very short of adequate land area for expansion purposes. It was decided that, in order to gain this land, it was either necessary to expand into the river or to acquire additional land from the City of Annapolis.

Q: And that would mean taking over properties?

Adm. M.: That would mean taking over properties, some of it historically natured, and the city was very reluctant to release this land. As a matter of fact, it caused a great deal of concern among the people of Annapolis when we talked in particular of the three blocks just outside of the Maryland Avenue gate, where there's a slight indentation into the city, and which adjoins the Naval Academy.

It was finally decided to go ahead with the land fill, and during the period that I was there fifty-four and a half acres of additional usable land were acquired by filling in Dewey Basin and an area in the Severn River outboard of Farragut Field.

Q: Was this financed by the Naval Academy, this operation of filling in?

Adm. M.: This was financed by the government, at the request of the Naval Academy, along with funds for other purposes - the same way we acquired funds for other purposes.

Q: Inasmuch as the government was doing this, was it necessary to get any approval for this kind of operation, the filling in of water space?

Adm. M.: Of course, we had to get the usual clearance from the Navy, the Secretary of the Navy and so forth, but I'm not fully acquainted with the requirements from other areas of the government for filling this in. Anyway, it was all cleared and the work was begun. It took almost a year to conduct this work.

Dewey Basin, which no longer exists, was a basin between - stretching between Bancroft Hall and the old power plant, which was a water area and was used at that time for docking small boats, particularly small sailing craft.

This area was filled in as well as a large area on the other side of Farragut Field, that is, on the seaward side of Farragut Field. Do you follow me?

Q: Yes. Did they also fill in adjacent to the hospital?

Adm. M.: That was a fill several years prior to this. That was a fill on Hospital Point. The Naval Academy needed this land for two major purposes. One was, with the expanding brigade of midshipmen, more area was needed for athletic purposes, and with the expectation and hope of adding additional necessary buildings, we had to provide land from somewhere because we just didn't have it inside the Naval Academy gates, the way the land was laid out at this time. You notice now a great deal of this land has been used by new construction which is going on at the present time.

Actually, no real expansion of the Naval Academy could be accomplished until this fill was done, although all of the fill was not used for new buildings. It's still largely used for athletics.

Q: Inasmuch as the subject was broached at the time to take over certain properties from the City of Annapolis and this caused a furor and was finally rejected, does this mean that no such attempt would be made again?

Adm. M.: No. I think the attempt could possibly be made again, but knowing how the Annapolitans feel about it, I think it would be a very brave superintendent who would try it again! I actually did not get into any conflict with the city during my time. It started before I arrived and really came to a head in Admiral Davidson's tour, which followed mine. I did not actually get involved in the direct attempt to acquire this land.

The land that was acquired by filling in has since served a very useful purpose as playing fields for various athletic squads, as practice fields for the same squads, and somewhat for the area required for new buildings, which have been built since then.

Q: Does it make it more difficult to erect big buildings on filled land than it would have been otherwise?

Adm. M.: It definitely does because it requires longer pilings to get down to solid ground to support the buildings. It's not impossible. It's done worldwide. But it does make the problem a little bit more difficult and naturally it costs more money. It would be cheaper to build on firm ground, but if you don't have it, I guess you have to pay for it.

Among other things that were done during this period was the rehabilitation of the old wings of Bancroft Hall. The whole building was really in deplorable shape, but after much talking and discussion with Congress, we finally obtained the money to rehabilitate all the old wings. This was done in groups, starting with the center of Bancroft Hall and the third wing. Later, the first and second, fourth, fifth, and sixth were all rehabilitated and modernized.

Q: Was this the principal emphasis, modernization?

Adm. M.: Modernization and rehabilitation, completely.

Also work commenced in April of 1959 to erect two new wings to Bancroft Hall, wings 7 and 8, which are now connected with the Library-Assembly Building. Wings 7 and 8 and the Library-Assembly Building are partially erected on some of the filled-in land on Worden Field. At the time of building these wings, it was very difficult to persuade the authorities to give us adequate funds to use the same type stone for the structures as the old wings of Bancroft Hall. At that time, they wanted to use white brick, instead of granite, but eventually we won the point and got the granite for the last two wings, which means that they all match now.

Q: The granite came from Georgia, did it?

Adm. M.: The granite, I believe, came from Maine or New Hampshire. Anyway, New England.

Q: And, I assume, was much more expensive than the white brick?

Adm. M.: Oh, it's much more expensive.

One minor thing that was added to the Naval Academy at that time was the temporary wooden footbridge between Isherwood Hall and Hospital Point. The bridge still stands there today, although at the time it was erected it was considered to be temporary. The purpose of the bridge was to eliminate the long route across the vehicular bridge and Hubbard Hall and round the cemetery for midshipmen engaging in athletics at Hospital Point, thereby increasing the time for athletics each day.

A major item of construction which was completed during my time as superintendent was the Navy-Marine Corps Memorial Stadium. This stadium was built by funds donated by the alumni and various organizations, such as the Athletic Association, in order to acquire this stadium.

Q: Was the fund-raising accomplished in your regime?

Adm. M.: The fund-raising was primarily accomplished during

Admiral Smedberg's regime and he was the coordinator for the whole drive. The success of the drive is his and his efforts and ability in doing this. There were many delays in the construction of the stadium. Originally the idea was conceived about 1950, but in the meantime the price went up many, many times and eventually the cost was in the neighborhood of $3,000,000.

Q: Was it necessary to have the money in hand before construction could begin?

Adm. M.: No. Construction began - this, again, happened before my time - when they'd collected about two-thirds of the funds. It's interesting to note here that some of the funds were raised by having memorial chairs placed in the stadium which individuals could subscribe to in memory of their relatives, primarily naval officers.

Q: That was certainly a needed addition, wasn't it?

Adm. M.: Yes, it was.

To answer your question a minute ago. It was determined that when $1,750,000 had been received, they would put out for bids. The contract was awarded in 1958 and it was scheduled for completion 15 August 1959. The stadium was dedicated on 26 September 1959 on the occasion of the Navy-

William and Mary football game. I had the great pleasure of conducting the dedication ceremony and making the introductory remarks and introducing the speaker. The speaker was Admiral Arleigh Burke, Chief of Naval Operations. Also present were the Secretary of the Navy and a number of officials from Washington.

The dedication plaque reads:

> This stadium is dedicated to those who have served and will serve, upholders of the traditions and renown of the Navy and Marine Corps of the United States. May it be a perpetual reminder of the Navy and Marine Corps as organizations of men trained to work hard and play hard, in war defenders of our freedom, in peace molders of our youth.

Q: Admiral, the acquisition of the land on which the stadium is located, was this included in the price of $3,000,000?

Adm. M.: Yes. The Athletic Association had owned some of this land for a number of years.

Q: Oh, they had? In anticipation?

Adm. M.: In anticipation of this, and preliminary work had been done back as far as fifteen years before this, like excavating the ground, things like that. I can't say just how much money went from each of these little endeavors into the total.

Among other things in the way of facilities that were accomplished during this period was moving the Navy Exchange gas station from the main Academy grounds to North Severn, air-conditioning of the commissioned officers' mess, rehabilitation of the steam and hot water distribution system, rehabilitation of the officers' mess basement area, and a number of other essential maintenance items.

Q: On the whole, how often does a job of rehabilitation of such facilities become necessary? What period of time?

Adm. M.: I think it's difficult to say, but in this case it had been a great many years. As a matter of fact, probably no major rehabilitation had been done to Bancroft Hall since it was built, except for minor work done in connection with every-day maintenance. It was very badly in need of upkeep throughout. This money, I think, was very well spent. The men living in Bancroft Hall today have much better living facilities than I had when I was a midshipman.

Q: With the rehabilitation of Bancroft Hall went the construction of the present mess hall?

Adm. M.: No. With the rehabilitation the extension of the mess hall was included. The mess hall now is in the shape of a T. Before this it was just the top of the T, one long section, and they added the stem that sticks out towards the water.

During the building of wings 7 and 8 and the rehabilitation of the old wings, it became a major problem how to take care of the brigade of midshipmen, which numbered, in summer, at that time around 3,800, during the period of construction. When wings 7 and 8 were completed they were immediately occupied, and two of the old wings were vacated for rehabilitation. This rotation continued until all the wings were rehabilitated and completed. Then the brigade moved into all the new quarters.

Q: Do you want to talk about the Distinguished Visitors Program when you were superintendent?

Adm. M.: The Naval Academy has always been a point of interest for distinguished visitors to Washington, and the authorities in Washington have invariably scheduled the Naval Academy for a visit during some point of the prominent visitor's period in the Washington area.

In 1959 we had the Duke of Sparta, who was then Prince Constantine of Greece, later King of Greece. King Hussein I of Jordan paid the Academy a visit. Rear Admiral Sung, the then superintendent of the Chinese Naval Academy, was here. All of the foreign military and naval attaches were visitors to the Naval Academy during the two years.

Q: You mean all of those stationed in Washington?

Adm. M.: All of those stationed in Washington, excuse me. Of course, the Secretary of the Navy, the Honorable Thomas S. Gates, and the Honorable William B. Franke, later Secretary of the Navy, paid innumerable visits to the Academy for one reason or another.

In addition to those that I have named, a great number of other lower ranking foriegn military officers and civilians came to the Academy. These occasions almost invariably required a parade of the midshipmen in their honor and luncheon at the Superintendent's Quarters.

Q: For heads of state and people of that sort was anything additional provided in the way of entertainment?

Adm. M.: There were no heads of state here.

Q: Hussein was.

Adm. M.: You're right, Hussein was. But no, there was nothing additional provided. The entertainment usually involved a luncheon, a meeting of any midshipmen that happened to be members of the brigade from the visiting VIP's country, then later a parade and reception in his honor, the reception being held at the Superintendent's Quarters.

Interview No. 9 with Vice Admiral Charles L. Melson, U.S. Navy
(Retired)

Place: His residence in Providence, Annapolis, Maryland

Date: Monday morning, 27 March 1972

Subject: Biography

By: John T. Mason, Jr.

Q: Admiral, you say you'd like to add a bit of information about the building program at the Academy. Do you want to talk about the over-all plan that was in being?

Adm. M.: The Naval Academy has had a master building program to provide for expansion of the Academy, but, due to the lack of funds which are provided by Congress, it has never been fully implemented. The result has been that it has been implemented piece by piece over the years, with a number of changes entering into the plan as time passes by.

Q: Was it ever intended to be carried out at one time?

Adm. M.: The ideal way would be for it to be implemented all at one time, but the costs involved were too much for Congress and we could only get a piece at a time. The result has been that, while there is a plan, the various changes that have been put into the plan have caused it to deviate a great deal from the basic plan originally conceived.

Q: I suppose you're referring to types of building materials and so forth?

Adm. M.: No, I'm referring to buildings, the actual structures themselves, and their location primarily. As you know and we've discussed before, there's always been a great shortage of land area at the Naval Academy. Now this has been partially rectified by the filling in of certain areas like Dewey Basin and out into the river to provide additional land space, and we hope that this will eventually help to solve the basic problem of land shortage and allow the Academy to expand in somewhat the way that it was originally planned.

This basically covers the master building plan which I talked about the details of somewhat before this, but I won't go into those details here.

Q: Were you instrumental in drawing up this master building plan? Was it done in your regime?

Adm. M.: No, the master building plan was conceived some time back around 1948 by the Manning Board, and since then I guess every superintendent has had a crack at modifying it according to his thoughts and desires and according to the needs of the Academy at his time.

Q: What was the Manning Board?

Adm. M.: The Manning Board - I'm not sure I remember the details, but it was a board appointed by the Secretary of the Navy, I believe, to study the Naval Academy and to determine its future needs.

Q: This was post war?

Adm. M.: It was a post-war board - and to try and develop an orderly plan of expansion for the Academy. It served its purpose well because over the years it has been a guideline for us all to work with and, although we have deviated from it, we have deviated mostly from necessity, sometimes by desire, and I think that all the changes have been good.

Now, I'd like to cover briefly the entrance requirements for the Naval Academy.

Q: They were revised in your time, were they?

Adm. M.: The entrance requirements were revised by Admiral Smedberg shortly before my arrival to provide for admission by college entrance board examination. This was placed in effect my first summer as superintendent, in other words in the summer of 1958. All the fourth class admitted that year were admitted under this plan. They came in under the CEEB, so-called.

Q: How large a percentage of an incoming class would be affected by this?

Adm. M.: All. I don't desire to get into the details of how the CEEB works, but, briefly, all applicants take the same examination and they're all graded according to certain standards and they attain a certain score. Then they are put in order or precedence according to their score, then the Academic Board decides on a cut point on the score and everybody above the cut point gets in. Then if they do not get enough applicants on this first step, it's possible to change the cut point so as to drop it a little lower and pick up a few more people. This way they continue their work until they get the total number of applicants they want, which by taking the top group are the best qualified academically.

The following year I put a new plan into effect, which we called The Whole Man concept. In doing this, we tried to take into consideration all the other factors which would influence a young man coming into the Naval Academy to become the type of naval officers that we thought desirable. In this procedure we gave due weight to the CEEB exam, but we also gave weight to high-school records, including academic performance in high school, the recommendation of his principal as to the type of boy he was, his extracurricular activities before he entered the Naval Academy, and his athletic record, which naturally comes under extracurricular activities, in determining his final grade before the cut point.

Q: So it wasn't all dependent on a single examination or series of examinations?

Adm. M.: Before this it had depended entirely on the mental examination plus the physical exam to determine his physical qualifications. In the new system, or The Whole Man procedure, we took a look at the boy in all of his activities, everything he had done that we could find which would give us a better idea how to judge him and mark him and put him in the proper sequence in the study to determine who was qualified to come in.

I am under the impression that during the time that I was there this procedure worked very well and it's my understanding that it's still in effect.

Q: Was there any noticeable change in the quality of the lad admitted?

Adm. M.: That's very difficult to say. We naturally think that there was, and I believe there was. But it's pretty hard to put this down in black and white because you can't quite put your finger on it. But we believed that this system gave us the best choice of the several thousands of boys who were trying to get into the Naval Academy each year. For instance, in the year that I was just speaking of there were over 4,000 applications. Today there are even more. But these additional factors gave us a means of eliminating some of the ones who didn't quite measure up in order to get somebody who was a little bit better qualified.

Q: And I suppose the entire system served to eliminate any political pressure being applied to get a boy in?

Adm. M.: We hoped it would and I think it did, but there's always the exception. I don't believe it applied to very many but there's always a little extra pressure here and there and sometimes the dividing line is overlooked a little bit.

Q: When the senator was powerful enough!

I might ask as to the inspiration for the development of The Whole Man concept, where was this idea generated?

Adm. M.: It was generated in my staff, the Academic Board. We were always seeking means of trying to measure one boy against the other to determine who was the best qualified and who was not so well qualified, and it just seemed to us in studying the problem that we just had to consider everything we could find out about the boy. While some boys did well in academics they fell down in other areas. While some were good in extracurricular activities, like athletics, they fell down on the academic side.

It's interesting to note that one of the best criteria we had, when everything else failed, was the high school principal's recommendation. Usually, this carried a lot of weight because it proved to be quite a good measure of what a boy could do and couldn't do.

Q: The principal had four years to observe him!

Adm. M.: Yes, and they usually were pretty good. We realized, though, that a principal's recommendation might be flavored a little bit, too, so we tried to consider that. But usually the principal had a pretty good recommendation.

Q: It has been said, I believe, in many quarters that a lad's athletic prowess sometimes perhaps carried undue weight in obtaining admission to the Academy for him. Would you talk about that?

Adm. M.: I'm afraid I'm getting on a little dangerous ground when I get into that, but anyway here goes. Naturally, the

Academy at one time and perhaps to a certain extent even today, like many other schools, went in search of outstanding athletes. Sometimes in the search certain rules were overlooked in order to get a particularly good full back or quarterback or an end, or in other sports, basketball, and so forth, a good center, but while the desire and the need for good atletic teams at the Naval Academy existed, it was not quite a fair way to approach this, considering all the boys who were trying to get in. I might say that there's been considerable change in this in recent years, and that the boy's prowess as an athlete is not a governing factor today as it was at one time.

The Naval Academy, to the best of my knowledge, has never paid athletes or done anything of that nature which there's so much discussion of in the papers today, but they did lean over a little bit backwards to get good boys, and they had to if they were going to stay in the athletic competition that they were in. Today they're not involved in these very competitive trials that they were ten or twelve years ago.

Q: You mean the football schedule today isn't equal to what it was?

Adm. M.: That's correct, but there are other sports this

applies to also. There are still people who want the Naval Academy to be Number One in football in the country, and I might say for myself I'd like to see it, too. But in order to do that you have to give up other things whose value should be fully considered before you decide to go along with this program.

Q: I would think too, Sir, that a boy admitted because of his athletic abilities and not necessarily his intellectual attainments might be a problem through his whole school career. How does he adjust?

Adm. M.: That is quite true, and at one time there were extra instruction periods for athletes - certain athletes - only. They were coached almost all the way through their four years at the Naval Academy. I can't really say that this is harmful to them or harmful to the Academy. Any harm it does is the competition of people, because they're all in competition to graduate and become officers in the Navy. Some fall by the wayside. If they don't make the grade, they don't get a commission. It's a very difficult thing to decide which is the better course to pursue, except that logic says, I believe, that you should give every man a fair chance, and the athlete who's getting this extra help is getting more than his fair share compared to the other boys who also have some difficulties in the academics.

I'll touch on it later, but this entered a little bit into our coaching problem. When I speak about sports, I'll touch on this a little bit more. You had to try and have a system that was fair to everybody and going to produce good naval officers. Now, it's said by many people, and I think it's quite true, that athletes make good officers because they become sort of natural leaders due to their training in various sports.

Q: They're disciplined.

Adm. M.: That's quite true. Many of our outstanding leaders have been football players and basketball players and lacrosse players at the Academy. But at the same time there are a lot of other men who are good leaders but did not necessarily get the same publicity, so therefore we didn't hear as much about them.

I do think that athletics in whatever form you take it is good for a military man. I think it should be encouraged at the Academy and I think we should keep in competition with other schools, because I do think it provides something in a man's character that makes him a good naval officer. I won't say that this is necessarily so, but I say that it is there and it's good to have it.

Q: Admiral, in your time as superintendent, did the Academy

have a system of providing scholarships to promising lads for a year in a prep school prior to entrance?

Adm. M.: There were certain arrangements by which boys could get scholarships to prep schools before entering the Naval Academy, and many of them did it. By the NCAA rules, though, this type of help from official sources was forbidden, not only for the Naval Academy but for all schools. So any help that they got had to come from outside sources. It's always been a very touchy problem and I noticed that it was emphasized in this weekend's paper in regard to Florida State University, which has done so well in this basketball program. It's not exactly scholarships they're talking about, but it is assistance that these boys got from their schools in order that they could play basketball and win championships in honor of the school.

Q: Well, the type of scholarship I'm referring to, was it offered exclusively to boys who were athletically inclined, or were there other virtues that were seized upon?

(No answer to that question.)

Adm. M.: You put me on the spot on that one.

The mission of the Naval Academy had been the subject of a great deal of study by me from the time I reported as superintendent. I gave it to the Academic Board to study and produce a mission which better suited what we were trying to do at the Naval Academy.

Q: What caused you to focus on this?

Adm. M.: Because we were making these changes in the curriculum and in the organization, and we wanted to make sure this all tied together with the mission.

The Academic Board came up with a new mission for the Naval Academy, to do what I thought it should do in respect to what we were trying out at the Academy. The mission of the Naval Academy, if I may quote, prior to this time reads as follows:

> "Through study and practical instruction provide the misdhipmen with a basic education and knowledge of the naval profession, to develop them morally, mentally, and physically, and by precept and example to indoctrinate them with the highest ideals of duty, honor, and loyalty in order that the naval service may be provided with graduates who are capable junior officers in whom has been developed the capacity and foundation for future development in mind and character, leading towards a readiness to assume the highest responsibilities of citizenship and government."

I felt that this mission was too long, to begin with,

and it didn't stress the things that I thought were important at that time. The new mission, which the Academic Board developed, reads as follows:

> "To develop midshipmen morally, mentally, and physically and to imbue them with the highest ideals of duty, honor, and loyalty, in order to provide graduates who are dedicated to a career of naval service and have potential for future development in mind and character to assume the highest responsibilities of command, citizenship, and government."

This was approved by the Secretary of the Navy on the 11th of March 1960. It may seem at first to be merely a repetition of what went on in the old mission, but to us it seemed to provide a mission that we could follow better under the circumstances we were under then.

Q: We talked earlier about the concept of a previous superintendent who felt that one aspect of the educational experience there should be to train a man to be a gentleman as well as a naval officer. How does that fit into this new concept developed in your time?

Adm. M.: Well, I think that's covered when we say "the highest ideals of duty, honor, and loyalty." I think that sort of covers all of that area. At least, we thought it did and that was our purpose in so doing.

I believe there's a new mission been recently developed. I'm not familiar with it, but there probably is.

Q: Since this has been to the fore in the last few years, what was your attitude towards the chapel services and how they tie into this whole picture?

Adm. M.: The chapel service - in speaking to you about this, I know you're well versed in this particular field as well as many others - supposedly was nondenominational, although the formality of the chapel service is a little bit after the Catholic or the Episcopal service, and I felt it met our needs and did what we wanted in the religious field. I'm speaking now of the Protestant service, and I'm sure the Catholic service provided the same. I was very well satisfied at the time I was there with the religious services, where provided, and I felt they met all of our needs at that time.

Q: In most recent years, of course, there's an attempt to eliminate the required attendance, and this was refuted and successfully so by the present superintendent on the basis that this experience was necessary to a young man in the development of leadership qualities and in an understanding of the needs of his men.

Adm. M.: I concur with him fully in this respect. I do

not believe the Naval Academy is a place where young men should be allowed to follow entirely their own pursuits and not go to chapel and have certain religious preferences. I believe in all the Constitution says regarding freedom of religion and so forth, but I feel that here in this Academy it's necessary for the proper development of a military leader.

Q: There are then limits on permissiveness?

Adm. M.: That's correct. There are limits on other things, too, not just that they have to attend chapel. They do not have the freedom of the town, the freedom to go and come as they please. They're regimented in many ways and I see no reason for religion not to be included in these as long as it does not violate the individual's desire to worship in his own way. I realize that there are many young men who take advantage of this to just not go to church, period. We've had many examples of that, and I'm sure the present superintendent can quote many examples of this. But I think that church service is a requirement for the proper development of religious feelings and thoughts of all these young men, because it's not just themselves that they are going to be responsible for. In their time, they're going to be responsible for many, many other men and what they do, and I think they need this training as well as any of the other training.

Q: That was the thesis that prevailed, apparently, in the courts.

Adm. M.: Well, as I said, I concur heartily in everything that Calvert's done in this respect. My understanding is that at the moment it's not a dead issue, that it's still subject to the action of the Appeals Court. Unless they have been called within the last two months, I think they're still waiting for a final call on this for a decision.

I have a number of items which I would like to get into the record, which are small in nature but indicate change and progress, and I'm going to put some of them on now just to get them in the record.

The first one happens to be a very insignificant one, but it has caused a great deal of discussion among Naval Academy people. In 1960 we changed the style and format of the diploma indicating graduation from the Naval Academy. The diploma issued in 1959, and which had been issued by the Naval Academy for over 100 years, was a large sheepskin, engraved, and a very beautiful job done, to a smaller engraved certificate which could be put into a folder. This change was made primarily because midshipmen leaving and going to sea had difficulty with this large rolled sheepskin. It sort of got in their way. We followed the current and what other schools were doing in going to this smaller type certificate in a blue, hard-backed binder which could be easily

Melson #9 - 294

carried.

In addition to that, a midshipman's first set of orders as a commissioned officer could be enclosed in one side of this folder, so when he graduated he had both pieces of paper in a small, hard-backed, attractive folder, which was easy for him to handle.

Q: Admiral, was the availability of sheepskin and the cost of sheepskin in the year 1959 also a factor?

Adm. M.: It was, because the cost was going up all the time, and these other diplomas were much cheaper in spite of the fact that we had the additional fact of the folder to put it in. But the engraving and the cost of the material were just going sky high. That was a factor, but not a major factor.

On January 9, 1960, I visited the Mexican Naval Academy on the occasion of their graduation exercises. Admiral Arleigh Burke ordered me to attend this exercise and to take Mrs. Melson and my aides and a representative midshipman. He provided his personally assigned plane for the trip, and we left the Naval Academy on the 9th of January, as I stated before, and proceeded to Mexico City, where we picked up the American Ambassador, Robert C. Hill, and his wife and flew on to Vera Cruz, the location of the Mexican Naval Academy.

We had with us Midshipman A. K. Thompson, the Brigade Commander, a five-striper, as a representative of the midshipmen of the brigade. Midshipman Thompson, incidentally was from Texas and very fluent in Spanish. We also carried with us a bronze plaque, similar to the one installed in the terrace of Bancroft Hall now, to present to the Mexican Naval Academy.

The day after we arrived the graduation exercises were held, which all of my party attended, and Midshipman Thompson made the presentation to the Mexican Naval Academy, all in spoken Spanish and it was very well received. We spent that night in Vera Cruz -- it was the second night we were on the trip - and flew back to Mexico City the next morning, where we dropped Ambassador Hill and his wife and spent one night before proceeding on back to the Naval Academy. It was a delightful trip throughout and I think it did a lot to help relations between the Mexican and American navies.

Q: How large an academy do they have? What kind of a student body?

Adm. M.: I've forgotten the exact figures at this date, but I think it was about 300. They were very smart, well dressed, in uniform, of course, and gave indication of being quite an outstanding group of young Mexicans.

I haven't touched on the summer cruises made by the

midshipmen during the summers I was here. Prior to this time it had been customary to have a midshipman practice squadron each year, made up of two or three major ships and a number of destroyers, which took all the midshipmen on a cruise either to Europe, South America, or, sometimes, the West Coast.

During the time I was a midshipman I made a cruise to Europe, one to Atlantic Coast ports, and one to West Coast ports. Prior to coming to the Naval Academy I had been second in command of the midshipmen's cruise in 1957, which cruised to South American ports, and I took half of the cruising unit in to the port of Sao Paulo, Santos, which is also a coffee port. I quote this merely to indicate that I had been mixed up in midshipmen cruises before.

At this time, that is the summer of 1959, the ships were just not available to provide a large cruising unit to carry all of the midshipmen on a combined cruise. So they were spread out to various units of the fleet. The first class went to ships in the Sixth Fleet, the First Fleet, Second Fleet, and the Seventh Fleet. The other class midshipmen were spread out among active ships throughout the Navy, mostly on the East and West coasts.

The following summer, the same general procedure followed. The first class men were given jobs aboard ship as junior officers, while the other classes that were aboard ship did the work of seamen and petty officers. A large contingent of each class went to aviation summer, visiting Pensacola and Key West. This plan, while it was effective and produced good training, did not in my personal opinion provide the same thing as the whole brigade going to sea as a unit in ships of the fleet and operating as a unit while at sea.

Q: This became no longer possible because of the disappearance of the battleship?

Adm. M.: Partially, but the ships were so busy. They were busy in Korea, they were busy in the Med, and they just couldn't provide the ships for the cruises as they had in the past.

Q: Did not this dispersal idea put a greater strain on the teaching staff at the Academy?

Adm. M.: It did because the few people that we could scrape up at the Academy to send on the cruises were spread pretty thin among the various units of the fleet. Where when we had all the midshipmen in a few big ships and a few small ones, as a unit cruising, we could do a lot of instruction at sea with the Naval Academy instructors. Under the new system, while some was done, it was nowhere near as effective as it was when we had them all on one group.

Q: What about the intangible factor, the morale factor? I've often heard in the past that the cruise experience for midshipmen was a great boost, and those students who were wavering in the idea of pursuing a naval career were very often determined to do so as a result of their experience. It would be more spotty, would it not, in the fragmentation?

Adm. M.: I think it would be. Of course, one of the great attractions of the cruises were visits to foreign ports. Under this system which I've just described that was used in the summers of 1959 and 1960, it was fine for the first class who got to operate in ships of the fleets at sea, the First, and Second, and Sixth, and the Seventh. But I'm afraid some of the junior classes who got no farther than the coasts of the United States were not very thrilled with the cruise in any way. We had one unit that made a cruise up to Great Lakes, and while I think it was a good cruise and educational, I don't think they were particularly thrilled with it. A lot of them were going close to their own homes, if they lived in the West.

Q: Was there any attempt made to analyze the results of the different cruises? I mean the effect upon the boy?

Adm. M.: Oh, yes. After every cruise questionnaires were submitted to the boys to get their ideas and thoughts, and these were all consolidated and formed into a paper to give opinions as to what happened and what was the best way to do these things.

Q: Was this then contrasted with earlier cruises, the reports on this?

Adm. M.: Oh, yes.

Q: And what was the result?

Adm. M.: The result was not a great deal of change. I think the cruises were controlled mostly by the availability of ships, more than the desires of the people who were trying to conduct the cruises. Prior to the cruises I made every effort I could, with consultations with people in Washington, CNO, to get the maximum number and the best ships I could and outline the best cruise that I could. They listened to me but I didn't win out in all respects, simply because the ships were busy and they couldn't spare them for this particular training duty.

When we had the battleships it was ideal because the battleships lent themselves to handling large groups under these circumstances, and you could hold certain classes under way with a great deal of ease. And you could cruise far and wide at sea. Most of the cruises that were made to foreign ports were well received. The midshipmen enjoyed them and I think it was a great attraction to them to make these cruises.

Q: It wasn't considered at all feasible to bring one of the battleships out of moth balls for this particular reason?

Adm. M.: Money. Of course, I'm a great advocate of the battleship and think they should never have been put out of commission.

Q: Having been skipper of one, yes!

Adm. M.: But I'm afraid I have very little influence in that field! It would have been good to have a ship of that type because of its size. We have other ships that can handle large numbers of people, transports and so forth, but they do not have the attraction that a man of war does. Now, I know a lot of people object to that statement because they consider the amphibious ships as fighting ships, and I agree with them, but an armed man of war built for fighting at sea just has a certain attraction to it that the transport types do not have.

Q: Well, the transports don't provide the training facilities either, do they, in terms of gunnery and related things?

Adm. M.: No, they don't in that respect. They provide it in other ways but they can't provide everything in the way I feel it should be provided.

Q: The assignment of various of the midshipmen to Pensacola and other naval stations seems like a great improvement over the earlier aviation summer?

Adm. M.: Oh, yes, by far. I experienced an aviation summer and during the aviation summer which I spent here at the Naval Academy I went up in an airplane three times, and they were the old lumbering seaplane types. Now the boys who go to the various air stations in the summer get to fly in modern jets and they have certain opportunities to do some flying themselves, and it's quite good experience for them.

Q: This is not on this particular subject, but do you, as superintendent, pay particular attention to the attitude of the midshipmen toward a naval career after his graduation? I mean, is there some close watch kept on this, as the boys go through the four-year course?

Adm. M.: Yes. They receive continued indoctrination in the Navy and the desire to make the Navy a career. That's part of the job of the superintendent and his staff and the various officers assigned to the Naval Academy.

Q: What kind of a check can you make on this?

Adm. M.: The closest check you have are the company officers, who are very close to the midshipmen in their daily life and they, in their conversations with them and so forth, report back on their feelings on various matters and how they feel about a naval career, and occasionally in command lectures we get their feelings. The boys are very free about expressing themselves regarding the Navy and the Navy life, and they ask many, many questions on the subject, naturally.

Part of our job is to indoctrinate them into life in the Navy. As long as we have them we spend a lot of money on them. Of course, that doesn't work in all cases, but I think it does in perhaps 95 percent of the cases after the four-year period. Of course, there are some boys who come to the Naval Academy in the beginning with the idea of just getting the education that's offered and then quitting. Well, the two-year service rule has been in effect for seven years now.

Q: Was it in effect in your time as superintendent?

Adm. M.: Yes, in which they have to spend two years of active duty after graduating. There are various ways of getting around this. Not all of them try it and it doesn't work in every case, but there are ways like physical disability and things of that nature which they use to get out of the service.

It's interesting to note at this point, I think, that in some cases, particularly disciplinary cases, boys who have disciplinary problems in their first-class year and sometimes in their second-class year and don't graduate are required to serve out their time as enlisted men.

Q: Oh, they are, to serve out the balance of the - ?

Adm. M.: They can be required. This is not true in all cases. I know of one case which happened back in 1926 in which a Midshipman Zerkel refused to take - I think I'm correct in this - the oath of office on graduation and he was sent to sea for two years as a midshipman. But that doesn't exactly compare with the boy who has to go to sea as an enlisted man, who after he's gotten three and a half years of education decides he doesn't want to be in the Navy.

Q: Did you have during your regime any instances of a conscientious objector popping up?

Adm. M.: No, but of course we weren't seriously at war during the time I was superintendent, so that really didn't come up. We were on the fringes of a war.

Q: Yes.

Interview No. 10 with Vice Admiral Charles L. Melson, U.S. Navy
(Retired)

Place: His residence in Providence, Annapolis, Maryland
Date: Thursday morning, 6 April 1972
Subject: Biography
By: John T. Mason, Jr.

Q: All right, Sir. On this spring morning, things are looking up. Let's have another chapter on the Naval Academy.

Adm. M.: Everything is looking up except my chest at the moment!

Athletics are and have been an important part of the overall training program here at the Naval Academy. The physical facilities are among the best to be found in the nation. In addition to the various intercollegiate sports which the Naval Academy participates in, there are various intramural sports for those who do not take part in the major programs. The Naval Academy has always competed at very high levels in all the major sports, particularly football, basketball, baseball, and lacrosse. In addition to those, they compete in a number of minor sports.

During my tour here in 1958 to 1960 I would say that we had a better than average record in wins versus losses. In football, the major sport, we won 60 percent of the games in 1959 and about 65 percent of the games in 1960.

Q: Quite an increase!

Adm. M.: Better than it had been in the past. In 1958 we had a very unfortunate thing happen. We lost to Army in football. In 1959 we had a much better year and we beat Army by the largest score ever 2 to 12 - excuse me, that should read 43 to 12. This was really a major victory and one that was greatly appreciated by the brigade.

In addition, in that fall we won all of the fall sports and I had the privilege of hoisting the broomstick at the masthead opposite my flag at the Naval Academy. I was very proud of that occasion and I now have a picture of that hanging in my house.

Q: Tell me about that ceremony.

Adm. M.: There really is not much of a ceremony to it. Everybody comes back in great excitement when we win the last event of a particular season, and if we've won them all somebody hoists a broom up to the masthead. There's no ceremony to it.

Q: It's a rare occasion, however?

Adm. M.: A comparatively rare occasion and something that's very good here at the Naval Academy.

Q: Admiral, in your period at the Academy in what sports did the midshipmen actually excel?

Adm. M.: It's hard at this time for me to remember exactly in which sports they excelled during my period of time, but I would say they exceled particularly in lacrosse and, while they did well in football, they did not have an unbeaten season, but they compared favorably with their opponents of other schools. I might say at this time that the opponents of the Naval Academy during this period were major universities and colleges of the United States, such schools as West Point, the Air Force Academy, Notre Dame - the really big schools in athletics, and none of them were pushovers. One of the faults with Naval Academy athletics has been, I believe, that we schedule too many high-powered teams without any resting period in between. That is something that could be corrected, but somehow or other never seems to quite get corrected in the desire to play big teams with reputations and play them on favorable terms, and, incidentally, to make money.

As you may or may not know, Naval Academy athletics are not financed by government funds. Sports are financed by money from the Naval Academy Athletic Association. The

Athletic Association obtains its funds from the members of the Association by dues, by income from football games, and various minor sports. Football is naturally the largest provider of funds in this particular category. Therefore, it receives the most in return - But the equipment, the fields, and all parts of the athletic program are supported by funds from the Athletic Association, including the stadium. So in order to continue this program we must have money, and the money comes naturally from the various games, and football is the biggest producer of funds. Therefore, it's imperative to have a good team.

In addition to the varsity squads, the Athletic Association supports the intramural sports programs by providing the equipment to all the various company and battalion teams.

Q: I would think then that special care would be exercised in avoiding games with teams outside of the particular league in which the Naval Academy finds itself? I mean teams that are superior, in terms that some effort would be made to avoid consistently scheduling games with such teams?

Adm. M.: That's not quite correct, because we do consistently schedule games with teams which we only beat occasionally, and I might mention Notre Dame as being one of those teams. I don't know what the score card would show but we've probably beaten Notre Dame about once every eight times we've played them. But, there again, Notre Dame is a big money-producer on the football field.

Q: You mentioned lacrosse as being one of the sports that the Naval Academy does excel in and I guess they've always excelled in that area.

Adm. M.: The Naval Academy was one of the first teams to take up lacrosse in the country. I shouldn't say "first" but among the earlier teams to take up lacrosse, and it has been very consistent in the years gone by in the results we've had in lacrosse. They've usually produced winning teams, and that is something that hasn't fallen off even in the last few years, although other sports apparently have dropped considerably.

Q: Tennis is another area where the Academy has had a considerable record?

Adm. M.: In tennis the Naval Academy has done reasonably well over the years, but I might at this point also mention fencing, which people don't speak of very often, but fencing is one of the outstanding sports at the Naval Academy and the Naval Academy has always been in the top group of the winners and the outstanding teams in this particular sport. In years gone by, before this period, boxing was a great sport at the Naval Academy, and it's too bad that it was abolished as a collegiate sport because the Naval Academy always did well in boxing! At the present time, they're doing very well in wrestling and have done over the years.

You can go back and pick any sport and I think you'll find that the Naval Academy has been outstanding in it at some particular period of time, more so than not. Swimming is another example where it's been sort of up and down, but the swimming team has always been better than average.

Q: And rowing?

Adm. M.: The crew has its ups and downs, too, but it has had its fine years in the past, and I expect they will have them again in the future.

I think the athletic program at the Naval Academy is one of the outstanding athletic programs in the country. I think it does a lot for the midshipmen and I think that it has a lot to do with producing good officers and, if you look back in the record of the Navy, you'll find that most, not all, of the Navy leaders were athletes of some form or another. Nimitz played football, Halsey played football. Almost any number of them engaged in some type of athletics. I don't say that athletics is a requirement for a leader, because we have others who were not. There was Spruance, for instance, who was never known as a great athlete, and he's probably, in my book, the great leader of World War II in the Navy. But it goes without saying that sports does produce a competitive spirit on the part of the individuals who play, and I think that's good in people who have to lead men in battle and have to fight battles.

Q: And also, would you not say, it helps to provide sports leaders within the fleet and these have terrific morale-building value?

Adm. M.: Yes, indeed. Most of the athletes who leave the Naval Academy and go out in the fleet end up coaching some type team within the fleet, which gives them very close contact with the men in the fleet and they are able to transfer to them some of the competitive spirit that they learned at the Naval Academy, although these people have plenty of competitive spirit anyway!

One other sport I might mention in particular is gym. Over the years Navy has pretty well excelled in gymnastics. I could go on this way about each sport, I guess, but I don't think that's quite desirable, because they've all had their ups and downs and most of them had outstanding years at one time or another.

Q: Well, shall we introduce an entirely new subject? You wanted to talk about the Operation Information.

Adm. M.: Yes. Operation Information is a program which was started around 1960. The purpose of the program was to have midshipmen present to people throughout the nation a picture of the Naval Academy as they see it, giving the mission and some description of life and what occurs here at the Academy. The program was started off and has continued over the years by having midshipmen going home on Christmas leave make appointments with various organizations in their home towns and home areas to speak to that organization on the subject of the Navy and the Naval Academy in particular. These organizations, such as the Chamber of Commerce, the Lions Club, etc., were all very receptive to the idea and the Naval Academy people helped organize and get appointments for these midshipmen to speak. Usually, the midshipmen left three or four days earlier on Christmas leave than the rest of the class in order to compensate a little bit for the time they spent on this program, and it apparently has paid off over the years in its public information program.

Q: Is there a selection made of boys to do this - a careful selection?

Adm. M.: Yes, the selection is very carefully made by the company officers and the commandant of midshipmen, to take into consideration the speaking ability of the boy, his knowledge and how he stands in his class, and how good a representative of the Naval Academy he is. So far, as I say, the results have been very good. I can't give anything more definite as to the results.

Q: Did this program begin in your regime?

Adm. M.: No, it started about 1960 - excuse me, about 1955. I believe it started under Admiral Smedberg.

While I was here, and I understand for some time before I arrived, Admiral Rickover showed great interest in the Naval Academy and the Naval Academy programs. He, of course, is interested more in the nuclear education of midshipmen than anything else, but anyway he thought that he was becoming a great educator and he should be able to tell all people how to run their institutions of learning.

He had asked several times before I arrived to come down to the Naval Academy and speak, which for one reason or another he was never given permission to do. He brought the subject up again after I became superintendent, and Admiral Smith, who was then the Chief of Naval Personnel, -

Q: What Smith was that?

Adm. M.: H. P. Smith, later commander-in-chief of the fleet.

Admiral Smith asked me to please arrange a visit for Admiral Rickover to the Naval Academy. I was against Rickover speaking to the midshipmen as a body, and I suggested that if Rickover would come down we would be glad to brief him on the Naval Academy and its curriculum. As a result of this, a date was set and Admiral Rickover came down.

We met in a board room down in the Marine Engineering Department. Present were Admiral Rickover and myself, the Commandant, the Secretary of the Academic Board, and the various heads of departments. Prior to this I had arranged that the heads of departments would brief Admiral Rickover during this meeting with details of what their departments did and how they ran their departments and so forth and so on, and requested comments. However, the Secretary of the Academic Board opened up the meeting by stating that he was there to brief him, meaning Admiral Rickover, on the Naval Academy curriculum and that various heads of department would describe their courses.

With that, Admiral Rickover said he didn't come down to listen, he came down to talk, and he proceeded to talk. Needless to say, the conference didn't last very long. I soon arranged to break it up and take Admiral Rickover on a short tour of the Naval Academy, and with that he left for Washington.

Q: It wasn't a conference at all, was it!

Adm. M.: It turned out not to be a conference at all and

Admiral Rickover, as far as I know, went back to Washington and I never heard from him again.

I merely put this in the record to indicate that he was at one time given an opportunity to find out what was going on at the Naval Academy, but we didn't have him down to hear a lecture on his philosophy about education.

Q: And that's what he really wanted to put across?

Adm. M.: Apparently, yes. Anyway, it was a very short, ineffective conference.

Q: Now perhaps you want to introduce the subject of the speakers?

Adm. M.: Yes. At various times during the year at the Naval Academy there are occasions when prominent people are invited to speak at the Naval Academy. The most outstanding time for speakers to be invited, in my estimation, is to speak to the graduating class at graduation.

At graduation in 1959, we, as always in the past, started out with the President and worked down the list to find a speaker. This has always been a more or less standard procedure, and occasionally it works that you get the President. President Truman was down here, President Eisenhower was here, and others of whom I don't have a record at the moment.

Q: I suppose they come when they want to use it as a forum for a pronouncement or something?

Adm. M.: Possibly so, but I really think they have a great interest in the service academies and they probably would like to come more often, except with three academies graduating each year now it's rather difficult to get around. So now it's very rarely that they speak at the academies.

Anyway, in 1959 we ended up with the Secretary of the Navy, The Honorable William B. Franke, as the speaker for graduation. Mr. Franke did a very excellent job and I might say he's a very close friend of the Naval Academy.

In 1960 we went through the usual routine to find a speaker for graduation, and we ended up with Henry Cabot Lodge, who I had known prior to this and who also did a very fine job as a graduation speaker.

Another occasion when we invited prominent speakers was to speak to the first class. Usually every Friday night during academic year during this period - and I mean during the period that I was superintendent - we had a speaker to speak on some particular subject on which he was well acquainted. This, in a sense, is part of the curriculum. The idea was to bring in these prominent people who could speak on the subject which was closest to them, about world affairs, and to give the midshipmen an opportunity to get different viewpoints. While most of the speakers spoke on political matters, there were others who spoke of the arts -

Q: Are they free to choose their own subject?

Adm. M.: No, they were not entirely free. They were given certain limitations, certains areas we asked them to speak in, and naturally in inviting a man we knew what his background was and would invite him to speak on a subject that was close to him, something that he knew the most about.

This is a very fine program and it worked out very well.

Q: This is required attendance?

Adm. M.: It's required attendance, and I might say that most of the officers at the Naval Academy on duty would attend these lectures, too, because they were really top-level people.

Q: Are outsiders permitted?

Adm. M.: No. It is, I guess, what you'd called a closed forum? Is that a correct way to put it? The only attendees were the midshipmen, the officers attached to the Naval Academy, and their wives. I might say that it was usually a full house. Of course, among the midshipmen, we had the usual group in the back row of the balcony that thought the proper thing to do was to sleep through these speakers' time on the podium.

It was particularly good for me because we usually entertained the speaker at dinner before the lecture and, in cases where he was not driving back to Washington that night, he was our house guest for the evening and it gave us an opportunity to chat with the individual privately, which meant a lot to me and my wife. This usually involved a small dinner party with some of the senior officers and their wives.

Q: Now you want to talk about the superintendents' conference in the year 1960.

Adm. M.: In 1959 Admiral Burke, then Chief of Naval Operations, decided there should be a closer relationship among the service academies. As a result of a meeting that they held, it was decided that the heads of the four schools, namely, the Naval Academy, West Point, the Air Force Academy, and the Coast Guard Academy, would meet to exchange views and ideas relative to the running and administration of their particular academy.

As a result of this, the first meeting was held in 1959 at the Coast Guard Academy, and in 1960 the Naval Academy was host to the other three superintendents. They arrived at the Naval Academy in the early spring, 1960, with various members of their staffs. The superintendents were all accommodated in my quarters and the staffs were put up at other places around the Academy, specially in the Officers' Club.

We had three days of meetings in which we discussed the various activities of the schools and the business regarding appointments, which is always critical to the three academies, and other items of general interest. These meetings proved to be extremely beneficial and gave us all insight into the operations of the other academies. A particularly valuable part was the opportunity to visit the other academies and to see for yourself what they were like, what they had, what they needed, and it gave us all a common ground in presenting our demands for funds to the government for future operations.

Q: Did this strengthen your requests for funds?

Adm. M.: Yes, it did. Of course, we all requested funds from our own departments, the Army, Navy, Air Force, and Treasury, but when they ended up before Congress they could see that we were all more or less aiming for the same thing and that these things were necessary, and not just the thought of one particular school. Of course, some schools had greater demands and different things they needed that the other schools didn't, which was very obvious, I think. But I think in the over-all it was very good - they still have these meetings, I might say.

Melson #11 - 320

Interview No. 11 with Vice Admiral Charles L. Melson, U.S. Navy
(Retired)

Place: His residence in Providence, Annapolis, Maryland
Date: Wednesday morning, 19 April 1972
Subject: Biography
By: John T. Mason, Jr.

Q: Sir, this morning we're going to talk some more about your period as superintendent of the Naval Academy. I think you want to talk about several different subjects pertaining to that period. Perhaps the first would be the Naval Institute?

Adm. M.: While I was here I was Vice President of the Naval Institute, which is a customary appointment for the superintendent of the Naval Academy. Being very much interested in the Academy and with the offices of the Naval Institute located in buildings on the Academy grounds, I naturally had a great deal of interest in the office space they had and their activities.

The Naval Institute is located on the second floor of the building which primarily was built for the Museum and for the Athletic Association. The Athletic Association and the Naval Institute share space on the second floor. The

Institute was in the process of expanding and becoming very cramped for space, as was the Museum, which has always been very cramped for space. Plans were drawn up to convert the then existing building into a building which would provide the additional space and accommodate the Naval Institute and Museum. The plans at that time - I don't believe they have changed - were for the Athletic Association to move out of the Museum Building into the Field House.

Q: Eventually?

Adm. M.: Eventually. The question of funds came up and I was in favor of and finally helped swing the vote towards converting the building into a combined headquarters for the two activities mentioned, with the Naval Institute and the Athletic Association supplying the necessary funds for the transformation. I do not remember now the exact division of funds, but I believe that the Naval Institute supplied the largest part of the funds for this conversion. Unfortunately, I did not stay at the Academy long enough to see the conversion completed -

Q: Was it more than a conversion? Was there an addition to the building?

Adm. M.: Conversion and addition to the building. Since

that time I have visited the building and I find that both of them, the Museum and the Naval Institute, are very happy with the spaces they now have, and of course when the Athletic Association does eventually move out, the Naval Institute, I presume, will benefit by this additional space.

During my period as superintendent and at the time of providing funds for the conversion for an addition to the building, the President of the Naval Institute was Admiral Arleigh Burke, followed by Admiral Jerauld Wright, retired.

Q: How did Jerauld Wright happen to be President? Usually it's the chief of naval operations.

Adm. M.: I've forgotten the exact details of how it came about that Jerry was selected as President, but at that time he was a four-star admiral in command of the Atlantic forces. In other words, commander-in-chief of the Atlantic, and was a very senior member of the naval forces, next to the Chief of Naval Operations, naturally.

Q: Now you want to tell me about the murals in Bancroft Hall.

Adm. M.: Around the top, or the ceiling, of Memorial Hall in Bancroft Hall is a series of eight lunettes. The plan was to have murals painted in each of these lunettes and be presented by different individuals. Admiral and Mrs. Thomas C. Hart presented three murals for this purpose, the first two being while I was superintendent. The first mural, the Battle of Lake Erie, was started by Charles R. Patterson, the artist, who died before its completion in 1958. The picture was finished in 1959 by Mr. Howard French, who tried to achieve the same pattern of painting as Mr. Patterson.

Mr. French also painted a second mural which was presented by different individuals. Admiral and Mrs. Thomas C. Hart presented three murals for this purpose, the first two being while I was superintendent. The first mural, the Battle of Lake Erie, was started by Charles R. Patterson, the artist, who died before its completion in 1958. The picture was finished in 1959 by Mr. Howard French, who tried to achieve the same pattern of painting as Mr. Patterson.

Mr. French also painted a second mural which was presented by the Harts to the Naval Academy and showed the first foreign salute to the Stars and Stripes. Both of these murals were in memory of their son, Lieutenant Commander Thomas Cummins Hart, USN, who died in 1945.

A third mural, showing the USS _Hartford_ and the yacht _America_ at sea, was presented in honor of the memory of their son, Lieutenant Commander Thomas C. Hart, Jr.

Q: You had something to do with the dedication of these?

Adm. M.: These first two murals were dedicated, with Admiral and Mrs. Hart present, and I accepted the murals in the name of the Naval Academy in Memorial Hall.

Q: This was not an ordinary experience because it doesn't happen very often?

Adm. M.: It doesn't happen very often because there are not many lunettes! I'm not sure today, but I think they're all filled. It's interesting to note that French and Patterson have painted all to date - between the two artists they've painted all the murals that now exist.

Q: Now you want to say something about the brigade?

Adm. M.: The brigade of midshipmen numbered about 3,800 fine young men. I liked to think of them as being the cream of young Americans. of young American manhood. The brigade at the end of the summer, after the plebe class had been accepted, sometimes went as high as 3,900, but due to attrition in the following academic year it usually reduced itself to around 3,600 by the time of the following graduation.

To me it was one of the greatest experiences that I've had in the Navy to be superintendent of the Naval Academy during this period. We did accomplish a number of items which I've spoken about before, such as validation, electives, "whole man" concept for admission, and I have a feeling of some accomplishment in this respect. The young men that I had dealings with were loyal, upright, and fine examples of American manhood. Like any large group of men, there was an occasional bad actor or one who did not measure up to the standards demanded by the honor code and the academic department, but they did not last very long. They usually were dismissed fairly early each year.

The mission, which has been quoted earlier, stated what we expected each of these men to be ready to do on their graduation, and I feel that most of them have lived up to our expectations. A great number of these young men are in the fleet today and this particular group are in the lieutenant-lieutenant commander bracket. They're flying planes, they're out on the ships, commanding some of the smaller ships and are giving a good account of themselves. The spirit shown by these youngsters while at the Academy was probably most visible at sport activities where they had a chance to vent some of their enthusiasm, but I'm sure they are just as enthusiastic out in the fleet today as they were here at the Naval Academy. That's not a very good speech - but!

Q: Tell me about the other hat you wore, the Severn River Command.

Adm. M.: The superintendent of the Naval Academy during the period from 1958 to 1960, which covered the period I was here, had additional duty as commandant of the Severn River Naval Command. The Severn River Naval Command was composed at that time of the Naval Academy, the small craft facility, air facility, the Naval Hospital, and the Naval Experimental Station.

This was a military command and the superintendent of the Naval Academy, as the commandant of Severn River Naval Command, had full responsibility for the military activities of the commands mentioned. Such commands as the Experimental Station, of course, were primarily involved in research and development and were controlled in other than military matters by their parent bureaus, in this case the Bureau of Engineering. The Naval Air Facility was here primarily for the training of midshipmen. They had a number of seaplanes assigned and in the spring and summer normally had a large complement of yellow single-float planes, which were commonly known as Yellow Pearls.

During the summer period it was customary to give all midshipmen certain flight training in these particular planes.

The Naval Hospital is here primarily to support the Naval Academy and to take care of the midshipmen medically and physically.

Q: They also take care of retired naval people in the area?

Adm. M.: That is incidental to their primary mission. Their primary mission is for active-duty people, primarily midshipmen.

The small-craft facility took care of the upkeep and repair of the boats assigned to the Naval Academy for training purposes. These boats consist of schooners, yawls, half-raters, motor boats, motor launches, and other small craft. They were here to train midshipmen in maneuvers, boat handling and sailing.

While these commands did not represent a great deal of extra labor, they did provide a coordinated training command for the Naval Academy. It's my understanding today that they are no longer assigned under the superintendent of the Naval Academy in a military sense, but are assigned to him for coordination. This does not involve military command directly.

Q: And who has the military command now?

Adm. M.: As I understand it now, the individual commanding officer is responsible to the parent bureau. Calvert, of course, being the senior naval officer here has the responsibility for coordination, which is almost the same thing as military command. It's hard to differentiate between the two, but when we had the Severn River Naval Command Admiral Hill's authority was much more direct than it is today under the coordination policy.

Q: Why would a change like that be made?

Adm. M.: I really can't answer the question because I'm not sure. It's a thing that took place in general throughout the Navy to provide for coordination between the different commands rather than military command.

Q: During your time, since you had one element of this command which had to do with aviation for training, what relationship did you have with, say, Pensacola?

Adm. M.: We had no direct official relationship with Pensacola, other than we used to send midshipmen there for training during the summer as well as the ones we kept here at the Naval Academy, the senior class, part of the first class usually went to Pensacola for training.

Q: You made those arrangements through the Bureau of Aeronautics?

Adm. M.: Yes, correct. That is, through the Bureau direct to Pensacola. The same thing applied to midshipmen who went out in submarines. We made our arrangements for them with ComSubLant, and this was all basically covered in OpNav's basic operations plan for the year, which we all followed. They provided in this basic operating plan for training midshipmen at sea, both in the air and on the surface, and

Melson #11 - 329

in submarines.

Q: What portion of your time was involved in this conglomerate command?

Adm. M.: Oh, as an estimate, about 5 percent. The greatest part of my time was in the Naval Academy and this other was more or less incidental to running the Naval Academy.

Q: Did you have a separate staff for this purpose?

Adm. M.: Not entirely so. Most of the Naval Academy staff had additional duties assigned to them. Like in my case I was superintendent of the Naval Academy and commander of the Severn River Naval Command. My administrative officer, the captain who was the administrative officer of the Naval Academy, was also chief of staff of the Severn River Naval Command. The two jobs were combined. Today the job is held by Captain Foster - I've forgotten his exact title, but he is in a sense the administrative officer of the Naval Academy. I don't believe he has anything to do much with these other commands.

One other thing connected with these commands. As the military commander, I had to conduct a military inspection of each of these activities each year, which Calvert does not have to do today. Each year I made a military inspection of the hospital, the Experimental Station, the Naval

Station, and all the associated activities.

Q: Which was time-consuming, wasn't it?

Adm. M.: Very time-consuming. That was sandwiched in. But that only happened once a year, but it took a full day for each command. It took much more time for the staff who had to write up a report.

Q: On July 14, 1960, you took over a new command, the command of the First Fleet, having said farewell to Annapolis?

Adm. M.: On the date you mentioned, July 14th, I relieved Vice Admiral Sharp as commander of the First Fleet. Admiral Sharp is a classmate of mine at the Naval Academy and we're very close friends.

Q: That's U.S. Grant Sharp?

Adm. M.: U.S. Grant Sharp, who later became CinCPac.
My wife and I moved into quarters at North Island, which has an interesting angle to it, in that the senior quarters on North Island had always been occupied by aviators. When I was ordered out, CNO directed that I occupy a certain set of quarters which, at that time, were occupied by ComAirPac, and this was the cause of a little ill-

feeling because ComAirPac had to move across the street in order for me to occupy Quarters D on North Island. Anyway, I was quite happy with the assignment of quarters. They were beautiful quarters and they were assigned as permanent quarters for the commander of the First Fleet.

The First Fleet is not an operational fleet in the same sense that the Sixth and Seventh Fleets are. The First Fleet as well as the Second Fleet, at this time, were more or less training fleets charged with the responsibility of training individual units for service overseas in the Sixth and Seventh Fleet. The First Fleet was also charged with being prepared to sail with the units assigned at the time to the assistance of the Seventh Fleet when and if required.

Vessels which returned from deployment overseas with the Seventh Fleet were usually granted a period in the neighborhood of thirty days for rest and recreation, and then ordered to a shipyard for repair and upkeep for a limited period of time, varying between thirty and sixty days, and then to their particular type commander for training. In this case, I refer to ComAirLant, ComPhibLant, ComCruDesPac, or ComSubPac.

After a period of training under the type commander, where they receive training in their particular phase of warfare, gunnery, torpedoes, aviation, etc., they then reported to the commander of the First Fleet who took charge of the individual units and trained them in combined operations as a fleet in the various aspects of warfare, such as amphibious landing, shore bombardment, ASW work, etc. This period with the First Fleet was a period in which they were being prepared to be re-deployed overseas and join, in this case, the Seventh Fleet.

This training took the form of various exercises along the coast, cruising in formation together, re-fueling at sea, replenishment at sea, shore bombardment on San Clemente Island, ASW work in the exercise areas off the coast, amphibious operations along the coast of California, particularly in the Camp Pendleton area.

When a ship had completed its training, it was inspected by members of my staff and, based on their performance in the past, was pronounced ready to be deployed. All of this had to fit a pre-determined deployment schedule which had been worked out by CinCPacFlt for each of the ships which said they had to be ready to go overseas and relieve another ship at a certain specified time. So we were working within a very limited time interval to get the ships ready.

In addition to this training, the First Fleet was occasionally called upon to perform certain social and political functions, such as attending the Rose Festival in Portland, Oregon, as a fleet and attending celebrations that occurred occasionally in San Francisco when they wanted ships of the fleet present.

All of this was very interesting and provided plenty for us to do. When I first reported to the First Fleet, the commander of the First Fleet and his staff were shore-based in a building at the Naval Air Station, North Island. I felt that the time the First Fleet should become a more active fleet, and to become more active the commander and his staff had to get to sea so he could visit units of the fleet in daily training outside of the operating area. After a great deal of agitation and plugging and making a few people unhappy, I finally got CNO to designate a cruiser flagship to the commander of the First Fleet on a permanent basis.

This took some doing, as every cruiser was in great demand for deployment to the Far East at that time, and with the limited number of cruisers avaiable CNO was very reluctant to tie up one ship for flagship purposes.

Q: It had to be a cruiser?

Adm. M.: A cruiser is the only ship that had adequate quarters for the staff assigned to Commander, First Fleet, to embark all his staff aboard. A destroyer or a destroyer escort or a smaller vessel just didn't have the space.

Q: What about one of those command ships?

Adm. M.: They were all in demand by the amphibious forces, and there weren't very many of those, either. They were in great demand. ComPhibLant had his fingers on those. The cruiser made the correct type flagship.

In cases where we were required to act as a fleet, CinCPac usually assigned a cruiser as temporary flagship for the particular operation. One of the first operations that took place after I arrived was the Pacific Festival in San Francisco. All of the First Fleet was detailed to attend this particular festival and participate in it. The USS Los Angeles was assigned as my flagship and I led the First Fleet into the bay for the festival on board this ship. The ships anchored in San Francisco Bay and participated to the extent of detailing men for parades, having open ship for visitors during the period of their stay. Admiral Sides was then Commander-in-Chief, Pacific Fleet, and came to San Francisco for a visit during this period, and was on board the Los Angeles for a number of events, including a review of the fleet while he was there.

I might say that the ships in this particular group consisted of one heavy cruiser, one guided-missile cruiser, one carrier, and a number of destroyers and destroyer escorts.

Shortly after we returned to San Diego from this particular visit to San Francisco, CNO designated the USS Helena as the First Fleet flagship and she arrived in San Diego, and the First Fleet staff transferred in to the ship.

Q: She was on a permanent basis?

Adm. M.: She was assigned on a permanent basis. She'd had certain modifications made in the office space to accommodate the staff for the purposes required. Our berth when we were in port at San Diego was at a pier in North Island, which was very convenient for me because my home was only a half block away.

President Eisenhower paid a visit to San Diego in October of 1960 and it was my pleasure to assist in his entertainment. He inspected North Island and I took him for a ride in the barge in San Diego Bay on a review of the First Fleet which were moored and at anchor at that time. The ships were all full dressed and the sides were manned. We steamed up and down the rows of ships, with the President sitting on top of the cabin of my barge. After the review I delivered him to the Commandant of the Eleventh Naval District on the San Diego side of the bay.

Q: Are there any recollections of his visit that are of interest?

Adm. M.: None in particular, except he sat on the cabin of the barge beside me, up high where all the people could see him, and, of course, being the President he was cheered right well as he went past up and down the line and more or less a type of fleet review.

Q: His naval aide at that time was Pete Aurand?

Adm. M.: Pete Aurand. I don't remember anything other of particular interest, except it was a very pleasant visit with the President. I was quite honored to be able to have the opportunity to talk with him for a short time.

In December of 1960, the 14th to be exact, I spoke at the graduation exercises at the General Line and Naval Science School in Monterey, California. Mrs. Melson and I drove to Monterey for this occasion and spent a delightful three days as guests of Admiral Yeomans.

I might mention at this point that the commanding officer of the Helena when she reported to duty was Captain Kauffman -

Q: Draper Kauffman?

Adm. M.: Draper Kauffman, who was later to become superintendent of the Naval Academy. At the time he was with me there was no indication of this assignment.

While in San Diego we, of course, had many official and unofficial visitors and were entertained a great deal by the people of San Diego and of Los Angeles. One of the big occasions was the Navy Ball on the 22nd of April 1961 in Los Angeles. Admiral Sides attended the ball - Admiral and Mrs. Sides. It was a very delightful affair. We had various dishes on the menu named in our honor. In my case it was, and I quote, "Crabs supreme, sauce verte, Admiral Melson." Admiral Sides, and I quote had "Tia Maria mousse, Admiral Sides."

In my quarters at North Island I had a small guest house which was outside the quarters, but very convenient to the facilities in the house. This guest house naturally attracted a lot of visitors, mostly travelers from Washington who stopped there at one time or another.

In between these various times of which I am speaking now, we went to sea on short trips, short training exercises of one or two days, sometimes three or four days, but they were all conducted mostly in southern Californian waters and kept us all very busy and very active.

The next big event in which we participated, I believe, was the Portland, Oregon, Rose Festival. I attended the Rose Restival in the Helena and we had a very interesting trip past the light ship, up the river, to Portland itself. The river is very narrow and it made it quite interesting going underneath the bridges and so forth to the approaches to Portland.

In Portland Governor Mark Hatfield was one of our VIP visitors, the governor and his wife. Also while we were at this festival I was crowned Knight of the Peace Robes.

Q: Why did the Navy get involved in this festival?

Adm. M.: Well, as I stated a little earlier I believe, the

Navy is called upon on occasion to furnish ships for various festivals and various really political in nature affairs that take place up and down the coast, and they provided ships for atmosphere and color, and also for a number of enlisted men and officers to go ashore and spend money, I guess. They were all very entertaining and it made good ports to visit and it gave the men a chance to go ashore and see these various towns. It was customary on the West Coast for any big event to invite Navy units to participate. That's how I became a Knight of Peace Rose.

The ships that visited Portland were several destroyers, amphibious ships, for a total of fifteen ships, in addition the Royal Canadian Navy sent down three ships to take part in the festival.

In August of 1961 a group of ships was designated to sail to the Far East to relieve ships on duty with the Seventh Fleet. It had been customary for these ships to sail in small groups or individually to the Far East for this purpose, but I felt that we were missing a splendid opportunity for training at sea as a task force when we had occasion for a number of ships to go to the Far East at about the same time. So I arranged for the group of ships due to sail in the middle of August to sail together, and I took advantage of the opportunity to witness the training by accompanying them in the Helena.

We sailed from San Diego in early August, stopped in

Pearl Harbor for a few days, where we picked up five more ships, and then we proceeded to sail for the Far East. It was the first time in four years that there had been a task fleet sailing for the Far East.

Q: Was it difficult to reverse the custom of the Navy in achieving this?

Adm. M.: No. It all seemed so logical that no, no problem at all.

Eight ships were in the group that left from San Diego, including the Helena. The Los Angeles joined and in Pearl Harbor we were joined by a carrier and two divisions of destroyers. The trip to Far Eastern waters was very successful and really gave the ships an excellent opportunity to test task force operations, because the minute they arrived with the Seventh Fleet they would be in close-order formation most of the time, and this gave the people the training that they needed. As always when they deployed like this, there were many new men and new officers aboard and few of them knew very much about task force formation.

Shortly before we reached Japan the fleet split up to join various units of the Seventh Fleet and that left the flagship alone. We went on to Japan and had a visit in Yokosuka, where I saw Admiral Griffin, conferred with him about fleet operations, and got criticisms and comments on the readiness of the ships which had trained under me as to their readiness to join the fleet. From Yokosuka we sailed for Hong Kong for a short visit, which was interrupted by a typhoon which passed directly over Hong Kong but fortunately it didn't do any damage or cause any concern to us because we were moored to a buoy out in the middle of Hong Kong Harbor.

From Hong Kong we sailed for Manila for a short visit, then on to Guam, a second visit to Pearl Harbor, and back to San Diego.

The trip provided training for my own staff and for the men and officers of the flagship, in addition to showing the flag at several ports. I considered it a very successful and very useful cruise. Whether this practice had been adhered to since I do not know.

A lot of these thing are of interest to me individually but I don't think they'd be of interest for the record.

The next event of interest that happened after returning to San Diego was that I had the pleasure of reviewing the recruit parade at Recruit Training Command at San Diego. This was a very interesting visit to the training center in the sense that I had an opportunity to see the training that the "boots" received before they were sent out to the fleet.

Q: These are enlisted men?

Adm. M.: These are enlisted men. I attended the parade where they did a very fine job.

Shortly thereafter we received word that President Kennedy would visit San Diego on the 17th or 18th of November, this still being 1961, and CNO directed the First Fleet to put on a demonstration for the benefit of President Kennedy. The responsibility for the demonstration was assigned to Commander, First Fleet. Shortly after receiving this word, there was an intense period of planning and checking on what ships would be available, what ships were present, and what we would do, how we'd put on a show, and how much time was allowed - trying to do all we could in a very short period of time.

My staff was very busily engaged in this programming and I'll say now that they just did a very excellent job. However, just before the scheduled visit of President Kennedy, Speaker Sam Rayburn died. The President was already on his trip to the West Coast and the First Fleet review in his honor. The President decided that he had to cancel out on the fleet review because the timing was such that he would have to go to Rayburn's furneral. He sent me a very fine message which I have here when he decided that he'd have to cancel the visit to the fleet, and wanted me to express to the members of the fleet his regret at not being there for the review.

Q: It must have been very disappointing, having worked this up?

Melson #11 - 342

Adm. M.: Yes, but I talked to Admiral Anderson, who was CNO at that time, and we decided to go ahead with the planned fleet review but in his honor instead of the President's. All the plans had been laid and we were ready to go ahead. It seemed a shame to cancel the exercise just a day or two before it was supposed to happen. So Admiral Anderson became the reviewing officer and we put on the demonstration out of San Diego for him.

The demonstration consisted of various activities of submarines - with submarines - aircraft and carriers did a lot of flying. I might say that the Kitty Hawk, which was a brand new ship at this time, acted as my flagship during this exercise, and the ship which embarked Admiral Anderson for the review.

We conducted exercises outside of San Diego en route to the Long Beach area. In the Long Beach area we conducted an amphibious operation, and Admiral Anderson, and I flew ashore by helicopter to witness the landing from the land side. I was happy with the way the demonstration went off and received a message of congratulations from Admiral Anderson after he returned to Washington on the conduct of the exercise.

Attending the exercise as guests of the Chief of Naval Operations were all the naval attaches and military attaches from Washington. They all were aboard the flagship and watched the landing, and I note that the Chinese Nationalist Officer, named Captain Chih, was a very interested observer. Captain

Chih was the Chinese Nationalist naval attache in Washington at this time.

Q: Had these men been invited in preparation for the President?

Adm. M.: Yes. They originally had been invited, as you say, to be there for the President's visit, and when we decided not to cancel, of course, this went on. You can see why we wanted to continue the exercise. We didn't want to cancel out all these people who had already made their plans and were in the San Diego area.

Q: Was the Russian naval attache permitted to come out there?

Adm. M.: I don't know, but he wasn't there. I didn't realize it at the time, but I had met Captain Chih while I was superintendent of the Naval Academy when he visited the Naval Academy in company with the other naval attaches. He was, as I said, present on this particular visit to the fleet, and later he was to become superintendent of the Chinese Naval Academy in Taiwan and was present at the time I was out there on duty.

In the early spring of 1962 I was notified by the Chief of Naval Operations that I had been nominated to become commander of the Taiwan Defense Command upon completion of my tour with the First Fleet. I debated this for some time, as

Melson #11 - 344

I wasn't sure whether I was ready to go to Taiwan for an extended tour, but decided that it was in my best interest to go.

Q: What were your reservations?

Adm. M.: My reservation was simply whether I wanted to go out of the country for that long a time - I and my wife - we were worried about our children, but we decided that we could manage all right so we agreed to it, as much as we were allowed to make our own decisions!

My relief was to be Admiral R.T.S. Keith, who had command of the Pacific destroyer force and was also stationed in San Diego.

Q: Roger Taylor Keith!

Adm. M.: Roger Taylor Keith, that's correct. In May I was detached as commander of the First Fleet and, after a month's leave, which I spent visiting our children, we proceeded to Taiwan, arriving there in late May of 1962.

Q: You flew out?

Adm. M.: We flew out, but we spent a few days in Honolulu with Admiral Sides and enjoyed the beach a little bit while

I became indoctrinated into matters concerning Taiwan. We had a very interesting and fine trip out. We went out by commercial aircraft to Yokosuka, where we were met by Commander, Seventh Fleet's plane which took us down to Taiwan.

Q: About your briefing in Pearl, was there a great deal that you had to acquire in the way of learning before you went to Taiwan?

Adm. M.: Yes, there was a great deal of background information on Taiwan that I needed. I was fairly familiar with the situation in the Western Pacific and I had some briefing on a previous trip out from Admiral Griffin up in Tokyo, but there was a lot about the island itself and the people on it that I had to become acquainted with, and that was included in the briefing given me by Admiral Sides' people in Honolulu.

Q: Sides was CinCPacFlt?

Adm. M.: CinCPacFlt.

Q: Did you get involved with Felt?

Adm. M.: I was involved with Felt. Admiral Felt was CinCPac, and actually I would report to Admiral Felt as my senior as Commander, Taiwan Defense Command. But the reason I saw a lot of Sides is that I'd just left Sides' command and he invited me to stay with him! That made a difference. But I was briefed by both CinCPac and CinCPacFlt people. They were both involved in the briefing, which was very fair and very good and I appreciated it after I arrived in Taiwan.

Melson #12 - 347

Interview No. 12 with Vice Admiral Charles L. Melson, U.S. Navy
(Retired)

Place: His residence in Providence, Annapolis, Maryland

Date: Wednesday morning, 3 May, 1972

Subject: Biography

By: John T. Mason, Jr.

Q: Admiral, this morning I believe our chapter is going to be on the Taiwan Defense Command, which you assumed in May of 1962?

Adm. M.: I arrived in Taiwan in the middle of May 1962 from Tokyo. En route from the West Coast of the United States to Taiwan I stopped in Hawaii for a briefing by Admiral Felt and his staff, as he would be my immediate senior on this new assignment. I also stopped in Tokyo, where I was briefed by Ambassador Reischauer, who was then our ambassador to Japan.

Q: Did Felt or Reischauer have any specific instructions, or any specific ideas which they wanted you to carry out?

Adm. M.: No, not directly. The instructions were mostly very general and covered more the state of affairs rather than any direction as to how to proceed.

Q: It was kind of a briefing then?

Adm. M.: It really was. It was bringing me up to date on what was going on in that part of the world.

I finally left Tokyo in Commander, Seventh Fleet's plane with Mrs. Melson in company with me and arrived in Taipei the same day. In Taipei we were welcomed by the full guard, band, and military detachment, gun salutes, and by General Peng Ming Chi. General Peng was the chief of staff of the armed forces of Taiwan.

Q: Whom were you relieving?

Adm. M.: I'll come to that. And by Admiral Ni, the commander-in-chief of the Chinese Navy, and by Mr. Ralph N. Clough, counseler for the ambassador - for the embassy - and the deputy chief of the mission, there not being an ambassador in Taiwan at that time. Also greeting me was Admiral Roland N. Smoot - Vice Admiral Roland N. Smoot, that is - who was commander of the Taiwan Defense Command and whom I was to relieve. I might add that meetings of this kind in Taiwan by the Chinese, all the wives and families usually attend these ceremonies, so it's quite a gallant gathering.

After the ceremony we were taken to the Seven Seas Villa which was to be our temporary quarters for a short time after arrival, until our house on Grass Mountain was prepared and cleaned and ready.

Melson #12 - 349

Q: Seven Seas Villa, was that a hotel?

Adm. M.: Seven Seas Villa was a villa owned by the Chinese Navy and used as a guest house by them. It was located down town.

After my arrival I had a great number of meetings and briefings with Admiral Smoot and his staff. Admiral Smoot took me around to visit all the senior Chinese officials and military personnel. I might add at this point that the Taiwan Defense Command was a unified command and that my staff, which I had just met, consisted of officers of all U. S. services. It was a comparatively small staff, but very well organized and well prepared to do what it was supposed to do.

I might put in at this point that the duties of the Taiwan Defense Command, other than planning, were not very extensive during times of peace. It existed primarily to take charge of all military forces in Taiwan in the event of hostilities in that area, in which case I would have full military command. Otherwise, it was a case of planning for the future, inspecting activities, inspecting the Chinese forces, and in general keeping control of U.S. military activities on the island.

Q: Admiral, once the plans were made for future operations, what was there to do in that area?

Adm. M.: It was a matter of continually updating, and the

greatest part of the effort was devoted to gleaning intelligence and reporting intelligence. I had a fairly large intelligence unit on my staff and we kept in contact with the movements on the Chinese mainland and what was going on in the sea area off Taiwan. Surprising as it may seem, this was quite a busy job.

Q: Those intelligence people on your staff, were they Defense Department Intelligence?

Adm. M.: Military - Air Force, Navy, and Army. We also had a CIA man attached to the Intelligence.

Q: A single man?

Adm. M.: From the local unit. He was liaison with the local CIA unit. The CIA had a very large unit in Taiwan and it was quite active in many respects, which I can't go into here because I really don't know all of them, although I was the senior military officer on the island. I might also add at this point the ambassador usually is somewhat in ignorance of what the CIA people are doing.

Q: Your liaison man, then, didn't keep you fully informed?

Adm. M.: No, he didn't keep us fully informed of their activities. He only informed us of the activities he thought we should - that is, the head of the CIA unit - thought we should know, and incidentally to pick up any information we might furnish to take back to his unit. It was not altogether satisfactory arrangement from the military point of view, but it seemed to work.

Q: How did the ambassador feel about this?

Adm. M.: Well, at this time there was no ambassador in residence. The former ambassador had gone home and his relief had not arrived.

Q: Who was this? Admiral Kirk?

Adm. M.: Yes.

Q: He'd gone home?

Adm. M.: No, no. Admiral Kirk was the new one coming in. Admiral Kirk arrived shortly after I did in 1962, and he and Lydia took up their residence in the embassy. Admiral Kirk, as you probably well know, had been in the diplomatic service for some time after leaving the Navy. He retired as a full admiral. He had been ambassador to the U.S.S.R. and to Belgium.

Ambassador Kirk is a very fine man to work with. He knew what he wanted and expressed it in no uncertain terms.

On top of that he is a very pleasant individual, a charming man to deal with. I can't say too much about Mrs. Kirk. She is one of the best.

I'd better go back again. I'm getting a little ahead of myself.

After we'd made all the routine calls and I'm met everyone, Smoot had done his duty in turning the job over to me, he departed the island and left the Taiwan Defense Command in my hands. On the 29th of May I was taken by Mr. Ralph Clough for my first meeting with The Gimo. This, to me, was a very interesting experience because I had heard so much of The Gimo and to actually meet with him and have a cup of tea and a cake was something that can only be classified as very unusual and interesting. While we were talking, through an interpreter I might add, Madame came in and I had the opportunity of meeting Madame Chiang kai-Chek, who, as you probably know, had been Mei-ling Soong. The audience lasted for about thirty minutes, after which I was dismissed.

As a matter of interest at this point, the interpreter for this occasion was a Chinese known as Jimmy Shen, who is now the Chinese Nationalist ambassador to the United States in Washington, D.C.

My headquarters were in an old Japanese hotel located in the lower part of Taipei and, while it was not as up to date as we like to have our headquarters, it did serve its purpose. I had a DC-3 at my disposal, which was very useful.

I was active in the following months in visiting the other Chinese cities and military units.

Our quarters were finally ready, within a month, and consisted of a very nice house on top of Grass Mountain with a fine view over the valley surrounding Taipei.

Q: Was this a new structure, or a re-furbished one?

Adm. M.: A relatively new structure. It had a very strange history, as a matter of fact. It apparently had been built for the senior military officer assigned to Taipei about ten years before that, and in some way it had been unsatisfactory and discarded and been played back and forth. Finally, Admiral Smoot was the one who moved into it more or less on a permanent basis and I followed after him. It was a Chinese house. It had plenty of room, plenty of servants' quarters, and a delightful view. I just don't understand why some of the previous people didn't live in it. The house was located on top of a mountain, which involved about a half-hour trip through Chinese traffic going to the office and back every day, but that was an experience you shouldn't miss.

In late fall, after Ambassador Kirk had arrived, I attended several audiences that he had with The Gimo. In nearly every case, Madame was present and although there was an official interpreter present, she did a lot of the interpreting and, reading between the lines, I felt that she helped make a lot of the decisions right there at the time of the audience, as far as the Chinese were concerned.

Q: By her interpretations?

Adm. M.: By her interpretations. All these audiences were very interesting and I enjoyed going to them. Sometimes they were not too pleasant because of the matters being discussed, but they were interesting.

Ambassador Kirk could be very tough in his dealings with The Gimo and was very tough with him. I got the impression that Ambassador Kirk disliked The Gimo as an individual and, looking back over what The Gimo had done in his past history, that I can very well understand. On the other side, of course, The Gimo was always asking for more money or more assistance. He was always wanting something and we had very little to give. But Ambassador Kirk handled him very well through all these meetings that I attended with him, and I felt that he came out on top in most of them.

Q: Can you give me an illustration of some of the subject matter?

Adm. M.: Well, they usually wanted military help in the form of money or ships or planes or things of that nature. Occasionally he wanted economic assistance, which involved dollars, of course. Each year a certain amount of economic assistance was granted to Taiwan, which varied from year to year, depending on the amount appropriated by our Congress. I've forgotten the exact figures but, going back, they were getting something in the neighborhood of 150 million dollars a year at the beginning of my tour in Taiwan. When I left they were getting 90 million, a considerable reduction, and today they're getting zero, as far as money's concerned. But The Gimo wanted airplanes. He wanted more airplanes, he wanted better airplanes, he wanted the newest airplanes, and he was never satisfied with what he received. So that was a big bone of contention between Ambassador Kirk and The Gimo.

Q: Was he able to assimilate the things he asked for? I mean did he have the force to man them?

Adm. M.: All the military equipment that was loaned, this was all considered a loan very substantially, to Taiwan was under constant surveillance by the people of MAAG, who were very closely related to the Chinese units which used this equipment. They're the ones who made the report as to whether - to the ambassador - as to whether they felt the Chinese needed them, whether they could operate them, whether they had the people to man the equipment, and whether they could be usefully used and whether their training permitted their use of this equipment. Of course, the final decision in all these cases was only reached after a great deal of discussion between the embassy and MAAG, my command, and also Washington. Any reduction in any of these things that we had given the Chinese from year to year always caused The Gimo to get up on his hind legs and want it back and ask for more at the same time.

It was difficult to try to satisfy him because he was never satisfied.

Q: I take it the MAAG unit wasn't under your command?

Adm. M.: No. I might spend a minute on that, on command relationships. There was the MAAG, which had three units under it. It had the Navy unit, the Air Force unit, and the Army unit, which handled the various activities. ComUSTDC had no direct command authority over any of these units. As I said earlier, it was only in time of war or action on the coast that I would become in command of these units. It was a peculiar relationship and I objected to it. I talked to Admiral Felt a number of times about it, and he agreed with me, and said, "Look at my own command. It's the same thing in CinCPac. They're all individual units, and I don't command them directly." He was talking about the RPac and AirPac, those forces. They still come under their basic command in Washington, and it's only in time of actual war that he gets straight military command. Does that agree with what Felt told you?

Q: Yes.

Adm. M.: In a sense I was a smaller unit in the same position he was, so I never got the other commands.

Ambassador Kirk, I felt, was a sick man when he arrived in Taiwan. He was not a strong man. He hadn't been there very long before he became very ill and had to be sent home early in 1963. Again, we were without an ambassador for a period of a month or so.

Q: He was only actually on duty for a period of about six months, wasn't he?

Adm. M.: Yes, that's right. I'll try to find the exact dates. I don't have it. He was there for Christmas of that year and they left shortly thereafter. Shortly after he had returned to the States Admiral Jerauld Wright was designated the ambassador to Taiwan. He arrived shortly thereafter. I felt very fortunate in my case in having Admiral Wright assigned as the ambassador, because I had been on his staff in Norfolk, I'd known him personally and his wife for a number of years, and it set up a nice situation for me as far as my own life was concerned.

Ambassador Wright was just as stubborn and determined as Ambassador Kirk in his dealings with The Gimo, and The Gimo got very little out of Ambassador Wright in their various meetings.

Q: I would imagine that this was a part of their orders!

Adm. M.: I suspect it was. It was a question always keeping The Gimo happy, but fending him off, not giving him too much. I might say that I felt that between Admiral Kirk and Admiral Wright they both handled the situation very well and made good ambassadors under very difficult circumstances. I don't imagine that the Chinese were very fond of either one, but they really did their jobs.

Part of my duties consisted of visiting the many Chinese military units and inspecting them in their areas, that included the Army, Navy, and Air Force, and, of course, the Marine Corps. They were all very well equipped, drilled, and trained, but the elite are really the Chinese Marines. They were a very active, smart force. All of the Chinese forces were very active in the field, in training, and getting ready for a war which they felt would come, in accordance with The Gimo's declaration that they must return and recapture the mainland, the China he had formerly ruled. That hasn't occurred, but they're still drilling, and becoming more proficient, presumably.

Q: Were the Marines especially proficient in amphibious operations?

Adm. M.: The Marines were trained in amphibious operations and they had regular amphibious operations the year round. They probably made more landings on the coast of Taiwan than we ever made anywhere! They were constantly landing.

Of course, there's more to this than just training. They had to do something with all these people under arms. They had to keep them busy. They couldn't let them sit around, or they'd become discontented. Also, they had to satisfy the MAAG people that they were utilizing the equipment which they'd received from us.

On one occasion I accompanied Admiral Ni on a trip to sea aboard a destroyer in a division of four ships. This demonstration was put on primarily for my benefit and consisted of steaming in formation, shooting their guns, making smoke screens, and doing those things which destroyers normally do. They were reasonably efficient. How they would react under enemy fire is a different matter. These ships perhaps saw more action than any other part of the Chinese armed forces, because they were constantly on patrol in the area to the west of Taiwan and off the off-shore islands. And occasionally they had clashes with Red Chinese gunboats. None of this was very serious, but they did occur.

Q: Were they largely former U. S. ships?

Adm. M.: All the ships of the Chinese Nationalist Navy were

former U. S. ships which had been loaned to the Chinese government. In addition to the destroyers, they had several DEs and a great number of landing type craft, amphibious craft.

I feel that it must have been very monotonous to keep up this steady training, day in and day out, since roughly 1950 to fight a war which will probably never be fought. It could become very boring.

Q: Did you sense any of that feeling among the Chinese forces?

Adm. M.: No, but I'd better explain a minute about the Chinese forces.

The Chinese forces are composed of two groups of individuals. One were mainly Chinese who had come over from the mainland in 1949. They were the hard core of all the armed forces. Most of the officers were from that group. Then the main body were the Taiwanese, but they were not in any command positions, except for one or two perhaps, but they were the main body of the armed forces. I had very little chance to talk with them. I never got that close to them. Whenever I was around them there was always somebody, some top Chinese, along. I never had a chance to get into the lower ranks.

Q: Did they seem to differ from the mainland Chinese?

Adm. M.: Not a great deal. In appearance you couldn't tell

the two apart. Their feelings, they seldom expressed, because if they expressed feelings contrary to the government they didn't last very long. They were put away. They dropped from sight for a while. Of course, there is a Taiwanese Freedom Movement. A lot of them perhaps are members of that, but they are very careful not to publicize it -

One trip I made was out to the off-shore islands, Quemoy and Matsu, normally just referred to as "the off-shore islands." Both of these islands are very heavily fortified. They have coast artillery pieces which they obtained from us and have been installed in underground fortifications. They have built fortifications along all of the coastline. They've installed a great number of guns of various calibers, and the islands are usually manned by somewhere in the neighborhood of 60,000 to 70,000 of what they call the trained troops. I might say that these troops rotate from the mainland. I don't know exactly how often -

Q: You mean rotate from Taiwan itself?

Adm. M.: From Taiwan itself to the islands. In other words, they go out to the islands for six or eight months and then are relieved. They keep rotating.

They keep the other islands around Quemoy and Matsu under constant surveillance, presumably looking for an attempt to invade the islands and recapture them. Of course, the islands were invaded once before by the Red Chinese and the Nationalists drove them off.

Q: Are there civilians on those islands?

Adm. M.: Oh yes, there are civilians on the islands. They live, they raise rice and various other such things that the Chinese raise in that area, and they go about their business every day although at this time the Red Chinese were shelling the islands every other day. These people had become used to it, I guess. They'd been under fire for ten years or so, and they went about their daily tasks just like there was nothing else going on.

Q: How far are they from the mainland of China?

Adm. M.: Well, you could almost throw a potato from Quemoy to the mainland. It's a narrow body of water. And from their watchtower you can see people moving around and going about their daily chores. It really is very close.

Q: One would almost think it would be untenable if the mainland Chinese really wanted to come out?

Adm. M.: I don't know. The island is very heavily fortified, and anything the Red Chinese did would be returned in kind from Quemoy. Of course, I imagine that if the Chinese wanted to devote enough force to it they could overcome Quemoy and Matsu, but also Quemoy and Matsu are protected by a treaty that we have with the Taiwanese for the protection of the off-shore islands. If the islands were attacked, then we would be obliged to help defend them, which means that we would bring ships in presumably to bombard the Red Chinese, and that is something we really don't want to do, have no desire to do.

I'm not sure of the status of that treaty at the moment, but I don't believe it's fully effective now.

The islands are a very interesting place to visit. They are lush and green. The civilians are very busily engaged in farming, agriculture, and they make various things like straw baskets and things of that nature which they sell back in Taiwan. They're kept quite busy. The guards, the lookouts, on the island, of course, are on the lookout all the time for infiltrators from the mainland who might try to get on the islands for spying or other purposes.

I also paid a visit to the Penghus, which we know as the Pescadores. This group of islands is part way between Taiwan and Quemoy and, at the moment, holds no particular military significance. The Nationalist Chinese have a fairly large force stationed on the islands to protect them from the Red Chinese. As you may know, it was a submarine base for the Japanese during the last war and could presumably be used for that again by anybody who occupied the islands. Other than being a beautiful little group of islands, I found no particular significance in these particular places.

Q: They have actually not figured in any of the difficulties of the past?

Adm. M.: Not as such, no. If it were to come to pass that there would be a military activity between Taiwan and the Red Chinese, undoubtedly they would be used because they would be a good base just half-way across the channel - not quite half-way.

Q: And the channel in its width is what?

Adm. M.: About ten miles. No, it's more than that, excuse me. One hundred miles, ninety-some to be exact.

Among the other places that I visited were the three service academies, the Naval Academy the Military Academy, and the Air Force Academy. These three academies were modeled very closely after our own academies here in the States. The uniforms are equivalent and the training is somewhat similar to ours, but not quite as extensive.

The Naval Academy I visited a number of times, and as Admiral Ni had turned over a cottage at the academy to me for my use when required. I might say that The Gimo used it occasionally, too. But it gave us a place to go down in the southern part of the island with my wife and spend a few days, play golf, and not have to stay in a Chinese hotel. It was a very nice house located right on the Naval Academy grounds, with Chinese servants and, while the facilities were not the most modern, it was still quite adequate. From there I could make numerous side inspection trips to the Military Academy and to the Air Force Academy, which were also in that general area, and to the Army units in the southern part of Taiwan, particularly the amphibious forces.

Of course, at the Naval Academy because I had once been superintendent of our Naval Academy they were quite interested in anything I had to say about the academy, so I received the full treatment. I dined with the midshipmen in their mess hall and went to their classrooms. I spoke to the brigade, I witnessed their various parades, training and drills and found a great deal of interest.

Q: What sort of a student body did they have?

Adm. M.: In size, about 300, which is quite large really for the size of their navy, but like everything else in Taiwan their military training is overdone a bit, considering the size of the country and the number of people involved. But, there again, they have to keep their people occupied. If they can't work, they serve in the military services.

The Naval Academy also is just a few miles from Tsoying, which is a naval base for the Chinese Navy in southern Taiwan. In company with various Chinese officials, generally General Chiang-Ching-ko, who was the oldest son of The Gimo, I visited a number of places in the island, including Sun-Moon Lake, which is a summer resort, and Huliaen, where we were escorted through the countryside and entertained in various ways. All these trips were very interesting, particularly in view of the beautiful scenery. Sun-Moon Lake and Huliaen are up in the mountains, a very good spot to visit.

Almost everywhere we went I had to play golf. Fortunately, in Taipei they had a very fine 18-hole golf course called Tamsui, and I played golf there regularly twice a week as a rule with General Sanborn, who was the chief of MAAG, an Air Force officer, General Peng-ming-chi, who was the chief of staff of the armed forces, and General S. K. Hu, who was the senior aide and interpreter to The Gimo. We played regularly every Wednesday and once at the weekend at Tamsui. There was always an occasion when someone like General Peng would kick his ball out of the bush to get a better lie before you arrived on the spot! But the Chinese love golf and on visits to Tsoying I usually had to play with Admiral Ni and some of his officers, and it was very helpful in our relationships.

Of course, being so close to Hong Kong an occasional trip was almost mandatory. We flew regular flights from

Melson #12 - 367

Taipei to Hong Kong -

Q: In the DC-3?

Adm. M.: In the DC-3 and also in a plane that MAAG had to take various families to Hong Kong for a health and recreation visit. This gave most of the people who lived there a chance to visit Hong Kong at least once during their tour and, if they were lucky, sometimes twice. Having this plane at my disposal, I took the opportunity to go more often, but when I did go I usually took other people with me so we could have a planeload. It's only about a two-hour-and-a-half trip. We never had any difficulty but I always felt a little nervous when flying out around the tip of southern China that something would go wrong and we'd have to land on an airfield in Red China, but fortunately this never happened.

One interesting thing which I failed to mention about the trip to Matsu and Quemoy - of course, we flew there, and for the first half of the trip we flew about 8,000 feet, but as we got closer to the mainland and to the islands we usually dropped down to around 200 to 300 feet, just over the water. This was to be below the Red Chinese radar, to keep from being tracked in. No one had ever been attacked, but you could never tell when they would be. Flying that low is not my cup of tea, over the water!

I had no direct responsibilities to the commander of the

Seventh Fleet but I did have a small unit attached to my staff from his staff. It usually consisted of a captain aviator and one other. This was just to form a liaison between the Seventh Fleet and Taiwan. Part of my duties would be to support the Seventh Fleet, if required, in whatever way I could. This could be logistics or communications or otherwise. Occasionally, our commands had some conflict and I remember one occasion when it was reported that Red Chinese submarines were operating in the Taiwan straits. My staff duty officer called me one morning about three o'clock to report that a Red Chinese submarine was operating just off the west coast of Taiwan and to tell me that he had sent orders to a Seventh Fleet destroyer in the vicinity to track it down. This was a violation of my relationship with the Seventh Fleet, in that I had no authority over the ships of fleet, except in extreme emergency, which I did not consider this to be.

So I told the staff duty officer to immediately cancel his orders to the Seventh Fleet destroyer, which he did. But Commander, Seventh Fleet, who at that time was Vice Admiral Moorer, came through very quickly with a message to the effect that I was exceeding my authority in ordering ships of his units to do certain tasks. I explained the circumstances to him and heard no more about it.

Q: In case a Red Chinese submarine had been apprehended, what action could be taken?

Adm. M.: Well, if the Nationalist Chinese were on the scene they would have taken over and conducted any attacks on the submarine. My proper course of action, which I would have taken if I had been aware of it earlier, would have been to request Commander, Seventh Fleet, to direct some of his units to search out and attack as required. I could lay this only to poor staff training in my case. I won't mention the service of the officer attached who gave the orders for that particular movement!

Q: On occasion, Commander, Seventh Fleet, made visits to Taiwan, did he not?

Adm. M.: Yes, and I'll cover that after my next paragraph of this. He was a very frequent visitor to Taiwan, as a matter of fact. He usually came down to call on The Gimo maybe twice a year at least, and other times on occasion he came in if he happened to be in the vicinity. Admiral Moorer was in several times while I was there and he had a close relationship with my command and also the Chinese.

On one occasion the carrier Kitty Hawk paid a visit to taiwan and I arranged for The Gimo and Madame to go aboard the Kitty Hawk for a visit. Admiral Moorer was present on the Kitty Hawk at the time. I went out with some members of my staff and escorted Madame and The Gimo to the ship, where they spent a few hours and witnessed the launching and recovery of aircraft and some of the other maneuvers that the ship went through.

I might insert here that years before, in 1953 when I had command of the New Jersey I stopped by Taiwan on the way from Hong Kong back to Korea and picked up some midshipmen of the Chinese Naval Academy and took them on a six-hour demonstration cruise on the New Jersey. Things of this nature occurred quite frequently as ships were available and passing in the area, more as a gesture of friendship than anything else.

Q: Did you during your period on Taiwan have any problem with U. S. atomic-powered submarines coming in to Chinese ports?

Adm. M.: No.

Q: A lot of this fear had been resolved by that time?

Adm. M.: Well, they didn't come in to Taiwan to begin with, so we weren't really involved in any way at that time.

We had numerous visitors in Taiwan. I think everybody from Washington who made a trip to the Far East stopped in Taiwan for a visit. This, of course, necessitated a lot of entertaining on my part as well as the Chinese, and I sometimes felt that it was an unnecessary burden and expense for the Chinese to have to entertain this constant stream of visitors through Taipei. I know it was a drain on me, although I had a reasonable contingency fund to cover such matters. The time and the physical effort involved in entertaining a great many visitors was something I didn't appreciate. I was happy to see people because we were isolated from the United States, but for many people who came through, I think it would be hard to justify the reason for their visit.

Q: You mean congressional junkets and things of that sort?

Adm. M.: There were constant congressional visits, there were constant visits from the other activities of the government. All these visitors had to be accommodated, put up, and entertained to a certain extent, depending on their particular rank in Washington. There were a great number of visits from military personnel. I can't particularly complain about our own Navy because I felt that their visits were mostly justified. We had frequent visits every year from CinCPac, who used to stop by on his rounds of the Far East, and CNO was there several times - Admiral Anderson at that time - and the other military services sent their senior people through there quite frequently.

But I still feel, as I said, some of them would find it very hard to justify the reason for their visit. Nevertheless, although it was a strain from time to time, we did enjoy seeing a lot of these people. It sounds like I contradicted myself, but I hope you understand.

Q: What about your visits off island? You spoke about going to Hong Kong. Did you go to Okinawa?

Adm. M.: Yes, I made two visits to Okinawa. One was a short, official visit, to visit the Seventh Fleet people who had a heavy patrol craft group assigned there. I went there once to visit with them. The other time I stopped by to visit en route to Japan.

While I was in Taiwan I unfortunately experienced a health problem involving a cyst on my kidney. I finally went to the naval hospital in Yokosuka to be operated on, and while I was up there I paid a short visit to Commander, Seventh Fleet, but I spent most of my time in the hospital so I saw very little. I flew up and back with Mrs. Melson in a Navy plane and was absent from the post only a very short time. As a matter of fact, I was back on the golf course in two weeks!

Q: You said earlier that you had liaison from the CIA on your staff. Did you make any visits to the CIA headquarters in Taiwan?

Adm. M.: Oh, yes. The CIA representative at the time was a Mr. W. T. Nelson, a very fine person and a very good friend of mine. We used to exchange visits between headquarters quite frequently and I felt he kept me as fully informed on matters that were going on as he could within the limits of his directives. They were known as a subsidiary to the Naval Air Station - that was their excuse for being in Taiwan, and they had rather a large group and they had their own mess, so I used to frequent their mess to have good American food once in a while, rather than Chinese. Of course, I had good American food at home too, but you do have to go out. When we had the excuse to entertain visiting men, including Chinese, we always went to CIA headquarters.

Q: I think you want to deal a bit with some of the Chinese personalities with whom you met?

Adm. M.: I had occasion to see The Gimo, President of the Republic of China, a number of times, both informally and formally. We never reached a close relationship. As a matter of fact, I don't believe he was really close to any foreigner. I think that he was, in a way, a very hard, tough man, probably brought about by his early experience on the mainland, and he was pursuing a hopeless quest for return to power on the mainland of China.

Q: Do you think he pursued this with conviction?

Adm. M.: From all outward indications, he did. But I don't see how he could do this under the circumstances without having some question about his success, the way things were going in the country. I think he was too smart a man to think that he was winning, but I also feel that he was very loyal to the several million Chinese who came over from the mainland with him, and he did not want to seem to weaken in his resolve to return to the mainland because of them. He didn't want to let them down, and leave them no hope for the future.

The mainland Chinese in Taiwan were mostly military types, and they held on to their military jobs with the pay with the hope and expectation of returning to China in their military capacity. Their pay was very small. If, for any reason, The Gimo indicated a lack of hope of returning to the mainland and threw these people out of the armed forces into the stream of life in Taiwan, there would be no place for them to go - that is, for the majority of them - and they'd just be beggars on the land.

Q: They're almost an army in exile, aren't they?

Adm. M.: They were an army in exile. Frankly, that's about what they were. I'm speaking of the mainland Chinese who were in the army. I think The Gimo kept up his outward appearance of expecting to return to the mainland primarily to support them. Of course, I imagine he always had some little glimmer of hope that something would happen and he could return, that the United States would help him put a landing force on the mainland of China, which they were not about to do, but he kept plugging away at it, I think hoping.

I do not believe that The Gimo was a kind man. I think he had no compunction about life, about killing people, about ordering them executed, which in a way is the general Chinese philosophy. Death doesn't mean much to them. He was nice to me in many little ways, but nothing in particular, more or less the normal courtesies.

General Chiang Ching-ko, the oldest son of The Gimo, was a very close friend of mine and I saw a great deal of him. We traveled about the island together. He came back to the States to visit me while I was at the War College, spent three days in the quarters there with us, and I think he has a great deal of ability. He's carried as a general in the Chinese Nationalist Army, but right now he is the premier and I think that when his father dies he will probably succeed him. However, Chiang-Ching-ko is plagued by diabetes, high blood pressure, and is not a well man. He used to drink a great deal but he has since stopped drinking and I presume his health has improved somewhat.

His younger brother is Chiang-wei-go —

Q: Are these sons of Madame?

Adm. M.: No, these are not sons of Madame. The older brother, Chiang-Ching-ko, is the son of a Chinese wife, Chiang's first wife. Chiang-wei-go is a son of The Gimo and a Japanese wife.

Q: And both of them, I take it, were educated in Moscow?

Adm. M.: Chiang-ching-ko was educated in Moscow, but Chiang-wei-go was not. Perhaps it isn't fair to say that Chiang-ching-ko was educated in Russia, but he spent some time there and he was at one time a representative of the Russian government in the southern part of China. He held various jobs in the Chinese mainland government until the time that they were all deported from - or rather had to leave - mainland China. He married a Russian girl and they have two sons, the older son named Alan is quite a wild young man and he has a great deal of difficulty restraining him. He was in trouble a number of times while I was there.

Q: What is Chiang-ching-ko's political philosophy? Did you glean that?

Adm. M.: Well, he supports his father. He supports the return to the mainland, at least he does while his father is alive. But somehow or other I believe that he's smart enough to see the light and probably might go for an independent Taiwan - or independence for the Taiwanese people. Of course, with him in a position of power. But whether he would do that or not, I don't know. He has strong backing among the mainland Chinese, particularly the retired army people in Taiwan, and works very hard for their welfare. Just what he will do with this turn of events I don't know. I think anything that happens now depends on the death of The Gimo. Nothing much will happen until he dies, then there could be quite an upheaval. I'm not sure whether Chiang-ching-ko is in a powerful enough position to control the country after The Gimo dies.

You have to remember, too, that most of The Gimo's supporters are damned near as old as he is, so they'll die off slowly too about the same time.

The present Vice President of China is C. K. Yen. C. K. Yen is contrary to the general run of people in the government. He is a civilian type. He's been in the Nationalist Chinese government for some time, during part of the time that they were on the mainland and came to Taiwan with The Gimo. He's a very well educated, very likeable, and very competent individual, and he's in his second or third term as vice president now. I think he will do a lot to stabilize - to keep the government stabilized.

Admiral Ni, whom I knew quite well, originally came to Taiwan in command of a destroyer with The Gimo as his passenger when they left mainland China in 1949. Ni is a northern Chinese, a big man, very likeable, and quite competent. After he left the assignment as Chief of Naval Operations of Nationalist China he fleeted on up to become the personal chief of staff to The Gimo and is now retired. He stands in well with The Gimo and I suppose having brought him out of China has something to do with it. I feel that he's one of the strong powers in the government today.

Are there any others you can think of?

Q: You might include Madame.

Adm. M.: Yes. Madame Chiang-kai-shek, whose maiden name was Mei-ling Soong, is the daughter of a Chinese financier. She was educated in the United States and is a very capable individual. She is likeable, a very strong personality, and is quite capable of controlling the Nationalist government through The Gimo. I feel that she is responsible for many of the decisions The Gimo makes.

Q: She's a much younger person?

Adm. M.: She's younger than he is. I'm not quite sure how old she is. I also feel there's possibly a streak of cruelty that runs in her, which is probably again a Chinese trait rather than something that I feel is peculiar to her.

In our associations with Madame we liked her quite well and she was very pleasant to deal with.

While I'm talking about Madame it might be well to mention the illness suffered by both Madame and The Gimo.

In the first year that I was in Taiwan The Gimo suffered from an infection of the urinary tract and, although they have a very splendid hospital which is modern in every respect and a staff of doctors, The Gimo requested assistance - that is medical assistance - from the United States. I had a doctor flown down, a Navy medical doctor, who specialized in this particular illness. He came down and prescribed for The Gimo and assisted in an operation from which he successfully recovered.

About a year later Madame had a somewhat similar problem and had medical assistance flown in to advise in the case of her treatment. I think they were both very receptive to this help they received and it probably was responsble for their quick recovery, and as far as I know they have had no ill effects since - ill aftereffects, I should say.

It might be of interest to mention the various receptions that The Gimo held. He occasionally entertained for foreign dignitaries, and for these receptions he invited senior people of other governments present in Taipei, such as the various ministers, depending on the visitors, and he nearly always included the ambassador and myself to these receptions, with our wives. Madame, of course, was there to act as hostess.

The Gimo usually sat in a large chair next to the wall. His interpreter sat on a high stool back of him and the guest of honor stood next to him - next to The Gimo, that is - so they could talk together and the interpreter would interpret their remarks back and forth. Madame would to to the other end of the room, which incidentally was a rather large room, and gather all the ladies around her. The other men in the party would line up on chairs running out from the wall with The Gimo and his guest and listen in as best they could to the conversation.

During the course of the reception various Chinese cookies and goodies would be served along with Chinese tea. At an appropriate time the senior military officer present would usually take his leave, which was the signal for everyone to depart.

They were interesting in the aspect of how they were conducted with these two separate groups gathered. There was very little intermingling between the men and the women. They were gathered in these two separate groups and had their conversations. Madame would entertain the ladies, and the men would try to listen to what was going on! Drinking tea!

Q: It must have been a satisfactory sort of duty, but still one that you wouldn't want to prolong?

Adm. M.: It was very pleasant, very interesting duty, but I

must say here and now that I was very pleased to get a call from Washington in April of 1964 telling me that I was going as President of the Naval War College that summer.

Q: I should think so, an assignment like that! The climate, I understand, on Taiwan is not the best, is it for a Westerner?

Adm. M.: No, it gets extremely hot and humid in the summer, and, of course, you're subject to having frequent typhoons. Sometimes they'd pass directly over the island and sometimes they didn't, but nevertheless you're in the band of typhoons on the coast, and during that season it's warm and humid and rather unpleasant. Living up on Grass Mountain is not too unpleasant because it's high enough to get a breeze and you could be comfortable. But going down into down with lots of Chinese and other people around you was not a very pleasant experience, from the point of view of the heat.

Q: Did you use air-conditioning to any extent?

Adm. M.: Only to a limited extent. In my quarters I think I had three portable air-conditioners, the window type. There was no general air-conditioning at that time. Now they're putting in hotels in Taipei which, I believe, are all air-conditioned.

After a round of farewell parties for the Chinese as well as the American colony, we departed Taipei in the chief of MAAG's airplane for Tokyo. Admiral Gettner had arrived two days before and I had turned my command over to him.

After a couple of days in Tokyo we flew commercially back to the States, stopping off in Pearl Harbor for a debriefing at CinCPac's headquarters, then took a month's leave in the States before reporting to Newport.

Q: Was Felt still there?

Adm. M.: I was just trying to think who was there. Sharp, of course.

Melson #13 - 383

Interview No. 13 with Vice Admiral Charles L. Melson, U.S. Navy
(Retired)

Place: His residence in Providence, Annapolis, Maryland
Date: Tuesday morning, 13 June 1972
Subject: Biography
By: John T. Mason, Jr.

Q: Well, Admiral, we're looking forward today to a most interesting chapter on your tour of duty as President of the Naval War College. You went there in July of 1964. Tell me about your appointment as President. Did it come as a surprise?

Adm. M.: I think I covered that partially in the last session, but I'll repeat it to be sure it's in the record.

Admiral Smedberg called me in Taiwan and inferred that I'd probably stay in Taiwan until I'd reached the age for retirement. Then, a couple of weeks later, he called again and stated that he knew that I had wanted to go to the War College and that the situation had cleared up now, and, if agreeable to me, I would be sent as President of the Naval War College. Nothing could have pleased me more and I assented to that very quickly.

Q: What made you want to go to the Naval War College? Did

you have some tangible objective in mind?

Adm. M.: I really had no tangible objective in mind, but I'd always enjoyed the War College - I'd been a student there - and I just thought it was doing a very fine job and that was what I wanted. And I thought it was a fine way to end my career, at the War College.

I arrived in Newport and relieved Count Austin on the 31st day of July 1964.

I might state at this point that, in passing through Washington en route to the War College, I stopped by to check in with the Chief of Naval Operations and also to call on the Secretary, the Secretary being Mr. Nitze at that time. Mr. Nitze questioned me at quite some length about what he had been briefed on this somewhat. Then he asked me, "What are you going to do to improve the War College?"

This question rather floored me in a way because I didn't feel I was that close to the War College that I could, at that time, recommend or consider any possible changes, and I replied in somewhat the same manner to Mr. Nitze. Whether he was pleased or not I don't know, but I just didn't feel that I should start talking about changes in the War College until I got there and knew what was going on, especially since I'd been out of the country for over two years.

Q: Sounds like a rather sensible idea!

Adm. M.: I'm not sure whether Mr. Nitze was pleased or not, but I suspect that he was hoping for change, and whether he wanted change for the sake of change or whether he really felt some changes needed to be made I don't know to this day.

Anyway, I tried to approach the War College with an open mind and do just what I thought best as time went on. I had relieved Count Austin, who I considered a very capable and excellent officer. I was very much surprised that he actually didn't get four stars, but he didn't and I relieved him, and he went on his way.

Q: He retired at that point, didn't he?

Adm. M.: He retired that day, the day of relief.

After a few days at the War College I began to make a survey of the general layout and the curriculum and what was going on, and tried to determine what was necessary for the coming school year, which started in September.

I found the War College then consisted of a senior course, a junior course, a command course, and a correspondence school. I decided to change this somewhat for the first year by changing the titles of the courses to the School of Naval Warfare, the School of Naval Command and Staff, and the Naval Command Staff and Correspondence School, dividing them up basically into four different schools. This was a very minor change, mostly a change in titles, but I felt it would be helpful in outlining the coming courses.

I had what I thought was a very competent staff at the War College. They were all senior naval officers, commanders and captains, and while none of them, except my chief of staff, were flag rank, I considered that they were all well qualified for what they were doing.

Admiral Nuessle, who has since died, was my chief of staff and he did a very fine job.

I started a review of all the courses then in effect, a routine review which carried on throughout the year, without making any great changes. We did make minor changes as we went along. We stuck basically to the same courses that had been carried on before.

Q: What was the main thrust of these courses?

Adm. M.: Basically, they started off with the study of history, a very brief study of history, then you developed into your warfare planning programs, and then you played war games, and then you wrote a term paper from a selection of limited subjects. That basically was the course. The difference between the School of Naval Warfare and the School of Naval Command and Staff was very slight, except mostly in the rank of the officers concerned, and the courses varied slightly in content, particularly in the early part of the course.

The Naval Command course was a foreign officers' course. We had approximately 25 foreign officers going to school at the War College. They all took the same course which paralleled the School of Naval Warfare course.

Q: These were all naval officers?

Adm. M.: All foreign naval officers. They represented some 25 countries. The majority were from South America, but there were students from China, Korea, Italy, Spain, Germany, Vietnam, the Philippines, Norway, Sweden, Turkey, and Greece, but as I said the largest single group were the South Americans.

Q: There were no Britishers?

Adm. M.: No. They'd had Britishers the year before, but there were none this year. There was a Canadian officer.

Q: I take it that they all spoke English?

Adm. M.: Oh, they spoke very fine English, for those who didn't speak very well we had a short course in English to help them out with the naval terms, in particular, which they had to use in the course. I might say they all did very well. I was very proud of this group of foreign officers who went through at the time I was there. They were knowledgeable, they spoke well, they took a great interest in the course, and, unlike many previous groups of foreign officers who had been on duty in Newport - not at the War College, they behaved themselves.

They used to have some trouble in Newport with the foreign officers who came up to go to the various destroyer schools because most of them were rather wealthy. They weren't in the Navy if they didn't have money, and most of them sported high-speed cars and what not and were the cause of considerable concern. But not a single one of these people in the War College class got into any difficulty. I'm very proud of that class because foreign officers did have a poor reputation in that respect.

Q: As playboys?

Adm. M.: As playboy types.

Q: That's curious. Does this reflect the prevailing conditions in those foreign navies?

Adm. M.: That I can't really state, whether it does or not. It simply shows that they had more money than they knew what to do with. Also, a number of these foreign naval officers from South America were pretty well heeled and that was the reason for having all this. But none of this was evident in this War College class. It may be that they were a little better breed than the ones who'd been at Newport before.

Q: Did they constitute another kind of problem for you? What about security and what about sensitive subjects being discussed in the school?

Adm. M.: They had their own classrooms, their own area in which they held their classes and studied. Only occasionally did they join in the main lectures at the Naval War College, and when they were invited to attend the main lectures at the Naval War College they were very careful that they were not on classified subjects, or subjects that they could not listen in on. Most of their publications were very well screened before they were issued to them. Of course, they did get certain classified information because we give it to their navies to begin with. But they were restricted in the stuff that they could get. They were a very social group. They liked to party and have a good time, but as I say they behaved themselves.

Q: Did they bring their wives with them?

Adm. M.: Yes, their families were there. They lived there. That made a big difference.

Q: I would think it would, yes.

Adm. M.: Some of the previous groups were there for very short periods of time without their families, and that probably caused them to indulge in a little bit more frivolity. We became very fond of most of the foreign officers. I say "most," I guess all of them, but some we were a little more fond of than others, particularly when their families were there and we all became very close.

Q: What about your teaching staff at the War College?

Adm. M.: The teaching staff consisted primarily of U. S. naval officers with the addition of several officers from other services, the Army, the Marines, and the Air Force, also from the State Department, the CIA - pardon me, the CIA man was not a teacher, he was a student. I'd like to cover the composition of the student body in a minute.

Then we had a limited number of civilian professors.

Q: Were they on loan from colleges and universities?

Adm. M.: No, we had a number who were assigned to the War College and were paid just like any other assigned civilian professor. Their number was very limited because our funds were limited with which we could hire them. In addition to that, we had the George Washington University unit which was not directly part of the War College but was there in the same building and conducted the George Washington University extension courses.

Q: Tell me about that.

Adm. M.: George Washington University established a unit at the War College. They held classes in the evening and odd hours when the students of the War College were not directly involved in War College studies. Students could enrol in these courses and obtain degrees in various fields like international law. That field was popular because it took less time, I think, but they ended up by receiving a master's degree.

Q: These were graduates?

Adm. M.: These were graduate studies.

Q: How did they happen to get involved in the school?

Adm. M.: George Washington was there when I arrived and I don't know how! I'm not being silly about this, but they were established at the War College several years back. Also the University of Rhode Island carried extension courses occasionally, in which students at the War College could enroll. The students were interested in these offerings because it was about this time that the stress on obtaining an advanced degree became so strong in the Navy, when the demand was for officers with degrees. All the officers who could, immediately took these extension courses where they ended up with a master's degree in some subject.

Personally, I didn't place a very great deal of credit in these degrees. It seemed to me that there was something lacking, and to give a man a degree while working on an outside course like that just seemed to me that he was missing something. He either wasn't doing his work at the War College, and that was my big objection, or he wasn't doing the proper amount of work on his course to get a degree. In other words, I felt the degrees were not demanding enough of the individual and that their standing wouldn't be very high in the educational world. I think I'm correct.

Q: That was the question I was about to ask. How could a man manage a course at the War College itself and then in the evening work for a master's degree?

Adm. M.: Well, I'll tell you. My first year at the War College this was a source of a great deal of concern to me. I spent a lot of time with the head of the George Washington course and with my own people going over "how can we allow

George Washington to set up a unit here in the War College and give degrees when we don't give degrees ourselves here, and they put so much stress on this it's bound to affect the War College?"

Well, the arguments went back and forth, pro and con, because the officers didn't want to give that up. They wanted to keep this George Washington course in. I was highly tempted to abolish it. As a matter of fact, my second year at the War College I had just about made up my mind I was going to abolish the George Washington course the following summer. By that time I'd left, though. But it seemed to me a conflict in what we were trying to do.

Do you feel that way about it?

Q: Well —

Adm. M.: Of course, you don't know the details.

Q: I don't know the details, but it would seem that if the course at the Naval War College is an extensive one requiring a lot of reading and so forth —

Adm. M.: They all did.

Q: —then it might be awfully difficult.

Adm. M.: Of course, in a way it's no different with the officers in the Pentagon today. They take extension courses at George Washington right here in Washington and work out degrees, but this is supposed to be in outside hours. But that's a little different from the War College where the War College and George Washington are so closely integrated. They're in one building and all of the classes were conducted in the late afternoon and evening. It just seemed to me it was interfering with the work that the students should do at the War College, and I was opposed to it for that reason.

Q: Was it largely your junior students at the War College who enrolled?

Adm. M.: The senior ones. The captains wanted to get a degree on their record. Not all of them. Don't misunderstand me, but most of them did, and that was because of pressures from the selection boards.

I'd like to go back for a minute now, if I may, and talk about the composition of the classes.

Both the senior class - rather, I'd better go back to the new terms, to the School of Naval Warfare and the School of Naval Command and Staff. The student bodies were composed of officers from various services. In the School of Naval Warfare there were naval officers, Marines, Air Force, Army, CIA, State - I think that's all - and with a smaller percentage some of these people were in the other course, the School of Naval Command and Staff.

I had on my staff a senior Army officer, a senior naval officer, and a senior State Department man, who were presumably my advisers in those areas.

My State Department man was Ambassador McClintock. He was our ambassador in Lebanon at the time of the crisis, if you remember the one I'm speaking about, and he's now ambassador, I believe, to some country in South America.

Speaking of these various people who were assigned, we had absolutely no conflict between the services at all. Everything went along smoothly. We all wore civilian clothes most of the time, except me. I usually wore uniform. But most of the students wore uniform all the time and they got along well together. No reason for any conflict really, but you'd expect there might be some.

Q: I expect the students from the Army and the Air Force had been through their own respective colleges?

Adm. M.: Most of them had, yes, that's correct. Most of them had had some previous schooling within their own commands.

The length of the course is normally ten months and it covered various aspects of sea power and military strategy and history, as brought out by those particular - in those particular areas. And, of course, there was a lot of planning done and war-gaming.

An interesting part of the War College is the Correspondence School. In the Correspondence School, which usually had a very heavy enrolment from officers at sea, they covered various aspects of the War College course in an abbreviated form. They had to submit papers and carry out problems on paper. At that time they received a certain credit in that they did not have to take the promotion exam in strategy and tactics. Now promotion exams have been abolished. I'm not sure how popular the correspondence courses are since promotion exams are no longer required.

Q: What induces a man to enroll in the correspondence course at the Naval War College?

Adm. M.: Just for education. That's about the only reason I can see for it now. Before he was seeking to eliminate the promotion exams the enrollment in the correspondence courses fell off considerably. That happened about the time I was there. But I think a lot of officers desire to improve themselves, get more knowledge, and this was a course they could take in installments aboard ship, anywhere they are. The courses are mailed to them. They go back to the War College, are corrected, and returned to them. They get graded and they get marked on their fitness report for it, that they have completed it.

Q: And this doesn't cost them anything, to enroll in this?

Adm. M.: No, it doesn't.

Q: Does it rule out a man's chances of being sent to the Naval War College later?

Adm. M.: No, it doesn't.

Q: Then you'd find that many of your students had taken such courses?

Adm. M.: Oh, yes. I had, for one. I think a lot of young officers take them. Among other things, it gives them something to do on these dreary nights at sea on long cruises and things like that, and when you have the duty. It's just like reading. You do a lot of reading in connection with the course. You're sent certain reference books to read and study, and, of course, to write about.

There is also a selective reading course in international law which they carry on.

Among other courses that the War College offers, they conduct a senior Reserve Officers' course which briefs Reserve officers on certain aspects of strategy and tactics.

And there's a Reserve Officers' Command and Staff course.

Q: This is not correspondence.

Adm. M.: No.

Q: This is for men who are in attendance?

Adm. M.: That's right. These are all short courses.

Q: How does a Reserve officer get sent there?

Adm. M.: When on two weeks of active duty he goes by his own request. No officer is sent there without requesting it. They also conduct a naval Reserve officers' school instructors seminar each year. These courses are conducted during their period of training. And there's a one-week course in fleet war games, and I might speak to that for a minute.

The Navy installed a Navy electronic warfare simulator in Sims Hall at the War College. The purpose of this installation, which was quite expensive, was to have an electronic means of playing war games. It had very large electronic display boards on which they could make electronic displays of various situations in a war and what not. It was quite effective. Occasionally, they held fleet war-gaming courses in which groups of officers came in from the fleet and played out a particular problem on this board. CinCLantFlt used to send people up. The Amphibious Force would send groups of their people who played these problems on the board before they went to sea to conduct an exercise.

In other words, the procedure was that the staff of a commander would work up an operation order. Then, if they wanted to, they could go to the War College, the same staff, and play out this operation order on this simulator. That way, they occasionally caught major mistakes in their planning before the forces ever went to sea and indulged in carrying out the same mistake. It was a check on their planning. I don't know how useful it is today, but while I was there a number of the staffs used it and considered it quite worthwhile.

Have you ever seen this?

Q: No.

Adm. M.: Sometime, go down to Sims Hall if you're up there and ask to see this electronic display board.

It might be well for a minute to talk about the method of instruction at the War College.

Reading played a major role. We had the facilities of the Mahan Library there, which is quite extensive for a War College type library. You found very little fiction in it.

While I was there we managed to build an extension on to that library, which expanded it quite a bit. Between reading and lectures and war-gaming, seminars, and consultations, research, and so forth, it was all individual effort. There was no classroom work, as such, unless you call a seminar or a lecture a type of classroom work. They depended a great deal on the lecturers who came in.

We had quite a wonderful series of people coming in to talk to the students at the War College.

Q: Did you have the major role in selecting these people?

Adm. M.: Yes. As a matter of fact, my staff made the recommendations to me, and if I agreed, it was my job, of course, to try and get them there. Sometimes the request went to CNO, sometimes to the State Department, depending on the individual. Sometimes direct to the individual, and you had certain funds at your disposal to pay expenses and what not. That was a big factor in getting any speaker - to say, "We'll pay your expenses."

Q: These people came from government?

Adm. M.: Yes.

Q: Did you have business people, too?

Adm. M.: Quite a mixture.

Q: Could I have just an illustration of the kind of people you had?

Adm. M.: Some of the speakers at the War College while I was there were Senator Saltonstall; Mr. Frank Pace, former Secretary of War; the CNO of the Norwegian Navy; an Air Force speaker on various aspects of air warfare; Admiral Ni, the commander-in-chief of the Chinese Navy; General Harold Johnson, who at that time was Chief of Staff of the Army; General Greene, the commandant of the Marine Corps; Mr. Lyman R. Kirkpatrick, the former deputy head of the CIA, who went to Brown University; Admiral Moorer; Admiral Austin, former President of the War College; Lieutenant General C. P. D. Cumont, of the Belgian Army — I'm quoting these just to give you some idea of the variety; Mr. Acheson, the former Secretary of State; Admiral Ward, who at that time was commander of the Second Fleet; Henry Cabot Lodge, who, interestingly enough, was graduation speaker at the Naval Academy here one year while I was here, so I think you can see why I got him. A number of our own flag officers who I won't go into and name. Admiral McCain.

Q: When men like this came did the students have a chance to chat with them privately? Did they stay for any length of time?

Adm. M.: No, the procedure usually was that they arrived in Quonset by air or at the commercial airport in Providence. We met them and brought them to the house. They spoke in the morning, as a rule. After speaking, I normally had a lunch at my house and invited a certain number of the staff and students. The number, of course, was limited but I rotated the invitations. The speakers usually left in the afternoon. Occasionally, some of them would spend the evening, to which they were welcome, but most of them were anxious to come and speak and go.

Occasionally, one of them brought his wife and they would spend the night.

As far as a general discussion period, except what occurred in the lecture hall - of course, at the end of each lecture they usually had a question and answer period - but that was as close as it came to being personal.

General Lemnitzer was there - oh, any number of people in military and civilian life, political life, were speakers at one time or another.

I found that the luncheons were a very useful way for the students to contact the speakers. It's true the number was limited, but I used to have anywhere from 25 to 30 people for lunch - a sit-down lunch. We'd have a cocktail before lunch, lunch, and after lunch there'd be a short period of coffee until the speaker had to leave. They were very informal and I think quite useful. Not as good as if you could have a large seminar type, but it was the best we could do, I think, under the circumstances.

Q: I suppose it would be difficult to induce many of these men to stay a full day and a night and make themselves available to the students.

Adm. M.: It depends on the person. Some would and some said they just didn't have time. But one thing about the War College is it's location is not conducive to people spending much time there unless they're there for some reason that requires it, because it's hard to get to, it's hard to get away from. I mean the traveling part of it is a little bit difficult. Military people had the best of it, in that they usually flew up from Washington. We flew them over by helicopter from Quonset Point and it took a minimum of time, but even they got hot pants and were ready to get back to Washington, so it just helped them get away faster.

But that is probably one of the most valuable parts of the whole course. We had a speaker almost every week throughout the academic year.

Q: Did you, as head of the War College, have any association with the heads of other service colleges?

Adm. M.: I was going to come to that shortly. We had a meeting of the heads of the colleges each year - Army War College, Naval War College, Air Command and Staff. The three of us met each, each year. One year they met at the War College while I was there, and the second year we met at the Army War College up in Carlisle, Pennsylvania. Those were very interesting and very instructive.

Q: Did you have anything to do with the Armed Forces Staff College?

Adm. M.: The National War College met with us, and the Armed Forces Staff College. All of them met.

Q: What came out of those meetings?

Adm. M.: It's hard to put my finger on something really constructive that came out, but we all discussed our problems and ways to combating our problems. A good many of our problems were similar, particularly in relation to funds and upkeep of the schools. The courses were considerably different in all the schools, so there wasn't too close a relationship as far as the courses were concerned. We all found out what the other fellow was doing, and I think we gained some constructive ideas in talking to other people.

Q: You mentioned funds, and limited funds, on one occasion. How generous was the Navy in supporting the Naval War College?

Adm. M.: Speaking as an ex-president, I'd say they were not very liberal! I felt that I had wonderful support in Washington. I knew the Secretary well. Arleigh Burke had gone and had done pretty well by me at the Naval Academy, and MacDonald, who was there then, had done as much as he could but there just wasn't any money available.

You compare that period - and I'm speaking of the period between 1950 and 1960, take a few years either way - money was very scarce. I guess we were recovering from the war and so forth. While there was adequate money for the day-by-day and routine maintenance and upkeep and things you had to do, there was very little extra money for improvements. This library extension at the War College was a minor item, but it took much effort to get the construction money. The small library they had was just bulging at the seams.

I go back and cite my time at the Naval Academy. We were scraping pennies the whole time I was here, just to keep the place running. Finally we got some money doled out to build two new wings to Bancroft Hall, to house an already overcrowded Bancroft Hall. And we got some money to fill in these two areas on the river to get additional ground space. If we hadn't obtained that space, they'd have been hard to put to find a place to put the new buildings they're building today. Money was just tight and it was hard to get.

Times changed in the last four or five years and rather unlimited funds were made available.

Q: To the War College?

Adm. M.: No, not the War College, to the Academy. I haven't been in communication with the War College, but I understand that they are very likely to get the funds for building there. As long as I mention it I may as well say that the whole time I was there I kept the Public Works officer, Captain Pratt, busy planning and laying out plans for extension to the facilities of the War College. We went over plans for extending the War College out to Fort Adams, which was then in Navy hands. I finally came to the conclusion and the decision that the only place for the War College was around the present main buildings. We drew up a number of plans on how we would expand. I understand now that's beginning to bear fruit and that they are going to, if they haven't already started.

And we were trying to get money to renovate Sims Hall. It was very, very tight. Now I understand it's going to be done. Sims Hall, I guess, means nothing to you, does it?

Q: So the plans that you made during your regime are being

carried our now.

Adm. M.: Not necessarily the same plans, but the basic idea is still there I think. I think the expansion plans call for building around the old buildings and adding to them. It was a fine old building, located in a nice spot up there, looking at the water. I didn't see any reason for moving it.

Q: A lovely location, looking out on Narragansett Bay.

Adm. M.: Yes, a beautiful spot.

Q: Will you speak about the endowed chairs for the professors?

Adm. M.: At the time I was there there were eight chairs set up, and I'll name them. The Alfred Thayer Mahan Chair of Maritime Strategy, the Chester W. Nimitz Chair of Social and Political Philosophy, the Ernest J. King Chair of Maritime History, the Chair of International Law, the Chair of Physical Sciences, the Milton E. Miles Chair of International Relations, Consultant in International Relations and Consultant in Economics.

These chairs were not continuous. They were intermittent in times that the chair was filled. The availability of funds having a great deal to do with it.

Q: Were they each and every one the result of a grant of moneys from somebody?

Adm. M.: No. They were established and that's the reason they weren't continuous. They didn't have the funds. It was only as the War College developed funds from one source or another that they were active.

Q: Who established them? Why were they established, as chairs?

Adm. M.: They were established by the War College because they felt the necessity of this particular subject having some emphasis and they needed somebody to continue them. Now, the Milton E. Miles Chair of International Relations was a continuous chair. That was filled all the time.

Q: That had an endowment then?

Adm. M.: No. It had a professor who was being paid by the government. I mean it was sort of - if we couldn't pay for it we couldn't fill it. That's what it amounted to, and occasionally we got money to fill these chairs.

Q: Was any effort made to reach out and get wealthy individuals to endow these chairs?

Adm. M.: No, I'm afraid we didn't do that, but we reached out to the Bureau of Personnel and asked for funds in order to have them occupied for a certain length of time, instead of being a continuing thing.

Q: Would you have had the freedom to do this, if you had been so inclined? To get some wealthy individual to give money?

Adm. M.: I question how we could have done it legally. This would have been a little different from the money to build a building or something like that. This is to pay an individual and I'm not sure how we could have accomplished that. Maybe it could be done. Maybe it is being done today. That I couldn't say.

All these chairs were established for a certain limited time. The time depended on how much money was available to pay the professor in it. The one for international relations was continuous because of an international law course. He was occupied there all the time. When he wasn't indulging in the study of international relations, he was working with the Naval Command course, the foreign officers' group. So we had to double up.

Melson #13 - 410

There was room for a great deal of improvement at the War College if the money became available. I hate to think that everything depends on money in this world, but that's just about it, isn't it?

I'd like to add at the end of this discussion on the Naval War College that I am very proud to have been President of this institution which had among its graduates such people as Ernie King, Chester Nimitz, Stephen B. Luce, Connolly, Raymond Spruance, Richard K. Turner, and many others. I consider it a great honor to have spent my time there and I hope that I benefited the War College, that I did some things that were useful and worthwhile while I was there.

I retired from the War College because of age on the 24th day of January 1966. This was a few months before my actual birthday, but I was under pressure from Vice Admiral Raborn, then the head of CIA, to join the CIA and become a member of the National Board of Estimates. As I say, I retired on the 24th of January and on the 1st of February I reported to the CIA.

Q: Would you clarify this in the biography – "transferred to the temporary disability retired list of the Navy, effective January 25."?

Adm. M.: Well, when an officer retires from the Navy, he retires either with physical disability or without – that's

Melson #13 - 411

an obvious statement. But in my case, I had rather severe physical disabilities as far as the record is concerned, so I retired to the temporary disability list initially. This meant that for a period of five years, these disabilities would be kept under observation, and at the end of that time I would be assigned a percentage disability and placed on the permanent retired list, which is what has happened in the past few years.

Q: It didn't mean that you were retired before retirement age?

Adm. M.: No. It just meant that I was kept on the disability list until the disabilities I had were stabilized so they could assign a percentage to it. I retired with a rather high percentage of disability, I'm sorry to say! But it's beneficial for tax purposes, but not very helpful in other ways.

I was with the CIA for almost two years and I enjoyed the work with the Board of National Estimates very much. It gave me an insight into the interior workings of the government, what was going on, and in a sense I was in the inner circle.

Q: Tell me about that. What does it involve?

Adm. M.: Well, I could speak briefly about it, I guess.

The Board of National Estimates is composed of a group of civilians with a few retired military officers on it, usually numbering 12 or 14, which sits in the CIA building and appraises and writes up estimates of a situation on all major happenings throughout the world that affect this government. If there's an uprising in India, a paper is written on how it might affect us, what our position will be, and so forth. If we become involved in an international situation with some other country, the Board writes up an estimate on bringing together all the facts, an estimate of the situation, and proposed course of action. These are all recommendations, you know, that go on up the line and eventually end up on the President's desk.

When the President makes a trip, they study all possibilities of danger to him, things that might happen on the trip, and write up an estimate, and make recommendations whether he should make the trip.

I found all this very interesting. Admiral Jerry Wright had preceded me on the Board, and I understand that Admiral Bluin — Vice Admiral Bluin who retired recently — has since succeeded me.

In October of 1967 — no, in August of 1967 my wife fell and broke her hip, and that changed the situation considerably for me. In the meantime, we were building a house in Annapolis as a permanent place to retire. We made the decision to continue building, in spite of her condition, and when the house was ready we moved down. I tried commuting for a while from Annapolis to the CIA building in northern Virginia, and I found that was a little too strenuous with the other things I had to do and other responsibilities I had at that time, so I retired.

Q: You were at your office every day during this period?

Adm. M.: I was leaving here at 5:30 or 5:45 every morning and not getting home till 6:30 or 7:00 o'clock every night, and after a couple of months of it I decided that that wasn't for me. In the meantime, it meant leaving Mrs. Melson here alone for a long day with a broken hip. She had been to the hospital and had her hip pinned and went through all that and was back home, but nevertheless she was going back and forth to the hospital.

So since then I've been fully retired, except for house labors!

Q: Well, I do thank you for all of this. I think it will be very worthwhile, when it gets transcribed and available.

Adm. M.: I've enjoyed doing it. I'm sure I've left gaps here and there, which I'll try to fill in.

Index

for

Series of interviews with

Vice Admiral Charles L. Melson

U. S. Navy (Ret.)

Anderson, Adm. George: Reviews the First Fleet at San Diego (1961) in place of President Kennedy, p. 342.

Anti-Submarine School: established in Miami, Florida (1942), p. 53-55.

Beary, VADM Donald B. (1948); becomes President of the National War College, p. 117.

Board of Visitors - U. S. Naval Academy: see entries under U. S. Naval Academy.

USS BOYLE: flagship for DD Div. 32, p 84; the landings on the South Coast of France, p. 88-91.

Brown, ADM Chas. R. (Cat): p 230-231.

Casco Bay: locale for Destroyer training in WW II, p. 72-3; 92-93.

USS CHAMPLIN (DD-601) Melson puts her in commission at Fall River shipyard, p. 63-4; equipped with SG radar, p 65; early escort jobs, p. 67-69; unit of follow-up force at Casablanca (Dec 1942), p 71-2; frequent training periods in Casco Bay, p 72-3; escorting convoy U CG-6, p 77-78; convoy to Oran via Bermuda, p 79; escort for British convoy, Gibraltar to Oran, p 81; additional Mediterranean operations, p 82-3; Melson (Jan. 1944) takes command of DD Div 32 and remains in CHAMPLIN as his flagship, p 84; Skipper killed in engagement with German SS off Nantucket, p 85; more escort work in the Mediterranean, p 86-7; paratrooper air convoy attacked by ships off Sicily, p. 100-1.

Chiang Ching-ko, General: eldest son of the Gimo, p. 375-6.

Chiang-kai Chek: Melson's first meeting with the Generalissimo, p. 352; the Gimos meetings with Ambassador Kirk, p. 354 ff; attitude of Adm. Wright, p. 357; visits Adm. Moorer's flagship, p 369; p. 373; description of receptions held by the Gimo, p. 379.

Chiang Kai-chek, Madam: p. 378-9; see also entries under Chiang.

Chiang-wei go: younger son of the Gimo and his Japanese wife, p. 376-7.

C. I. A.: maintained large contingent on Taiwan with liaison man on staff of Commander, Taiwan Defense Command, p. 350; p. 372. Melson retires from the Navy (1966) and serves for two years on the Board of National Estimate of the C. I. A. - duties and functions of the Board, p. 411-412.

CIncLant: Melson on duty as Assistant Chief of Staff for Plans (Feb. 1955) p. 194 ff; draws on Naval War College training, p. 199-200. Melson promoted to RADM (June, 1955) and becomes Deputy Chief of Staff to CincLant, p. 202.

Clark, ADM J. J. (Jocko): Commander, 7th Fleet, p. 167-8; 170, 174, 177, 184.

Clark, Gen. Mark: p. 171; 176-7.

U. S. Coast Guard: involvement in protection of merchant shipping a the Eastern Seaboard and the Gulf of Mexico, p 52-3.

ComBatCru: Melson serves as Chief of Staff (Oct. 1953), p. 187;

Melson

duty with the Sixth Fleet, p. 191-3; detached (Feb. 1955) for duty with CincLant, p. 193.

ComDesLant: Melson named as Operations Officer on staff of Commander Destroyers, Atlantic Fleet (Nov. 1944) - a special training command for duty on the East Coast, p. 92-95.

Convoy Duties: p. 67 ff.

CruDiv 4: Melson assumes command on March 17, 1957, p. 212; participates in NATO review with midshipmen on board, p. 213-217; visit to Brazil, p 217-218; Puerto Rico, p. 219. 223; NATO exercises, p. 224-226; duty with the 6th fleet, p. 227-229.

Culebra: p. 219-221.

DD - Div. 32: Melson in command in early 1944 - moves from CHAMPLIN to the BOYLE, p. 84.

USS DENEBOLA: flagship of Commander, Destroyers, Atlantic Fleet, p. 91-2, 96.

DesRon 20: Melson (July 1949) named as Commander, p. 126; sonar school, p. 127; travels to station via submarine, p. 127-8; DD BARTON is flagship, p. 128; p. 129-30.

Deyo, VADM Morton L.: p. 89-90.

USS DICKINSON: Melson serves as Engineer Officer, p. 29.

Distinguished Visitors Program: p. 275-77.

USS DUPONT: Melson has duty on her (1931-32), p. 26.

Eastern Sea Frontier: Melson's assignment as Asst. Operations Officer on staff of Adm. King for duty on ESF, p. 46 ff.

Eastern Sea Frontier: Melson' assignment as Asst. Operations Officer on staff of Adm. King for duty on ESF, p. 46 ff.

Eisenhower, President Dwight D.: visits San Diego and inspects the First Fleet, p. 335.

Felt, ADM. Donald: CncPac, p. 345, 356.

First Fleet: Melson (July 14, 1960) relieves Adm. Sharp in command p. 330 ff; duties, p 331-2; recollections of command years, p. 333-43.

Fleet Training Office - CNO: p 39 ff; annual competition, awards, p. 40-41.

France - landing on the South Coast in WW II (1944), p 88-91.

Franke, The Hon. Wm.: p. 237-8; speaker at N.A. graduation (1959), p. 315.

Harrison, Lt. Gen. W.K.: senior negotiator at time of the Korean truce, p. 180.

Hart, ADM. T. C.: presents murals to Naval Academy, p 322-324.

USS HELENA: CNO designates her as flagship for the Commander First Fleet, p. 334-335.

Hill, ADM Harry: p. 143-145; p. 239.

Hill, The Hon. Robert C.: Ambassador to Mexico (1960), p. 294-5.

Kimball, The Hon. Dan: SecNav, p. 123.

King, Fleet Admiral E. J.: Cinc-US Fleet: Melson assigned (1942) to his staff as Assistant Operations Officer with duty in connection with Eastern Sea Frontier, p. 46-52; use of PBY's, p. 56-57.; p. 59.

Kirk, Adm. Alan: Ambassador to Taiwan, p. 351-353, 357-8.

Korean War: BB NEW JERSEY participates, p. 164 ff; coastal train bombardment, p. 174-5.

Lee, VADM Willis A.: Deputy for Fleet Training (1940), p. 39, 44-45.

Libby, VADM R. E.: becomes ComBatCruLant, p. 188; 190-1.

USS LOS ANGELES: Cruiser serves as temporary flagship for Commander First Fleet, p. 334.

MAAG - Taiwan: role in handling Chinese requests for military equipment, p. 355; position of the MAAG unit in Taiwan, p. 356-7.

Massive Retaliation: p. 196-7.

McCorkle, RADM F. D.: skipper of the BB NEW JERSEY, p. 155-6.

USS MC CORMICK (DD 223): Melson assigned to her in Asiatic Fleet, p. 17-19; cruise with Governor General Dwight Davis in the Philippines, p. 22-23.

Melson, VADM Chas. L.: family data p. 1-3; early desire to attend the Naval Academy, p. 3-4; marriage, p. 31-32.

Mexican Naval Academy Dedication: p. 294-5.

USS MISSOURI - BB: grounded in Norfolk channel, p. 130.

Moorer, ADM Thomas: Commander, 7th Fleet, p. 388-9; visits to Taiwan, p. 369-70.

USS NAPA: sea going tug with Asiatic fleet, p. 17.

U. S. Naval Academy: entrance, p. 4-5; academy years, p. 6; first cruise, p. 7-8; student memories, p. 9-12; mission of the Academy, p. 11-12; Melson (May, 1950) becomes Admin-

Melson

istrative Aide and Chief of Staff to Adm. Harry Hill, p. 131-3; Board of Visitors, p. 134-5; Naval Station, p. 135-6; gift of yachts, p. 136-138; duties as Chief of Staff, p. 139 ff; the handling of tourists, p. 142, 148; Naval Academy Museum, p. 143; entertaining, p. 141, 146; status of the Commandant of Midshipmen, p. 148; Melson ordered as Superintendent of the Academy - June 27, 1958 - p. 234 ff. Melson prepares by spending five weeks in BuPers, p. 235 ff; liaison with other service academies, p. 241-248; re-statement of Melson's preparations for duty as Superintendent, p. 249 ff; the plebe class and method of enrollment, p. 254; curriculum changes, p. 255-265; building projects during Melson's tenure, p 266-275; Distinguished Visitors' Program, p. 275-77; additional information on the building program and the master plan, p. 278-280; Academy entrance requirements, p. 280-1; the 'whole man' concept, p. 281-284; consideration of athletic prowess in gaining entrance, p. 284-288; the mission of the Naval Academy as re-stated, p. 289-290; Summer cruises, p. 296 ff; athletics, p. 304-310; hoisting a broom to the masthead, p. 305; operation INFORMATION, p. 310-312; guest speakers, p. 314f (see also entry under Rickover); Superintendent's Conferences, p. 317-318; murals in Bancroft Hall, p. 322-3; the Brigade, p. 324-325; the Severn River Command, p. 325-330.

Naval Academy Preparatory School - Norfolk; p. 26-27; p. 29.

U. S. Naval Institute: p. 320-322.

Melson

Naval War College: Melson a student at the Naval War College (June 1947), p. 104-110; 114-115; Stays on as Secretary of the Naval War College, p. 116-117; War College REVIEW comes into existence, p. 117-8; correspondence courses, p. 119-125; Melson named as President of the War College (July 1964), p. 363; attitude towards new assignment, p. 384-6; foreign students, p. 387-390; George Washington University Extension Courses, p. 391-393; students, p. 394-5; Reserve Officers' Command and Staff courses, p. 398; electric warfare simulator, p. 398-399; Mahan Library facilities, p. 399; guest speakers, p. 400-402; conferences with heads of Service War Colleges, p. 404-5; money problems p. 405-6; endowed chairs, p. 407-409; retirement, 1966, p. 410.

Navy-Marine Corps Memorial Stadium: p. 271-2.

HMS NEWCASTLE: p. 177.

USS NEW JERSEY - BB: Melson given command in Oct. 1952, p. 152-4 ff; ship control school, p. 155; impressions of a big ship, p. 155-6, 158; p. 160-164; Korean assignment, p. 164 ff; flagship of Adm. J. J. Clark, p. 167, 170; joins TF 77, p. 169; targets, p. 171-2; (see also entries under TF 77); birthday celebration, p. 180; 182-3; end of Korean assignment, p. 185-6; p. 231-2.

Ni, Admiral (Chinese): p. 377.

Nitze, The Hon. Paul: As SecNav interviews Adm. Melson on the Naval War College appointment, p. 384.

USS NORTHAMPTON (CA 125): Melson assigned to number one gun

turret, p. 30-31.

USS PATTERSON: p. 35 ff; experiment in high pressure steam propulsion, p. 35-36; single engine room, p. 37-39.

USS PENGUIN: Melson assigned in February 1929 - eclipse expedition to Iloilo, p. 16.

USS PENNSYLVANIA: Melson assigned, p. 34-35.

Pescadores: p. 363.

Pirie, VADM R. B.: becomes Chief of Staff to CincLant, p. 203.

USS PITTSBURG: Melson reports to her in Jan., 1931 - trip to Norfolk, p. 22-23, 26.

Post Graduate School: June 1934 - p. 32-33.

The Queens - Cunarder transports Queen Mary and Queen Elizabeth, p. 70-71.

Quemoy and Matsu: p. 361-363.

Reed, RADM O. M.: ComDesLant (1944-45), p. 92; becomes ComBatDevFiv Flagship TEXAS, in 1945 - Melson becomes his Chief of Staff, p. 97; commander of a task force to bring the boys home, p. 98; Nov. 1945 ordered to command the 16th Fleet on the East Coast, brings Melson back as his Chief of Staff, p. 99.

USS REINA MERCEDES: Station ship at the Naval Academy, p. 135, 151.

Rhee, President Syngman: p. 177, 179, 185.

Rickover, ADM. Hyman: visit to the Naval Academy, p. 312-314.

SAC LANT: nature of command, p. 203-4; liquor mess in Norfolk, p. 205; problems of NATO command, p. 206 ff; manner in which SacLant plans were developed, p. 209-210.

Sasebo, Japan: the base for U. S. Battleships operating with the 7th Fleet, p. 168-9.

Severn River Naval Command: see entries under Naval Academy.

Sixteenth Fleet (Atlantic Reserve Fleet), p. 99, 101-104.

Smith, ADM. H. P.: Chief of Naval Personnel, p. 234.

Spurt Communications: p. 77.

TF 77: operating force of the 7th fleet in Korean waters, p. 169-170, p. 175, 179.

Taiwan Defense Command: Melson named to command (1962), p. 343-4; 347 ff; relieves Adm. Smoot, p. 348-9; duties of the command, 349; nature of the aid demanded by the Chinese, p. 354 ff; duty of the Commander to inspect Chinese units, p. 358-9; the Chinese military forces, p. 360-362; command relationship with the 7th fleet, p. 368; constant visitors from Washington, p. 370-1; Melson departs in April, 1964 for duty at the Naval War College, p. 381.

Taiwanese Naval Academy: p. 365-6.

USS TRENTON: first duty, p. 13-15; Asiatic station p. 15; Japanese flag incident and apologies offered, p. 24-25.

UCG - 6: convoy to North Africa, p. 77-80.

Wonson: p. 170-172.

Wooldridge, ADM E. T.: p. 187-189; 233.

Wright, ADM Jerauld: CincLant, p. 194; succeeds ADM Alan Kirk as Ambassador to Taiwan (1963), p. 357.

Yen, C. K.: Vice President of Taiwan, p. 377.

www.ingramcontent.com/pod-product-compliance
Lightning Source LLC
Chambersburg PA
CBHW080623170426
43209CB00007B/1501